Digerati

BOOKS BY JOHN BROCKMAN

AS AUTHOR

By the Late John Brockman

37

Afterwords

The Third Culture

AS EDITOR

About Bateson

Speculations

Doing Science

Way Of Knowing

Creativity

AS COEDITOR

How Things Are

<John Brockman>

Digerati

Encounters with the Cyber Elite

HardWired San Francisco

HardWired
520 Third Street, Fourth Floor
San Francisco, CA 94107

HardWired books are distributed to the trade by Publishers Group West.

Printed in the United States of America

First Edition 1996

10 9 8 7 6 5 4 3 2 1

ISBN 1-888869-04-6

Cover design by John Plunkett.
Text design by Susanna Dulkinys.

For my son – Max Brockman

Contents

PROLOGUE: 1966 xxi

McLuhan had pointed out that by inventing electric technology, we had externalized our central nervous systems; that is, our minds. Cage went further to say that we now had to presume that "there's only one mind, the one we all share." Cage pointed out that we had to go beyond private and personal mind-sets and undersand how radically things had changed. Mind had become socialized. "We can't change our minds without changing the world," he said. Mind as a man-made extension became our environment, which he characterized as "the collective consciousness," which we could tap into by creating "a global utilities network."

INTRODUCTION: CONTENT IN THE DIGITAL AGE xxvii

Value is in activity. Content *is no longer a noun.* Content *is context.* Content *is activity.* Content *is relationship, community.* Content *is not text or pictures as distinct from the interactive components that provide access to them.* Content *is the interactive quality.* Content *is a verb, a continuing process. Value on the Internet will be created through services, the selection of programming, the presence of other people, and assurance of authenticity — reliable information about sources of bits. In short, intellectual* processes *and* services *will appreciate; intellectual* assets *will depreciate.* Content *is information, and information is not a thing. Value is in activity.*

Editors are the original intelligent agents. We try to figure out what our customers do, and we succeed to the degree that we're able to give them what they want, compel them, give them an identity, and make them feel that they're part of a community.

Information is like a life jerky: dried up and not terribly communicative. Through information you come back to the vast set of phenomena that is creating the data in the first place. Experience and the universe itself are intimately bound up with one another. The purpose of the Internet and all its surrounding phenomena is to create a context where experience is universal, and the informational reduction is no longer necessary.

The peculiarity of the new devices on the Internet is that you've got a double acceleration or a double instability. First there's Moore's Law, the fact that the number of processors on a chip, and thus computer power, keeps doubling every eighteen months, decade after decade. Then there's Metcalfe's Law: the value of a net goes up as the square of the number of people on that net. That is to say the Net itself or any net — even one made up of faxes or cellular telephones — increases dramatically in value the more people are on it. You've got a double-runaway phenomenon. Throw into that the tools that suddenly turn up, like the World Wide Web, Mosaic, and later Netscape Navigator, which also can become dramatically empowering in short order. The Net is a major social event. Culture's got to change.

THE SEER: DAVID BUNNELL 29

There's a fundamental shift taking place, because information is no longer an object that has to be transported. In the digital world, information that traditionally took the form of newspapers, magazines, or books can instantaneously be transported anywhere. The implication is vast. It requires a different value system. How heavy a newspaper is and how much it costs to get it to somebody no longer determine the cover price. Suddenly that cost is zero.

THE THINKER: DOUG CARLSTON 39

You have to think of the convergence companies in terms of their multiplicity of functions. For film and television, the locus of control historically has been distribution. They have direct access to theaters in a way that independent producers can't match or onto the airwaves in a way not available to others. That distribution function has been the source of most of the profit in film and television over the years. Most film and television companies have been spinning off productive capability to small independent studios so they can fob off a lot of the risk and then pick and choose the more successful projects. Distribution is a whole new game on the Internet, and it's not clear how controllable it is. If the Net stays as anarchistic as it is now in terms of access, then distribution may not be a good way to control it. A better route may be controlling productive capability. In this case, the people who are going to succeed are the ones who get very good at investing in new products and new ideas, and at being right in a commercial sense.

THE IDEALIST: DENISE CARUSO 49

I refuse to use the word content. *It's insulting. Artists create art; writers write ideas. The word will continue to be used, though, because media has become such a huge commercial enterprise. Everything is becoming a commodity – including art, including ideas.*

THE STATESMAN: STEVE CASE 61

There's too much focus on technology in the industry, an obsession with bandwidth and the latest browsers. What's much more important is creating a magical interactive experience, for which the technology is certainly an enabler. Human creativity is really going to drive us.

THE GADFLY: JOHN C. DVORAK 73

The revolution is in the increased communication capability. This is a continuation of what started well before the Industrial Revolution. Genghis Khan was one of the first to grasp the concept of the necessity of quick transmittal of information. He had horses positioned every twenty miles, and when guys wore out a horse, they jumped on the next one and the next one. They made two hundred miles a day, which was a big deal back in the year 1200. Now we can do everything instantly, worldwide. It's frightening.

THE PATTERN-RECOGNIZER: ESTHER DYSON 81

A new kind of community, not a culture, is coming. The difference between a culture and a community is that a culture is one-way — you can absorb it by reading it, by watching it — but you have to invest back in a community. Absent this return investment, it's not really a community. People will be investing in sharing content and sending messages to each other, in spending time together, and, in part, that's what builds these communities.

THE SOFTWARE DEVELOPER: BILL GATES 93

Essentially, Netscape wants to take a browser and turn it into an operating system. We want to take an operating system and have enough Internet capability built in so that people continue to view Windows as the best way to use the Internet. That is what our customers expect us to do. Unless we're doing a better operating system and keeping the prices low, somebody else is going to come in. Nobody has a guaranteed situation as you look ahead a couple of years. Companies are moving as fast as they can, and the marketplace is the judge of who gets these things right. This competition is great for the end-user, because all the companies involved have very low prices and there is a lot of free software being made available.

THE CONSERVATIVE: DAVID GELERNTER 105

A community is not a community of disembodied spoken statements, in part because the most important aspect of the communication that people have is emotional, and one often communicates emotion not in terms of the text but as a subtext. The physical body is not irrelevant to a human community. The emotional subtext of human communication is crucial to human thought. It isn't a footnote. Too many computer scientists don't understand this.

THE DEFENDER: MIKE GODWIN 115

One of the difficulties we face now, and the cause of a backlash of fear of the medium, is the problem of pluralism. Most of us don't have to deal with the full range of opinions and ideas — from the inspiring to the obnoxious — that exist in the American landscape because the mainstream mass media filter them out. When you spend time on the Net, you discover that people are hungry to read and talk and that the political landscape is a lot richer than you ever thought it was. People hold beliefs that are orthogonal to the usual Democrat versus Republican scale.

THE GENIUS: W. DANIEL HILLIS 123

People are so tuned in to the near term that they aren't thinking in terms of decades. Yet, over the long run, we have a chance of fundamentally changing humanity. Many people sense this, but don't want to think about it because the change is too profound. Today, on the Internet the main event is the Web. A lot of people think that the Web is *the Internet, and they're missing something. The Internet is a brand-new fertile ground where things can grow, and the Web is the first thing that grew there. But the stuff growing there is in a very primitive form. The Web is the old media incorporated into the new medium. It both adds something to the Internet and takes something away.*

THE JUDGE: DAVID R. JOHNSON 133

What's happening on the Net is that the combined decisions made by a systems operator setting rules and the users who vote with their modems, by deciding which areas to frequent and how often, are creating competing environments where different rules and different laws obtain. It's the first time that I know of in the history of the world in which we've had Darwinian selection pressure on the law.

THE SEARCHER: BREWSTER KAHLE 145

A model that took some of the revenue from subscription payments and had a royalty structure paying money back to the content creators who made the Internet interesting would make for a more robust Internet. It would also enable providers with only a small niche to have an easy mechanism to make a little bit of money. We're getting there so far on the advertising model. We have to get the subscription model going.

THE SAINT: KEVIN KELLY 155

What we are talking about now is a communications revolution. That is exciting, because communication is the basis of culture. Culture is a process of communication among individuals and groups. We are amplifying and enhancing the foundations of culture and society with this communications revolution. All the dynamic and revolutionary effects we are going to see will come from these tiny chips being used in a communications mode.

THE PRODIGY: JARON LANIER 163

One of the processes that concerns me is what I call the "Karma Vertigo Effect." We have an extraordinary amount of what you could call karma in this generation, because this generation is creating the computer network and the infrastructure of computer software that will be running for a thousand years. I call it the Karma Vertigo Effect because when you realize how much karma we have in this generation, you get vertigo!

THE MARKETER: TED LEONSIS 175

In terms of marketing, would you rather be loved or needed? That's a question I ask all the time. Utilities are needed but they're not loved. So are cable companies and phone companies. If you're a brand that's loved, you don't even have to know who your customers are. Coke doesn't know who its customers are, but it has the most important shelf space — a position in a consumer's mind. We want to be a brand that's loved, and that's where word of mouth becomes very positive. We can send out a billion disks, but if members don't love us and tell their friends and relatives about us, we won't win.

THE SCRIBE: JOHN MARKOFF 187

A small anarchic community of wireheads and hackers made the mistake of giving fire to the masses. Nobody is going to give it back. It is paradise lost. This wonderful community is not a community anymore. It's a society. It is a city on the Net, and in the back alleys of this electronic city, people are getting rolled. It is no different than being in New York. Let me be a couch potato if this is what Internet activity is about.

THE FORCE: JOHN McCREA 197

At a technical level, VRML is a file format. At a higher level, it is a way of doing 3-D graphics over networks. 3-D graphics are coming to a Web where people have become comfortable with a page-centric view. But VRML will take the page-centric view and pop it into another dimension, with the potential to make the experience more like the physical world. This fundamental shift brings a sense of place to something that has absolutely evaporated the notion of space. While evaporation of space is a powerful concept, much of the information suddenly loses context. Introducing the notion of space to the Net via VRML has the potential to make it more compelling and appealing to a larger audience.

THE COMPETITOR: SCOTT McNEALY 207

At Sun we believe in the network-computing model. We're not wired up and married to the host-based centralized computing model, and we're not all tangled up in the desktop hairball — that is the desktop computing model of the Intel-Microsoft world. Everything from the first computer we shipped a long time ago goes out with a network interface, and every desktop, server, application, software product, and service product that we've ever offered has been network-centric.

THE PUBLISHER: JANE METCALFE 219

It's trite to say that Wired *is talking about the convergence of media, computers, and communications. What we are really talking about is a fundamental shift in society that is being led by technology but is infiltrating every aspect of society. Technology, invented in labs, gets absorbed by business, and as business takes it on, it starts to spread throughout society. Often, at that point, artists are attracted to it and pioneer it, champion it, stretch it, push the boundaries of it, and use it to bring a different message to the public. It's a three-pronged approach that has a multilayered response from the society it's impacting.* Wired *is really about this change. It's led by technology, absorbed by business, and spread by artists. But it's not about technology.*

THE WEBMASTER: KIP PARENT 229

A lot of corporate guys are saying that the Web is going to implode and that 40 percent of the companies on the Web today will be gone in six months. I think they are wrong. Interactive TV is what has imploded. We may very well see a merging of the ideas of interactive TV and the Web as we get broadband TCP/IP broadcasts via TV cables. We'll see a natural merging of the technology, but it'll be far better and far more powerful than people were thinking interactive TV would be in 1993. You're really going to have the opportunity to interact with it.

THE CITIZEN: HOWARD RHEINGOLD 237

I resent the shallowness of the critics who say that if you sit in front of a computer and participate in online conversations worldwide you are not leading an authentic life. I question the premise that one person can judge the authenticity of another person's life. Millions of people passively watch television all day long. Don't tell me that having an email relationship with someone on the other side of the world is less authentic than sitting alone and watching the tube. For many people, this new medium is a way of breaking out of the virtual world they already live in.

THE BUCCANEER: LOUIS ROSSETTO 247

The online services would like to believe they are content providers. Wrong. They have hosted content providers (and alienated a lot of them by not appreciating their contribution to increasing the service's user base), but they themselves are not content providers. It's like theater owners thinking they are operating studios. Media is not so easy.

THE ORACLE: PAUL SAFFO 259

For most of this century we have viewed communications as a conduit, a pipe between physical locations on the planet. What's happened now is that the conduit has become so big and interesting that communication has become more than a conduit, it has become a destination in its own right — what in the vernacular is called cyberspace.

THE RADICAL: BOB STEIN 269

The subtext of what's happening is that we are changing the way that humans communicate with each other. This transition is going to take much longer than people talk about, and it may be a hundred years, two hundred years, before it settles out. This profound shift is more significant than the invention of the printing press, and the deep implications of it won't be known for some time. A thousand years from now, humanity will look back at the late part of the twentieth century as the time when something big started.

THE SKEPTIC: CLIFF STOLL 277

When I'm online, I'm alone in a room, tapping on a keyboard, staring at a cathode-ray tube. I'm ignoring anyone else in the room. The nature of being online is that I can't be with someone else. Rather than bringing me closer to others, the time that I spend online isolates me from the most important people in my life, my family, my friends, my neighborhood, my community.

THE CATALYST: LINDA STONE 287

In real space, each place we go has a different sense of place. Places offer mood, personality, and context. When we choose where we want to take a walk or have dinner, carry on a conversation or shop, we do so based on how a place dovetails with how we're feeling, who we will be with or what we hope to accomplish. Likewise, how we dress and how we generally present ourselves impacts the impression we make on others. In part, our lives are a process of developing, tuning, and refining who we are...both to ourselves and to others. At the moment, our cyberspace identity is our email signature.

THE EVANGELIST: LEW TUCKER 295

When you talk about executable content, you face the following problem: how does the provider know what system the content is going to be viewed on? Today, software is system-dependent. Java is designed to be architecture-independent and run on almost all platforms. Application writers who write to the Java platform don't have to worry about the fact that the user is on a Windows system, a Unix system, or a VCR. Instead, from the developer's point of view, Java allows one to write to a single standard software platform, the Java Virtual Machine.

THE CYBERANALYST: SHERRY TURKLE 303

Many of these same ideas no longer seem abstract or esoteric when you immerse yourself in life on the Internet. For example, the idea that you are constituted by and through language is not an abstract idea if you're confronted with the necessity of creating a character in a MUD. You just have to do it. Your words are your deeds, your words are your body. And you feel these word-deeds and this word-body quite viscerally. Similarly, the idea of multiplicity as a way of thinking about identity is concretized when someone gets an Internet account, is asked to name five "handles" or nicknames for his activities on the system, and finds himself "being" Armani-boy in some online discussions, but Motorcycle-man, Too-serious, Aquinas, and Lipstick in others.

THE LOVER: DAVE WINER 315

What's nice about DaveNet *is that I don't need any money to do what I do. I don't require an editorial staff, and I don't need a printing press. Therefore I don't have anybody telling me what I can write. I also have a lead time that is the envy of every journalist in every other medium. If a news story comes out and I get it first, I can be out on the street in ten minutes. There's never been a medium like this, with that kind of immediacy. It changes the way news happens. It also changes the way opinion happens.*

THE IMPRESARIO: RICHARD SAUL WURMAN 327

When I pick up a book, if it's a novel, I know that I have so many more pages to read. I know where I am in the story. When I watch a movie that I know is two hours, I know that no matter what happens in the first five minutes, it's not the end of the movie. It's going to take two hours to go through the plot. I have a sense of where I am. This is not a trivial issue. It gives me a base. It's a centering thing.

EPILOGUE: 1996 333

"Dad," Max interrupted, "I don't mean to be disrespectful, but it's kids like me that are going to be the pioneers and make things happen. We're the digerati."

INDEX 340

Acknowledgments

I am grateful to Judy Herrick, who, for the past year, has presented me with thousands of pages of accurate transcriptions. I also want to thank a number of people at HardWired: Peter Rutten, the publisher, for his time and valuable suggestions; Donna Linden, production director, for her diligence and attentiveness; and Susanna Dulkinys, design director; Jennifer Colton, marketing director; Alex McOsker, marketing coordinator; Leslie Rossman, publicist; and Judith Dunham and Constance Hale, for their careful copy editing.

Thanks to Sarah Taylor at Brockman, Inc., who organized a great number of details in coordinating the final stages of the project.

Finally, special thanks and appreciation to Katinka Matson for her patience and support, and to our son, Max Brockman, who helped instigate the project, went on the road with me, videotaped many of the encounters, and assisted throughout.

Prologue

1966

"'Love Intermedia Kinetic Environments.' John Brockman speaking – partly kidding, but conveying the notion that Intermedia Kinetic Environments are In in the places where the action is – an Experience, an Event, an Environment, a humming electric world."

– *The New York Times*

Intermedia Kinetic Environment? What is that? A Java applet? A new OS platform from Microsoft's Advanced Technology and Research Division? A 4-D VRML file format?

Not quite. The date was September 4, 1966. I was sitting on a park bench on Labor Day weekend in Easthampton, Long Island, reading about myself on the front page of *The New York Times* Sunday "Arts & Leisure Section." I was wondering if the article would get me fired from my job at the New York Film Festival at Lincoln Center, where I was producing "expanded cinema" events. I was twenty-five years old.

New and exciting ideas and forms of expression were in the air. They came out of happenings, the dance world, underground movies, avant-garde theater. They came from artists engaged in experiment. Intermedia consisted more often than not of non-scripted, sometimes spontaneous, theatrical events by artists in which the audience was also a participant.

I arrived at this spot after managing the Film-Makers' Cinematheque, the home for underground cinema in 1965, where my mandate had been to produce a festival that expanded the form of cinema. I commissioned thirty performance pieces by world-class artists, dancers, poets, dramatists, and musicians. They were free to do anything they wanted, the only stipulation being that their piece incorporate cinema.

The result was the Expanded Cinema Festival, and it received major media attention. Within a year there were two *Life* covers and a *New York Times Magazine* cover on derivative works. *Intermedia,* the word I had coined and used as my logo, was hot. A number of legendary art-world figures became interested in the genre. Some of the people I worked with during that period included visual artists Les Levine, Claes Oldenburg, Robert Rauschenberg, Andy Warhol, Robert Whitman; kinetic artists Charlotte Moorman and Nam June Paik; happenings artists Allan Kaprow and Carolee Schneemann; dancer Tricia Brown; filmmakers Jack Smith, Stan Vanderbeek, Ed Emshwiller, and the Kuchar brothers; avant-garde dramatist Ken Dewey; poet Gerd Stern and the USCO group; musicians Lamonte Young and Terry Riley; and through Warhol, the music group The Velvet Underground.

One of the artists I got to know during the Festival was the poet Gerd Stern, who had, on occasion, collaborated with Marshall McLuhan, incorporating live McLuhan lectures into USCO intermedia performances. Gerd, with his unkempt hair and abundant beard, was an odd counterpoint to the buttoned-down classics professor from Toronto, but they got along famously. Through Gerd and other artists, McLuhan's ideas had begun to permeate the art world, though it would be several more years before they hit the mainstream.

Gerd introduced me to anthropologist Edmund Carpenter, McLuhan's collaborator, who in turn invited me to Fordham University in 1967 to meet McLuhan, Father John Culkin, and other members of that charmed circle of communications theorists. The discussion centered on the idea that we had gone beyond Freud's invention of the unconscious, and, for the first time, had rendered visible the conscious.

McLuhan turned me on to *The Mathematical Theory of Communication* by Bell Labs scientists Claude Shannon and Warren Weaver, which began: "The word *communication* will be used here in a very broad sense to include all of the procedures by which one mind may affect another. This, of course, involves not only written and oral speech, but also music, the pictorial arts, the theater, the ballet, and in fact all human behavior."

The composer John Cage had also picked up on this set of ideas. He convened weekly dinners during which he tried out his ideas, as well as his mushroom recipes, on a group of young artists, poets, and writers. I was fortunate to have been included at these dinners where we talked about media, communications, art, music, philosophy, the ideas of McLuhan and Norbert Wiener. McLuhan had pointed out that by inventing electric technology, we had externalized our central nervous systems; that is, our minds. Cage went further to say that we now had to presume that "there's only one mind, the one we all share." Cage pointed out that we had to go beyond private and personal mind-sets and understand how radically things had changed. Mind had become socialized. "We can't change our minds without changing the world," he said. Mind as a man-made extension became our environment, which he characterized as "the collective consciousness," which we could tap into by creating "a global utilities network."

Inspired also by architect-designer Buckminster Fuller, futurist John McHale, and cultural anthropologist Edward T. Hall, I began to read avidly in the field of information theory, cybernetics, and systems theory.

During this period I also seized on the opportunity to become the first "McLuhanesque" consultant and producer, and soon had a thriving business working with clients that included General Electric, Metromedia, Columbia Pictures, and Scott Paper.

I wrote a synthesis of these ideas in my first book, *By the Late John Brockman* (1969), taking information theory – the mathematical theory of communications – as a model for regarding all human experience. A main theme that has continued to inform my work over the years: new technologies = new perceptions.

New technologies = new perceptions. Reality is a man-made process. Our images of our world and of ourselves are, in part, the models resulting from our perceptions of the technologies we generate as products.

Man creates tools and then molds himself in their image. Seventeenth-century clockworks inspired mechanistic metaphors ("the heart is a pump") just as mid-twentieth-century developments in self-regulating engineering devices resulted in the cybernetic image ("the brain is computer"), a disturbing idea to some people at the time that is now considered almost passé.

Some people can't even bear to think about this new epistemology. It tears apart the fabric of our habitual thinking. Subject and object fuse. The individual self decreates. As Gregory Bateson noted, it is a world of pattern, of order, of resonances in which the individual mind is a subsystem of a larger order. Mind is intrinsic to the messages carried by the pathways within the larger system and intrinsic also in the pathways themselves.

Key to this radical rebooting of our mindsets is the term *information,* which, in this scheme, refers to regulation and control and has nothing to do with meaning, ideas, or data. Bateson explained to me that "information is a difference that makes a difference." A raindrop that hits the ground behind you contains no information. The raindrop that hits you on the nose has information. Information is a measure of effect. Systems of control utilize information if and when they react to change to maintain continuity.

These ideas laid the groundwork for my thinking about the current communications revolution. If Newtonian physics taught us that it is the parts that matter, we now inhabit a universe that interacts infinitely with itself, where importance lies in the patterns that connect the parts. This becomes problematic because how can a system describe itself without generating a spiralling ladder of recursive mirrors?

The answer? "Nobody knows, and you can't find out." The description of the plane of language is the plane that holds our descriptions. Language becomes a commission, a dance, a play, a song.

With the Internet and the World Wide Web, we are creating a new extension of ourselves in much the same way as Mary

Shelley's Dr. Frankenstein pieced together his creation. Only this creation is not an anthropomorphic being that moves through accretive portions of space in time. It is instead, an emergent electronic beast of such proportions that we can only imagine its qualities, its dimensions.

Can it be ourselves?

Edward T. Hall once pointed out to me that the most significant, the most critical inventions of man were not those ever considered to be inventions, but those that appeared to be innate and natural. His candidate for the most important invention was not the capture of fire, not the printing press, not the discovery of electricity, not the discovery of the structure of DNA. Mankind's most important invention was...talking.

To illustrate the point, he told a story about a group of prehistoric cavemen having a conversation.

"Guess what?" the first man said. "We're talking."

Silence. The others looked at him with suspicion.

"What's talking?" a second man asked.

"It's what we're all doing, right now. We're talking!"

"You're crazy," the third man replied. "I never heard of such a thing!"

"I'm not crazy," the first man said, "you're crazy. We're talking."

Talking, undoubtedly, was considered to be innate and natural until the first man rendered it visible by exclaiming, "We're talking," a moment of great significance in the process of evolution.

A new invention has emerged, a code for the collective conscious. I call it "DNI," or "distributed networked intelligence."

DNI is the collective externalized mind, the mind we all share. DNI is the infinite oscillation of our collective conscious interacting with itself, adding a fuller, richer dimension to what it means to be human.

I am the Internet. I am the World Wide Web. I am information. I am *content.*

It's not about computers. It's about human communication.

"We're talking."

Introduction

CONTENT IN THE DIGITAL AGE

In January 1995, I invited the chairman of a publishing division of one of the mega-media convergence companies to lunch to talk about book projects. He had another agenda. The Board of Directors of his corporate parent had just handed down a mandate to division heads: digitize all assets. My luncheon guest was faced with the dreary prospect of digitizing thousands of backlist titles.

"I can arrange to have the keystroking done in India or the Philippines," he said. "But, after the files are digitized, then what do I do with the content?" "John," he continued, "you work with content providers. Perhaps you have some insight into how I can repurpose these paper-based assets."

Keystroking? Repurposing? Content providers? Paper-based assets?

Ten years before, in 1983, I added a computer disk image next to the book on the logo of my literary agency and announced our transition as the first "literary and software agency." Because I had moved quickly when the personal computer market exploded I enjoyed a substantial success as the agent for software developers and computer book authors and packagers who wanted to work with the large, well-funded New York publishers.

This business experience, coupled with my intellectual curiosity regarding communications, alerted me that something big was beginning to happen. I wasn't about to sit on the sidelines and watch it go by.

Thus I began a series of what I termed "digerati dinners," in San Francisco, San Mateo, Los Angeles, Phoenix, Barcelona, London, Seattle, Palo Alto, Cannes, New York, Sausalito, Milan, Monterey, Paris, Napa Valley, and Munich.

The questions driving my curiosity involved ideas about content in the digital age, how new approaches to the theories of description and language are critical to a new understanding, and how the anesthesiology of common sense stands in our way.

Stewart Brand, founder of The Well (Whole Earth 'Lectronic Link) points out in the *GBN Book Club Newsletter* that "Bits are bits, not things. As the economy shifts from primarily distributing things to primarily distributing bits, it is being transformed almost unrecognizably. The whole nature and flow of value is shifting. Not only is the business environment altering radically, the function of business itself is morphing. But toward what?"

Esther Dyson, publisher of the influential computer industry newsletter *Release 1.0.* writes in "Intellectual Property on the Net" (December 1994): "the future world of electronic content and commerce...is...not the world most intellectual property owners have been planning for, contracting for, securing rights for." Those ten thousand backlist titles in the warehouse (aka "paper-based assets") are not assets in the electronic information economy. Content does not sit in a warehouse or on your library shelf.

Content is context.

"Information is an Activity," writes John Perry Barlow in *Wired* ("The Economy of Ideas: A Framework for Rethinking Patents and Copyrights in the Digital Age – Everything You Know About Intellectual Property is Wrong.") "Information Is a Verb, Not a Noun. Freed of its containers, information is obviously not a thing. In fact, it is something that happens in the field of interaction between minds or objects or other pieces of information."

John Perry, who is cofounder of The Electronic Frontier Foundation, uses a medieval model of storytelling to render visible the new digital model. When stories are passed from generation to generation there is no definitive version, no authorized authorship. Thus, "digital information, unconstrained by packaging, is a continuing process." He sees a diminishing value in the traditional importance of authorship. In this new environment, according to Barlow, "information is a relationship, meaning has value and is unique to each case."

Text supplanted by billable interactivity is the hallmark of the "new media." He notes that "as people move into the Net, and increasingly get their information directly from its point of production, unfiltered by centralized media, they will attempt to develop the same interactive ability to probe reality that only experience has provided them in the past. Live access to these distant 'eyes and ears' will be much easier to cordon than access to static bundles of stored but easily reproducible information."

Esther Dyson sums up the business realities implicit in this new order. She envisions content-based value on the Net created through "services (the *transformation* of bits rather than the bits themselves), the selection of content, the presence of other people, and assurance of authenticity – reliable information about sources of bits and their future flows. In short, intellectual *processes* and *services* appreciate; intellectual *assets* depreciate."

Esther makes the radical suggestion that "content (including software) will serve as advertising for services such as support, aggregation, filtering, assembly, and integration of content modules, or training – or it will be a by-product of paid-for relationships. The likely best defense for content providers is to exploit that situation – to distribute intellectual property free in order to sell services and relationships. The provider's task is to figure out what to charge for and what to give away free – all in the context of what other providers are doing and what customers expect. *This is not a moral decision but a business strategy.*"

The end-users, according to her scheme, might be given access to works on the Net for free. "The payments to creators," she writes, "are likely to come not from the viewers, readers, or listeners, but from companies who use the content as – or to deliver – advertising. The challenge for advertisers is not being paid, but making sure that their advertising messages are inextricable from the content. The intellectual activity of agents – talent scouts, advisors, creative packagers – will be valuable and richly rewarded."

Value is in activity. A total synthesis of all human knowledge will not result in fantastic amounts of data, or in huge libraries filled with books. Information is process. There's no value any more in amount, in quantity, in explanation.

Value is in activity. *Content* is no longer a noun. *Content* is context. *Content* is activity. *Content* is relationship, community. *Content* is not text or pictures as distinct from the interactive components that provide access to them. *Content* is the interactive quality. *Content* is a verb, a continuing process. Value on the Internet will be created through services, the selection of programming, the presence of other people, and assurance of authenticity – reliable information about sources of bits. In short, intellectual *processes* and *services* will appreciate; intellectual *assets* will depreciate. *Content* is information, and information is not a thing. Value is in activity.

A year later, in February of 1996, the four keynote speakers at an Internet conference held at the Jacob K. Javitz Center in New York were arguably the key players shaping the future of the Internet.

Bill Gates, CEO of Microsoft, presented his plan to embrace and extend the new open technologies and allow Microsoft customers to interact with the Web through the integration of new versions of Microsoft desktop applications and Microsoft Explorer, a proprietary Web browser.

Jim Clark, Netscape's chairman, envisioned a new era of communications engendered by the development of telephone and communications technologies.

Steve Case, CEO of America Online, disagreed with the conventional wisdom that "content is king." He believed the battleground would not be just content but also context and community.

Scott McNealy, CEO of Sun Microsystems, viewed the Internet as example and extension of his dictums that the network is the computer and the network is the business.

According to Dr. Eddie Currie (general manager of MITS in 1974 and thus one of the founding fathers of the personal computer revolution): "If there is a single truism of the evolution of computers, computer technology, the Internet, it is that no one knows where it is going or precisely what drives it or in what direction."

This is perhaps another way of saying that we have grabbed the tail of an electronic beast so large that we can't begin to imagine its size or the impact it will have. All approaches reveal a different aspect of the beast. Yet all agree: it's the next big thing.

What is the nature of this next big thing? What kind of vocabulary do we need to describe it? Who is driving it? Who can render it visible for us? How does it change our culture, and ourselves? These are some of the questions that this book explores through my encounters with the members of the "cyber elite" I present in this book.

The "digerati" in this book are *a* cyber elite, and it is not my intention to define the group as *the* cyber elite. They are, I believe, representative of a much larger group of cyber elite, and as a group they constitute a critical mass of the doers, thinkers, and writers, connected in ways they may not even appreciate, who have tremendous influence on the emerging communication revolution surrounding the growth of the Internet and the World Wide Web. Although they all happen to be Americans, their activities have a worldwide impact.

Stewart Brand points out that "elites are idea and execution factories. Elites make things happen; they drive culture, civilization. They are usually a group of people who are good at what they do, have gotten into a meritocracy with others like themselves and force each other to get better. They want status, but it's not status necessarily in the commonly agreed domain; it's status within the game that they are playing. They are open to new members, provided entrance is based on merit. They may not be the elite in five years."

The digerati evangelize, connect people, adapt quickly. They like to talk with their peers because it forces them to go to the top of their form and explain their most interesting new ideas. They give each other permission to be great. That's who they want to talk to about the things they are excited about because they want to see if it plays. They ask each other the questions they are asking themselves, and that's part of what makes this cyber elite work.

A common characteristic is personal authority that, by and large, is not derived from institutional affiliation. The digerati pay close attention to each other. Not all of them necessarily communicate with each other, but they are interconnected in various ways, and are in personal communication with me, and in varying degrees, through me to each other. There is one overriding consideration that makes them an elite: they are at the helm of some of the most important developments of our time and they are a tremendous influence.

The new communications technologies change the terrain of everything. Huge corporations are finding that their entire companies are changing. None are changing as much as Internet and software companies. And they have become the companies that really matter. The individuals and corporations that dismiss this set of developments do so at the risk of marginalizing themselves.

Many of the brightest people in recent years have gone into computing (hardware, networking, software, Internet, convergence media). The cutting edge is in exploring new communications, such as the World Wide Web, through the use of computers.

Emerging out of the digerati are new ideas about how human beings communicate with each other. As communications is the basis of civilization, this is a book not about computers, not about technology, not about things digital: this is a book about our culture and ourselves. The ideas presented here offer a new set of metaphors to describe ourselves, our minds, the world, and all of the things we know in it, and it is the individuals presenting these new ideas and images, the digerati in the book (as well as others), who are driving this revolution.

In today's world, technological advances are taking place at a rate unparalleled at any other time in history. The very nature of change itself has evolved so quickly that a hallmark of the twentieth century is the uncertainty with which we all live. The ideas and information included in this book are essential to anyone interested in knowing who we are, and where we are headed. Our models and metaphors are in a state of flux. Our world and all of the things that we know in it are being radically altered and transformed. This is a book about a group of people who are reinventing culture and civilization.

I present the digerati; they present themselves. They are not *on* the frontier, they are *the* frontier. They are:

The Pragmatist (Stewart Alsop), The Coyote (John Perry Barlow), The Scout (Stewart Brand), The Seer (David Bunnell), The Thinker (Doug Carlston), The Idealist (Denise Caruso), The Statesman (Steve Case), The Gadfly (John C. Dvorak), The Pattern-Recognizer (Esther Dyson), The Software Developer (Bill Gates), The Conservative (David Gelernter), The Defender (Mike Godwin), The Genius (W. Daniel Hillis), The Judge (David R. Johnson), The Searcher (Brewster Kahle), The Saint (Kevin Kelly), The Prodigy (Jaron Lanier), The Marketer (Ted Leonsis), The Scribe (John Markoff), The Force (John McCrea), The Competitor (Scott McNealy), The Publisher (Jane Metcalfe), The Webmaster (Kip Parent), The Buccaneer (Louis Rossetto), The Citizen (Howard Rheingold), The Oracle (Paul Saffo), The Radical (Bob Stein), The Skeptic (Cliff Stoll), The Catalyst (Linda Stone), The Evangelist (Lew Tucker), The Cyberanalyst (Sherry Turkle), The Lover (Dave Winer), and The Impresario (Richard Saul Wurman).

JOHN BROCKMAN *New York City*

Note to Readers

From August 1995 to April 1996, I videotaped one-on-one discussions with thirty-six digerati about their work and the work of others included in the book. I had a multilevel agenda: (1) to write a book; (2) to use the material I gathered to supply the foundation for building an ongoing Web site devoted to the digerati.

This is not a general survey or a work of journalism, but rather an oral presentation of a culture. The book is an exhibition of this new community in action, communicating their ideas to the public and to one another.

Three of the digerati who graciously took the time to talk to me did not make it into the final text strictly because of temporal considerations. I talked to them early in the interview process. In the six months it took to complete the manuscript, the ground we had covered changed dramatically. Their work is important; they are worth knowing about. They are: Greg Clark, President, News Technology Group, News Corporation, "The Physicist"; Stewart McBride, chairman and chief creative officer of United Digital Artists, "The Maestro"; and Jerry Michalski, managing editor of *Release 1.0*, "The Pilgrim."

The selection of digerati is subjective and idiosyncratic, and far from comprehensive. Indeed, several other entirely different casts of characters could be assembled under the same book title. There are a number of obvious people missing that I am very much aware of and, indeed, I invited their participation.

In this book I am presenting "the first generation" of digerati: they are the people who got us here; they may not be the ones who push the envelope and get us to the next plateau. The Web is breeding a whole new generation of movers and shakers.

About a third of the digerati in the book I work with professionally: some of those are clients of Brockman, Inc., my literary and software agency. Several others run companies that are customers. Most are friends. Although HardWired is the publisher, I have no connection to *Wired* magazine (except as a paid subscriber) and the book is neither an endorsement nor critique of what some have called the "*Wired* culture."

I have taken the editorial license to create a written narrative in the voices of the digerati from my videotapes. Although the participants have read, and in some cases edited, the transcriptions of their spoken words, there is no intention that the following chapters in any way represent their writing. For that, read their books and articles. I have also made the assumption that the views of the digerati are of more interest to readers than any interpretations I might offer. I have thus written myself (and my questions) out of the text. Finally, remarks made by the participants about each other are general in nature and were not made in response to the text.

Digerati

<Stewart Alsop>

The Pragmatist

The Oracle: <Paul Saffo> *Stewart Alsop has played a number of different roles in this business. Despite his considerable expertise, he works very hard to keep the perspective of the reasonable businessperson asking what exactly does this mean for me. It is very much in the intellectual tradition of his family to speak and write articulately about things in a way that makes sense to ordinary people.*

Stewart Alsop is a partner in New Enterprise Associates, a venture capital firm, and a contributing editor to *InfoWorld,* of which he is the former editor-in-chief. He is executive producer of Agenda, an annual conference for executives of the computer industry.

Stewart Alsop is excited. "It's changed my life. I don't watch television anymore. I watch only the Internet now. It's an interesting thing to look at. First of all, I have an ISDN line at home, so I can get faster access to the Internet. That's crucial. The Net is fundamental, very compelling."

Stewart has been in the publishing business for twenty years – as editorial director of *InfoWorld,* a key trade weekly; as the publisher of a newsletter, *PC Letter;* and as the director of Agenda, an annual conference for power players in the PC industry. Stewart is "The Pragmatist." He likes doing business. He likes making money. He likes creating things that people are willing to pay for.

I have known Stewart since 1983. Over the years, we have spent time together at numerous conferences, professional events, and social occasions. He is always affable. I enjoy his easy company and appreciate the unique way he looks at the industry.

He brings the perspective of one who has grown up in the environment of serious, no-nonsense journalism. His father was Stewart Alsop; his uncle, Joseph Alsop. He can edit and write. He reads and thinks.

Although Stewart was raised in the epicenter of the Eastern establishment, he grew up as a typical American boy, watching a lot of TV, avoiding his schoolwork, and otherwise making trouble. As an adult, he kept watching TV, two or three hours a day, and always felt productive. Now he surfs the World Wide Web two or three hours a night. He still feels productive, even though he recognizes that surfing the Web is beginning to yield the same level of content as watching television.

Stewart makes the point that the Web is a precursor. It hasn't changed our lives yet, but it promises to alter our lives substantially. "If you start drilling down on what the Internet represents, or what the World Wide Web represents," he says, "you can see the kinds of changes in behavior that accompanied the arrival of roads and cars, trains, or airplanes. The Internet is something that can create entirely new ways of putting together communities and transacting our lives on a daily basis. It's hard to say how the Internet will ultimately change our lives, because we can't see the end point of it."

According to Stewart, no one has figured out how to make money off the World Wide Web. There are three reasons: (1) there are no tools; (2) there are no customers; (3) the technology doesn't really work. But to say you can't make any money off the Web is like saying you couldn't make money off PC software in 1978. Stewart believes that if the Web is going to change our lives substantially, there are going to be plenty of ways to make money, and some will be the ways we already make money.

"*InfoWorld* is a publisher," Stewart notes, "and we're going to figure out how to sell advertising over the Net. We'll probably make just as much money or more than we do by printing. We'll figure that out, and so will other people in their particular business, whether it's movies or books. The trick is to figure out new ways to make money on the Internet by selling to your customers."

Stewart wears many hats with aplomb and style, and has achieved a degree of influence in the industry far out of proportion to *InfoWorld*'s limited circulation of 310,000. Why? Because he left

InfoWorld for eight years to publish an important newsletter, and because his Agenda conferences draw many of the major industry figures. Or maybe it's just because he's been around for so long; people keep score and realize how many times he has been right.

The Pragmatist: <Stewart Alsop> Editors are the original intelligent agents. We try to figure out what our customers do, and we succeed to the degree that we're able to give them what they want, compel them, give them an identity, and make them feel that they're part of a community. I'm used to newsstands where there might be a hundred publications. There are literally thousands of things on the Web – lots of competition – and you have to think about which things are going to stand out in a reader's mind and make a neural connection. It's not just a matter of things changing every day. Change has to be relevant to the readership. You have to decide whom you're trying to talk to and what community you're operating in.

The Web has made people throw their sanity out the window. Even rational people in the publishing business sit around talking about warm bodies: "We've got 6 million people using the Web" or "We've got 10 million people using the Web." Finally I say, "Wait a minute. Are we going to throw away everything we know about publishing because this technology exists and just count warm bodies again?" Our job as editors or providers is to attract a particular audience, develop a sense of community. So it doesn't matter how many warm bodies there are on the World Wide Web. If you're going to talk about developing a sense of community on the Web, then you have to figure out what community you're talking to. You have to engage in that transaction. It's still a business.

The fundamental problem is push versus pull. Web sites are pull: you have to go to them. Newspapers are push: they arrive at your doorstep. Even though books are mostly push, there's pull in that you as a publisher have to convince your customers to go somewhere to get them. That changes the nature of what you do. Baseball games are pull: you have to get in your car and go to the stadium to watch the baseball game. A complex of motivations is acting on the customer. You've got to think about the motivations that must exist and the processes that must occur before a product actually reaches the customer.

I hate the notion of *content,* because it generalizes the value of creative effort by applying a generic word to it. If you're a writer, you write; if you're a movie producer, you produce movies. Being a content guy doesn't say anything about you. Content is talked about as though it's something you can pick up off the floor and throw together, and people are going to be compelled by it. Although I don't like the word *content,* it is the only way, across multiple disciplines, to describe what it is that digital publishers do. The generic word has to be specific to the audience. You can't presume that you're going to be able to deliver your product to a particular audience. You have to understand what motivates that audience to buy.

When we consider the mega-media companies – the "convergence companies" that have been created through mergers and acquisitions, such as Disney, Viacom, Time Warner, and Newscorp – we must focus on a fundamental issue: in any particular creative effort, there has to be somebody who understands how to motivate customers. Jeffrey Katzenberg was great at Disney because he knew how to get people out of their chairs and into movie theaters. If you're Sumner Redstone of Viacom, you have to have people who know how to put on TV shows, people who know how to produce movies, people who know how to publish books. Fundamentally, it's still a question of how to get people compelled by the content.

If I were talking about interactive content to the people running the media conglomerates, I would give them this advice: "Don't worry about it. It's a speck on your horizon. There is nothing that's going to be financially interesting or compelling to you, and you should ignore the whole thing, unless you want to protect your company from technological obsolescence. In that sense, you need to be personally involved and understand your company's Internet initiative. But you don't do it for your board of directors, and you don't do it to satisfy your shareholders, and you don't do it because it's financially motivating. You do it because you understand it's going to affect all of your businesses in the future. You will make money on it in the future, and in order to do so, you have to participate in it, understand it, and be involved with it."

The economic value of the Web is equal to the value of television, which is a multibillion-dollar business that people are dying to buy into. There are distribution and entertainment opportunities in the Web. They may not look like what we are used to seeing, but a whole culture of people out there finds surfing the Web a lot of fun. These people are going to pay to do that.

THE SCRIBE: <JOHN MARKOFF> Stewart's role in the industry is to bring people together. Stewart was once my boss at *InfoWorld.* The son of a distinguished journalistic family, he came in and tried to take over *InfoWorld* and turn it into a boring trade publication. Three of us quit, but I managed to stay friends with him. He has good insights, he gives good quote. His conferences are well done. He's got a wry sense of humor. One of his problems is that this industry has just bubbled over with money so that he's been able to coast a little bit. I don't think Stewart's had to push himself as hard as he might have.

THE SEER: <DAVID BUNNELL> Alsop is a journalist in the true sense of the word. He is perceptive, skeptical, talented, and not for sale. His opinions are valued and interesting because he won't allow himself to be corrupted by all the forces that swirl around him. He is a breath of fresh air in a jaded industry.

THE PATTERN-RECOGNIZER: <ESTHER DYSON> Stewart Alsop is one of those people who is a year or two ahead of the marketplace, and he's got a very good nose for how people are going to think. He's probably the best weather forecaster I know.

THE IDEALIST: <DENISE CARUSO> Stewart Alsop gave me my start in this business; how can I say anything about him? He's truly a pragmatist. Of most people in the PC business, Stewart's the one guy who focuses on the customer. At least he used to when he was an editor. I hope his becoming a "vulture" capitalist doesn't change him.

THE GADFLY: <JOHN C. DVORAK> I'm kind of disappointed that Stewart became a venture capitalist recently. Now I have to see if there is a hidden agenda in what he's writing about. I can't believe he did it because he needed the money.

THE STATESMAN: <STEVE CASE> Stewart has always had a common man's view of technology, whether it was in the early days when he was writing for consumer-oriented business publications, or now, as he writes for industry trade publications. Somehow in the sea of announcements, with every company claiming the latest, greatest feature, he's had a deft touch in divining what's real and what's not real, and who's going to really make a difference. He's proven to be remarkably pragmatic over a very long period of time.

THE MARKETER: <TED LEONSIS> Stewart Alsop is an incredibly sharp thinker and the world's worst golfer. He wants to come off a lot meaner and tougher than he really is. You go have a beer with Stewart and you'll have a great time. What's interesting is the clarity in his thinking. Stewart's been right more than wrong, which is something you can't say for most of the people that have been in the business for fifteen years.

THE IMPRESARIO: <RICHARD SAUL WURMAN> Stewart has created and runs perhaps the best of the focused meetings. He backs it up with great style, incisive writing, and an indulgent show-biz attitude to the deep-pocket high rollers in the business. If I had to choose two conferences to attend, his would be the second.

<John Perry Barlow>

The Coyote

The Saint: <Kevin Kelly> *John Perry Barlow is resident senator of cyberspace, and he's probably the first politician to play cyberspace. He basically holds an unelected office: he is in many ways the spokesperson representing the Internet to the outside world, and not to everybody's liking. Barlow is a humanist and in part a mystic, but he is also very technically savvy and eloquent. He has a long career ahead of him as the senator from cyberspace.*

John Perry Barlow is cofounder of the Electronic Frontier Foundation, a former lyricist for the Grateful Dead, and a former Wyoming cattle rancher.

John Perry Barlow's writings resonate throughout the Internet and inform many of the debates springing up about freedom of expression and the challenges raised by the medium. John is "The Coyote."

Any email from John Perry is a cyber-event. His emails may tell you he is a "Cognitive Dissident," a cofounder of Electronic Frontier Foundation (EFF, a group dedicated to preserving civil liberties in cyberspace), and that his home(stead)page is *www.eff.org/~barlow.* Or the email may chronicle Barlow in meatspace – today he's in France at the Hotel Martinez in Cannes, but soon he'll be passing through Amsterdam, Winston-Salem, San Francisco, San Jose, and Pinedale, Wyoming.

He also spends time at the White House. He hangs out with the homeless on the Bowery. He lectures the world's business leaders at the Davos Economic Conference in Switzerland. He tells the CIA what to do. He's as comfortable traveling in *Air Force II* (probably waiting for an upgrade to *Air Force I*), as he is participating in an anonymous chat group on the Internet. He knows everybody worth knowing, and that includes an array of the world's most beautiful and intelligent women.

A woman with whom he was especially close might be mentioned in an email, along with John Perry's late friend and colleague, Jerry Garcia of the Grateful Dead: "In Memoriam, Dr. Cynthia Horner and Jerry Garcia." (Cynthia died of a heart attack in April 1994 on a flight from Los Angeles to New York, just a few hours after John dropped her off at the airport. She was a psychiatrist, vivacious and exciting. They were very much in love and intended to spend the rest of their lives together. She was two days shy of her thirtieth birthday. John was devastated.)

I met Cynthia twice, once in 1993 when John invited me to a meeting of the EFF at an East Village restaurant, and again at a fundraising dinner for the Dalai Lama. John was a changed man. He had gone from being a bit of a grouch to a happy, smiling guy.

Prior to those encounters, John had visited me in Connecticut on two occasions. One visit was to a weekend meeting of the Reality Club, where he was one of three speakers, the others being Buddhist scholar Robert Thurman of Columbia University and biologist Robert Weinberg of the Whitehead Institute at MIT, the discoverer of the oncogene. In his talk, John Perry laid out many of his ideas about what he considers to be a new communications revolution. His talk was well received by the group of luminaries present. (It's probably the cowboy outfit that lets him get away with quoting Jesuit philosopher Teilhard de Chardin.) He's authored numerous seminal screeds, including "The Economy of Ideas" and "A Declaration of Cyberspace Independence," but is unable to finish his book. (Thankfully, I do not represent him.)

My ultimate Barlovian moment occurred at a dinner, when I seated John Perry across from Lord George Weidenfeld, friend and advisor to prime ministers, presidents, and popes. For The Coyote, Weidenfeld was a man who played the game at a global level. As the evening unfolded, I watched and listened to the two raconteurs take measure of each other. I slipped into a state of awe and wonder as His Lordship and John Perry engaged in a ritual I would characterize as the incantation of the names: "Jackie Onassis." "Chaim Weizmann." "Jerry Garcia." "Harold Wilson." "Tim Leary." "Princess Diana." "Teilhard de Chardin." "John Paul II." "JFK, Jr." "Helmut Kohl." "Al Gore." Across the generations, the cultures, a close bond was formed. After coffee, as His Lordship rose to leave, John Perry stood, took his hand, looked at him with admiration and earnestness, and asked, "But, George, don't you think the sixteenth was a much more ironic century than the seventeenth?"

THE COYOTE: <JOHN PERRY BARLOW> The big error with information has been mistaking the container for the content. When we started turning information into a product post-Gutenberg, it was easy to think that the product was the book; we set up a huge industrial apparatus to create those objects, dealing with them like other manufactured goods. In terms of distribution, there wasn't a useful distinction to be made between books and toasters. We're still focused on this idea that information is a product, a property, a thing, that it's made out of atoms and not out of bits. We have failed to recognize that information occurs fluidly and interactively in the space between two areas of the mind, and exists only in that sense. Trying to own information in the standard property model doesn't work. Property is something that can be taken from you. If I own a horse and you steal it, I can't ride it anymore, and its value has been lost to me. But if I have an idea and you steal it, not only do I still have the same idea, but the fact that two people now have that idea makes it intrinsically more valuable. It has gained in value by virtue of your stealing it. The fundamental aspect of an information economy is its ability to fight entropy and to increase in value and complexity. We aren't going to be able to fully harness that economy until we start recognizing that.

Data differs from information. You can gather infinite sets of data with machines, but in order to convert data into information, a human mind has to process that data set and find it meaningful. That's the important difference between information and other kinds of products. Products of the physical world are generally themselves, regardless of their context. A toaster is a toaster is a toaster. In the informational world, however, each piece of information draws value from its direct relevance to the area of mind that is finding it meaningful or not meaningful. This is an aspect of information economy that's hard for people to wrap their heads around, because they're so used to having everything reduced to the common physical level.

The next layer is experience, which also differs from information. Experience is the real-time interactive relationship between the sensorium and all the phenomena that the sensorium has available to it, either by means of telecommunications or by means of presence within the context. Every synapse in my body is assessing my surrounding environment, is in an interactive relationship with it, is testing it, is on the alert – unlike information, which in most cases is something taken from the realm of experience and compressed into a format that eviscerates and alienates.

Information is like a life jerky: dried up and not terribly communicative. Through information you come back to the vast set of phenomena that is creating the data in the first place. Experience and the universe itself are intimately bound up with one another. The purpose of the Internet and all its surrounding phenomena is to create a context where experience is universal, and the informational reduction is no longer necessary. It becomes possible for me to ask questions in real time of phenomena that are taking place where my body is not. That's an important distinction, because people tend to develop their map of the world based on information, and most information is being generated by large accumulating engines that have a set of prime directives that are not necessarily in the service of accuracy or truth.

Intellectual property is an oxymoron. The intellect implies a relationship in the sense that if you have a distilled set of meaningful experiences, or the artifact of meaningful experiences, the way in which you communicate those to me, even if you're an old-style broadcaster, is by establishing some kind of relationship with me. In the broadcast model, that relationship was as asymmetrical as broadcasters could make it, and technology was what made it asymmetrical. In reality, if your objective is understanding, you want to simulate experience as much as possible, because that's where understanding comes from. What you want to do is to put yourself in a condition where you can ask as many questions of the information generator, the information source, as possible so that you can fine-tune the perceptions of the information source to match your remaining questions.

There has always been a relationship between the performer and the audience that hasn't been well mapped, but is extremely vivid to me. In the case of the Grateful Dead, for example, the audience was a very active part of the performance. They created the performance, in a sense. They knew what the band was going to play before the band did and almost telepathically communicated that to the band. Things of an informational nature should be regarded as are love or friendship. You would never claim to own your friendships. You would never regard them as property. An ideal informational exchange is more like friendship than it is like the exchange of physical goods.

People who think that there is a useful reason to stick with the intellectual-property model from the physical world need to think about an environment where there is no discernible difference between the principal article of commerce and speech. As long as you assume you need to contain that article of commerce in a property model, there is no way you can adhere to that model without diminishing freedom of expression. The point of copyright to begin with was to increase freedom of expression and distribution. We've now entered into a condition where it will have exactly the opposite effect.

The EFF defends the borders of cyberspace against hegemonic incursions by various power sources of the terrestrial world. The problem is that most of the major foci of power in the terrestrial world are artifacts of the Industrial Revolution. The nation-state was created to serve the needs and purposes of industry. After the decline of the industrial period, those relatively stable power relationships go up for grabs, and the institutions that feel their power waning will become all the more draconian in their efforts to assert it. That which cannot be held by common consensus is always held by force. We have to gear up for what I think of as a revolution.

Cyberspace is naturally anti-sovereign. We need to prepare ourselves for the efforts of the terrestrial governments to compromise that spirit, which they are now trying to do. Every government trying to control cyberspace is doing so under the pretext of its own cultural bogeymen. In the United States, we're sexually obsessed, largely because our media have been putting us in a constant priapic condition, and our religion and culture have been telling us that it's not OK to have a hard-on. We're in this terrible double bind. There's a huge cognitive dissonance between the images that we're bombarded with and the moral teachings that we're given by our established culture.

In Germany, they want to control cyberspace to keep the skin-heads from using it. In Iran, they want to control it to keep people from having infidel conversations or having inappropriate contact between the sexes. Every culture is going to try to use its primary bogeymen to give it an excuse to go into cyberspace and ride roughshod over it. The pornography issue in the United States is nothing but a stalking horse for control.

What we have here is attempted governance by the completely clueless, in a place they've never been, using tools that they don't possess. When I go to Washington I feel like Tom Paine must have felt when he visited the court of King George in about 1770. The audacity of these people to claim moral right to govern an area where they've never even been is stupefying.

THE ORACLE: <PAUL SAFFO> Barlow is cyber-coyote. His job is to be out there in the darkness beyond the end of the campfire reflecting back what's going on in the light and reminding us that there is change and chops in all directions.

THE DEFENDER: <MIKE GODWIN> Barlow took the frontier metaphor and enabled us to think about the online world as a place, like the original American frontier – a place in the process of being settled. At the same time, he observed that it is a place whose "aboriginal inhabitants" are being threatened by the unthinking encroachments of the settlers, and that in cyberspace we must avoid the mistakes we made a couple of centuries ago when we explored and exploited the actual physical frontiers of this country.

THE SOFTWARE DEVELOPER: <BILL GATES> There are some people, like Barlow, who are famous because they're famous.

THE STATESMAN: <STEVE CASE> Barlow is one of the more fascinating personalities in cyberspace. A lot of us are pretty dull. If you spend time with Barlow it's a wake-up call. It's an adrenaline rush to have a conversation with him.

THE LOVER: <DAVE WINER> I don't know what John Perry Barlow's game is. I don't know what he wants out of all this stuff. I guess it's not money, right? He says some outrageous things that are clearly not true and are dangerous. I read his "Declaration of Independence for Cyberspace," which was widely linked to and quoted on the Net around the time when the Communications Decency Act was coming out, and was totally appalled. Barlow implies that they can't get you in cyberspace. It's not true. It's clear that they can get you. People could take risks based on what he's said, and they could end up in jail, dead, or hurt.

THE SCRIBE: <JOHN MARKOFF> There is a phenomenon that began in the early '80s where people have been sucked into this industry. Barlow was sucked in, and he's nothing if not an opportunist. He has made a niche for himself. Barlow enjoys being close to people in power, and that's not very becoming. He's the kind of guy who likes to fly in *Air Force II.*

THE IMPRESARIO: <RICHARD SAUL WURMAN> My first impression of JPB – and I suspect most people's – is the now boring cowboy description. Boy, were we all wrong. Although slightly holier-than-thou for a daily dose, he's massively smart, clear, and passionate, and is everybody's strange choice for the conscience of the industry.

THE CITIZEN: <HOWARD RHEINGOLD> John Perry Barlow is an intellectual ecosystem of his own; his uniqueness has a lot to do with his appeal. His acute perception of the political realities of this new medium was crucial in forming what has become an increasingly formidable grassroots political force of people who believe in free expression because this medium has shown us its power. But I often wish he would choose his words more carefully. He has a weakness for rhetoric.

THE SEER: <DAVID BUNNELL> Barlow lives on the edge. He survives by being brilliant, iconoclastic, and entertaining to his hosts. He's the life of the party. His verbal skills and wit are legendary. I hope that the battle over Net censorship has given him motivation to stay focused long enough to do something meaningful with his talent. He runs a great 100-yard dash, but has not yet completed a marathon.

THE GADFLY: <JOHN C. DVORAK> John Perry Barlow has developed into a marvelous sound-bite man. He's got little jazzy riffs that he probably works on. But he's a lyricist, so I guess that makes sense. He's the poet among this crowd.

<Stewart Brand>

The Scout

The Citizen: <Howard Rheingold>

What's unrecognized about Stewart is that he's a designer. He designed The Well to be something that wouldn't require his running it. He designed the Whole Earth Review *and the* Whole Earth Catalog *to be self-sustaining communities. We need more mavericks like him. The world has become too much of an intellectual monoculture of people who belong to corporations and who don't question the established way of doing things.*

Stewart Brand is founder of the *Whole Earth Catalog*, cofounder of The Well, cofounder of Global Business Network, and author of *How Buildings Learn* (1994) and *The Media Lab: Inventing the Future at MIT* (1987).

A great deal of discussion regarding the Internet often seems to ask, What the hell is the Internet? Stewart likes to point out two reasons for that: it is new and it keeps changing. "It keeps changing," he notes, "partly because the technology is moving and partly because it is basically a grassroots phenomenon where the users are constantly reinventing the technology, constantly reinventing what would be fun to do on it, what would be useful to do on it. Each time you begin to think you have an idea what the Net is, it turns into something else. This was not the case with broadcast television or broadcast radio, which settled down within a couple of decades and then remained the same for twenty, thirty, forty years. The Net can't hold still for even ten months."

I first met Stewart thirty years ago at the headquarters of USCO ("us" company), an anonymous group of artists whose installations and events combined multiple audio and visual inputs, including film, slides, video, lighting, music, and random sounds. USCO's mantra, "We Are All One," had already been altered to "We Are All One...except Brockman" in order to accommodate my involvement. In 1963, the group had erected a Psychedelic Tabernacle in a church half an hour outside Manhattan in Garnerville, New York. It became an obligatory stop for every seeker and guru passing through the area. Stewart lived there (in the steeple) for a while.

Stewart was fascinated with the USCO community of artists – including painter Steve Durkee, poet Gerd Stern, and filmmaker Jud Yalkut – and with Rockland County neighbors such as John Cage and his crowd, all of whom were reading, studying, and debating Marshall McLuhan's ideas on communications. In fact, at one point USCO went on tour with McLuhan and provided an "intermedia" counterpoint to his talks.

Clearly, some of the interesting thinking about the Internet has its origins in ideas formulated by the artists of the '60s, which, wittingly or unwittingly, were carried forward by the enthusiastic young Lieutenant Brand. Considerations of form and content, context, community, and even the hacker ethic all were presaged in part by activities and discussions during that period.

Stewart, who preferred the term *multimedia* to *intermedia,* performed his own piece, "America Needs Indians," from 1964 to 1966 and performed "War: God" from 1967 to 1970. He organized The Trips Festival in January 1966 and created the Whole Earth button in March 1966 (it read: "Why Haven't We Seen a Photograph of the Whole Earth Yet?"). He is best known to my generation as the founder, editor, and publisher of the *Whole Earth Catalog.* I recall visiting him in Menlo Park, California, in 1968 while he was working on the original catalog. His wife at the time, Lois, a Native American mathematician, spent an entire day working on the catalog with a layout person while Stewart and I sat together reading and underlining a copy of Norbert Wiener's *Cybernetics.* I still have that copy.

Several months later, the oversized catalog arrived packed in a long tube. Reading it – or should I say devouring it? – was a memorable intellectual experience. More than any other book for me, the original *Whole Earth Catalog* captured the moment and defined the intellectual climate of the times. A subsequent edition, *The Last Whole Earth Catalog,* published in 1971, was a number-one best-seller and won Stewart the National Book Award.

During the '70s, Stewart often talked about his vision for what he called the *personal computer,* a term he is often credited with inventing, although he is quick to point out that Alan Kay deserves credit for its coinage. "Alan credits me for being the first to use it in print in '74 in my book *Two Cybernetic Frontiers,*" Stewart says. "I don't recall others using it as a term, and I didn't think I was doing a coinage, just describing the Xerox Alto in an epilogue in the book. By '75 I did use it as the name of a regular section in the *CoEvolution Quarterly,* well before personal computers existed."

As a friend, Stewart can be a challenge. I called him once in the '70s upon arriving at the San Francisco airport.

"Hi, I'm in town for a few days."

"Uh huh."

"What's happening?"

"Busy."

"Want to get together?"

"Nope."

What a charmer. For a cold fish, he has a special kind of charisma. Who else could grant an entire generation permission to wear sandals, hug trees, live off the land and be self-sufficient (i.e., poor), wear penknives on their belts – while at the same time pursuing the intellectual edges of our era?

In 1983, around the time IBM presented its first personal computer, Stewart and his colleagues at *CoEvolution Quarterly* quickly leapt at my suggestion that they seize the opportunity to carry their franchise into this new area. I presented their ten-page proposal for the *Whole Earth Software Catalog* to several publishers. Several days later, an editor from Doubleday called to make a preemptive offer of $1 million, which after several hours of negotiation became $1.3 million. A response was required within twelve hours or the offer would be withdrawn.

Stewart thought the offer "too much money." "It might screw us up," he said. Then he announced that he needed to talk to his financial advisor. At midnight, New York time, he finally phoned me. "Can't get ahold of him," he said. "Think I'll stay up tonight and do the *I Ching*. I'll call you in the morning."

The *I Ching?* Stewart had just been offered the largest advance in the history of publishing for a paperback original – and he was going to spend the night consulting the *I Ching* for a decision? Fortunately, the forces of ancient wisdom overcame the quixotic voices in Stewart's head. He went for it.

In 1983, Stewart sent Dick Farson and Darryl Iconogle of the Western Behavioral Science Institute to see me in New York about a piece of conferencing software called the Onion, which was being used on a bulletin board system called EIES (Electronic Information Exchange System) and run by Murray Turoff. When I demurred, Stewart told me I could be a player or I could choose to sit out the biggest development of the decade.

Sit it out I did, without regret, except I found that I had become a grayed-out area on Stewart's screen. Our typical '80s telephone conversation went as follows:

"Hi, what's up."

(tap-tap-tap-tap-tap) "Busy, talking to somebody online." (tap)

Stewart was right and wrong. It is the biggest development of the '90s, not the '80s. Inspired by EIES, in 1984 Stewart cofounded The Well (Whole Earth 'Lectronic Link), a computer teleconference system for the San Francisco Bay Area, considered a bellwether of the genre. But The Well was not for me. I couldn't deal with its clunky interface. Nor was I interested in the self-consciousness of the community, which, strangely, seemed to have adopted many of Stewart's linguistic mannerisms.

Over the past few years, sbb (his user name) has spent a great deal of his time making ideas safe for the Global 500 clients of Global Business Network (GBN), the consulting firm he cofounded in 1988 with futurist Peter Schwartz and philosopher Jay Ogilvy. He can now toss around the acronyms for major conglomerates as fluidly as he once threw a Frisbee. His place became secure in 1995 when the October 16 issue of *Fortune* ran a twelve-page profile of his pursuits entitled "The Electric Kool-Aid Management Consultant."

Stewart has evolved into a legendary figure, historic even, who is, year in and year out, the most interesting and influential thinker I know.

Stewart Brand is "The Scout."

THE SCOUT: <STEWART BRAND> There's a major disjunction between the speed of computer technology, biotechnology, and nanotechnology, on the one hand, and the speed of environmental direness and maybe civilizational direness, on the other. You used to be able to think in terms of many generations or many administrations. Winston Churchill liked that the monarchy emphasized generations. People who elect democratically think in much shorter terms.

Danny Hillis and I are putting together the Clock Library, to relengthen civilization's attention span. It will be a physical facility that is both a big slow charismatic clock and something we're calling "a library," which may or may not be recognized as a working library by the time it's actually been built. The Clock Library's function is to help people think about the depth of time both backwards and forwards, and take responsible relationship personally to that. The project is the exact analog of the photograph of the Earth from space from the Apollo spacecraft in the late 1960s, which almost instantly engendered the ecology movement. The trick is to find something that works for understanding time the way that photograph worked for understanding the Earth as a beautiful and fragile planet. The board members are Esther Dyson, Doug Carlston, Kevin Kelly, Danny Hillis, Paul Saffo, Mitch Kapor, Brian Eno, Peter Schwartz, and myself. People like them are flying very fast and are also thinking about having a place to land.

We want to make a clock that, as Danny says, "ticks once a year, bongs once a century, and cuckoos once every thousand years" – because we are living at the cutting edge of technology, constantly and rapidly creating new technological environments, becoming more and more aware that we've made the future opaque to ourselves. For instance, trying to imagine what the World Wide Web might be in fifteen years is a meaningless pursuit. Too much is going to happen between now and then in that domain to think usefully about it.

The peculiarity of the new devices on the Internet is that you've got a double acceleration or a double instability. First there's Moore's Law, the fact that the number of processors on a chip, and thus computer power, keeps doubling every eighteen months, decade after decade. Then there's Metcalfe's Law: the value of a net goes up as the square of the number of people on that net. That is to say the Net itself or any net – even one made up of faxes or cellular telephones – increases dramatically in value the more people are on it. You've got a double-runaway phenomenon. Throw into that the tools that suddenly turn up, like the World Wide Web, Mosaic, and later Netscape Navigator, which also can become dramatically empowering in short order. The Net is a major social event. Culture's got to change.

The theory of scaling says that when you change scale you change quality. It may not apply in familiar ways on the Net, because the Net is ground-up: it's grassroots, people connecting directly with one another. It's geodesic, rather than hierarchical, in that all of the players connect directly with each other instead of going through some leadership structure. The problems you get with growth and scale in hierarchical systems will not occur in geodesic grassroots systems like the Net. Something different will happen, and it's too early to discern what.

When there were three or four hundred of us on The Well, people started saying, "What happens when we get another hundred people on here? We're going to lose this wonderful sense of community." A few years later there were ten thousand people on The Well, and everyone was still bitching about the same problem. It turned out that scaling up a magnitude or two did not present the problems people thought it would. You get communities within communities. You get private conferences where there's a very intense community of thirty or forty or one hundred people who feel just as strongly about each other and the things they're interested in as they did when The Well was very small. A granularity keeps reasserting itself, and it may make some of the usual scaling problems irrelevant.

The Well computer teleconferencing system was essentially a gift from a friend who had some software to spare, a little bit of money, and a Vax minicomputer to loan. When it started in 1984, it was connected to *CoEvolution Quarterly*, which had a community feel, and it was another way for people who used the magazine to contact each other.

Within two years, it had attracted a particular group of people who were intensely interested in talking to each other online, the Deadheads. That was enough of a protocommunity for a real electronic community to take shape, where marriages and births and deaths and suicides and other profound personal changes all took place and were brought to life through the prism of this online connection. It worked as a community partly because it was set up as a regional system and partly because we insisted that people be identifiable. Anonymity was not allowed. Bright, eloquent people, both hackers and journalists, were involved from the very beginning.

Something else is going on here. To a large extent, value on the Internet is not being created by businesses, as much as they want all kinds of credit and money for creating this wonderful value. Inventors, folks who are coming up with new tools, are creating it. Some of them are well harnessed by businesses, but it turns out that businesses don't have to exist for them to harness themselves with the Net and get these things out there. For example, the person who created Eudora is a University of Illinois fellow who did it basically for himself and people he knew. In terms of quality, Eudora is visibly beyond any other email program. It makes you wonder what's wrong with companies, what prevents them from doing the right thing when a random person puts his exquisite tool out on the Net for free. This happened with Eudora, and later with Mosaic, which led to a commercial version, Netscape Navigator.

The inventors of these tools are not crazed codgers in basements. They are, by and large, young people with a sense of social and cultural responsibility who want things to be better for everybody. They are as valuable as our snazziest scientists, but are not accorded the respect or rewards of the snazzy scientists. They are taken for granted more than they should be. Something is wrong if we think inventors are a lower order of being than theoretical scientists.

People are surprised by the intensity and intimacy of online communication, but they shouldn't be. You could probably find a parallel for what's going on by comparing the correspondences and the books of past intellectuals. The quality of writing in their letters is often different and frequently better than that in their books. A letter has intimacy and eloquence because it's addressed to a known audience of people the author respects, whose opinions he or she cares about. It's not written for an enormous, anonymous audience, like the readership you would assume for a book. That intimacy makes for a much higher quality of writing and discourse. You could say it's the relationship that makes the difference. Speed that up, and you've got online teleconferencing.

THE DEFENDER: <MIKE GODWIN> Stewart Brand brings two important things to the table. The first is that he understands that human beings are tool-using creatures. It's important that we use the best tools, and that we understand our tools and the consequences of the tools we use. The second thing Stewart offers is his role as a contrarian – he's very much in the habit of taking the conventional wisdom and asking what the opposite view is. He forces people to question their assumptions about technology, society, and the relationship between the two.

THE GADFLY: <JOHN C. DVORAK> When you go to the roots of the New Age movement, which I think is a negative thing, you'll find Stewart in there kicking the old crankcase to get the engine started. He promoted a lot of the kind of touchy-feely parts of the New Age movement. He's the early touchy-feely guy. That stuff is crap. He is not a player anymore. I wish he were, though. He's an insightful guy, but I think he's left himself out of the picture.

THE IMPRESARIO: <RICHARD SAUL WURMAN> Early my idol, Stewart still impresses me with the power of what seems like some of his gentle choices. Although I'm an architect, I didn't know where he was going at first with his choice of the investigation of buildings. He appears so courageous to me as I limit my projects to the obvious and generic.

THE SCRIBE: <JOHN MARKOFF> Stewart understood the importance of personal computing before anybody else outside the very small hacker community did. He was the first reporter to reach the promised land and bring it back to the world. He has continued to reinvent himself; he has found new things to look at and hasn't stuck in the same circles, whether it's architecture, new media, or the personal computer. He also has a wonderful wry sense of humor.

THE PATTERN-RECOGNIZER: <ESTHER DYSON> He has had the courage and the open-mindedness to change over the course of his life. He is now one of the wisest, smartest, most sensible people I know. He has also become very kind.

THE COYOTE: <JOHN PERRY BARLOW> Stewart is a magnificent piece of informational arbitrage. He has contained within his personality a lot of contradictory impulses that make him very fertile. There's something very conservative about Stewart. He's a flinty, Presbyterian, military sort of guy. Yet he was also the organizer of the first "Acid Test." Whenever I see those kinds of contrasts, I know there's creative potential. The more the difference is, the greater difference it makes, the more voltage there is across the gap.

THE IDEALIST: <DENISE CARUSO> Stewart is so smart he's scary. I would love to spend a year wandering around inside of his brain. Opening doors. Opening trunks. Looking around in closets. If he could bottle the way he evaluates the world, I'd be first in line for a big dose.

THE CYBERANALYST: <SHERRY TURKLE> Stewart Brand has looked at evolving culture and recognized what was genuinely new. And he has been able to do this again and again, always seeing the world with fresh eyes. A great talent.

<DAVID BUNNELL>

THE SEER

THE SCRIBE: <JOHN MARKOFF> *David was present at the creation of the personal computer industry, and he had this wonderful insight. He essentially helped create the personal computer magazine industry.*

DAVID BUNNELL is founder of *PC Magazine, PC World, MacWorld, Personal Computing,* and *New Media,* and is president and CEO of Content.Com, Inc., a digital publishing company.

You wouldn't expect that the personal computer would have been invented and commercialized in 1974 by a company of twenty employees called MITS in Albuquerque. You would expect that the personal computer would have come out of the labs at IBM or Xerox PARC. But that's not what happened, and David Bunnell was present at the creation, having left his job as a sixth-grade teacher in the Chicago public schools to find his place in what he perceived to be a new and important industry.

"One of the more interesting things that happened," he recalls, "was that two fellows in Cambridge, Massachusetts, noticed the Altair on the cover of the January 1975 issue of *Popular Electronics* and got very excited about working at MITS to develop software for this first personal computer. Their names were Bill Gates and Paul Allen. They created a basic language program for the Altair and called us up and said, 'Gee, wouldn't you like to have Basic for the Altair?' The company president, Ed Roberts, who is regarded by many as the father of the personal computer, replied, 'Well, if you can show us that it works, we'd love to have it.'

"Paul Allen hopped on an airplane and flew to Albuquerque and demonstrated that Basic worked, even though Paul and Bill hadn't seen an Altair. They created the Basic language interpreter on a mainframe computer at Harvard University using an emulator for the 8080 Intel chip that was the brains of the Altair. The entire personal computer industry sprung out of MITS, and the Altair, and Paul Allen and Bill Gates."

That David happened to be at the right place at the right time and was able to take advantage of it was probably no accident. And that circumstance has been a hallmark of his career in the personal computer industry. He was not a technical person like everybody else; it was his job as a writer and an editor to interpret the personal computer for people who wanted to use it, to explain what you could do with it, and to help market it. That became his role not just at MITS but in the industry at large. At MITS, David and his colleagues created the first retail computer stores, the first computer conventions, the first publications. David is "The Seer," a player from the very beginning.

David is best known among his peers not for his stunning successes in promoting the personal computer magazine industry but for his idealistic and deeply humanistic vision. (Perhaps this just means that he's not quite as greedy as his counterparts in the computer revolution.) He devotes his considerable energies and resources to this end. One of his favorite projects is Computers and You, a program he founded at San Francisco's Glide Memorial Church to give hundreds of underprivileged kids and homeless adults computer training every day.

I met David in 1983. Together we made the front page of the *Wall Street Journal* when I, representing his magazine *PC World,* sold a line of computer books for a newsworthy sum to Simon & Schuster. This publishing deal was a prime example of the dictum that the people who make money in a gold rush are the ones selling eggs at $10 apiece.

I ran into him in March 1995 at the Intermedia show in San Francisco. Over a drink at the Clift Hotel, we decided to join forces and form a digital publishing company, Content.Com, Inc. As president and CEO, David would run the company out of San Francisco. As chairman, I would be in New York spending half my time on this new venture. Allen & Company, Incorporated, the New York media investment banking firm, became the third partner.

We recruited a board of advisors, many of whom are in this book, including: John Perry Barlow, Stewart Brand, Doug Carlston, John C. Dvorak, Esther Dyson, Danny Hillis, David R. Johnson, Jaron Lanier, Howard Rheingold, Paul Saffo, Cliff Stoll, and Sherry Turkle. Content.Com's opening announcement included its motto – *The default site for intelligent people on the Internet* – and stated the following:

> Content.Com, Inc., founded in September 1995, is a digital publishing company that will launch an Internet site envisioned as a virtual community, a "place" in cyberspace built around contemporary thinkers, writers, artists, musicians, filmmakers, technologists, and scientists, who represent their creative work, their lives, and the questions they are asking themselves.

In the Internet revolution, David sees the possibility of an optimistic future that can rescue us from the materialistic and misguided conceptions of a personal computer revolution gone wrong.

David and I have been talking several times a day for a year. He wears well. He's the real thing.

THE SEER: <DAVID BUNNELL> There's a misconception among major publishers – and some smaller publishers as well – who seem to feel that they have this tremendous asset because they're magazine publishers. Their magazines have been coming out every week for fifty years, and they have all this text, and somehow if it can just be digitized, they can put it online and sell it for lots of money. Book publishers have the rights to different books, and movie companies have the rights to films and have film libraries, and they think that this is a tremendous asset. Well, it's not. If anything, it's an impediment to the new media age. Just as it has been for upstart media in the past, the content for a particular medium has to be created fresh and has to take advantage of the capabilities and characteristics of the new medium. The idea that old media have any value in this new world is misguided.

People who understand the technology and the online experience are beginning to create content that's exclusive to that medium. It's not that different from when the film business started, when some of the early movies consisted of stationary cameras filming plays. You can't take a magazine or a book and put it online and expect that to be a robust experience and a valuable property. Content online is something that is continuous, changing, and evolving. It is something you react to; it's an experience, an intangible. It's not an object. It's more like a flow of information, a reaction to that information, a mixture of things. The people who are going to make a difference in the Internet and the online world understand this concept and can create entirely new and interesting content.

There's a fundamental shift taking place, because information is no longer an object that has to be transported. In the digital world, information that traditionally took the form of newspapers, magazines, or books can instantaneously be transported anywhere. The implication is vast. It requires a different value system. How heavy a newspaper is and how much it costs to get it to somebody no longer determines the cover price. Suddenly that cost is zero.

How do you think about charging for the substance of the newspaper, not the production costs of the newspaper? How do you create new models for the publishing and entertainment industries, and for communications? How does that impact governments, and societies, and cultures? It's bound to have a radical impact and transform our societies. Nobody knows how it's all going to turn out. It's scary, and perhaps that's the reason why the United States Congress is so frantically trying to control the Internet: they're afraid of what might happen if it's not controlled.

How do you make money on the Internet? You need multiple revenue streams. You need advertising revenue, transaction revenue, and subscription revenue. You need to be willing to sell Internet publishing services to your advertisers and outside clients. To achieve this goal, just follow "The Bunnell Eightfold Path to Internet Revenue and Profits."

1. Avoid the temptation simply to "put something up there on the Net." You'll end up with a business that is all costs and no revenue. Then you'll run out of money. You won't be happy.

2. Repeat business is king. It's not hard to create a site that tens of thousands of Net surfers will want to check out once. But it's difficult to create a site that thousands of people will return to routinely. In the future the real money will come from "destination sites" that can demonstrate loyal followings. Pass-through sites like Yahoo! are successful in attracting advertising because they get a lot of traffic, but no one stays at Yahoo! for long. Yahoo! is not a site that can engage you. (Yahoo! is working hard to fix this problem. They want to become both a pass-through site and a destination site.)

3. Build your content for the technology breakthroughs that are just around the corner. The most engaging sites a year from now will have lots of multimedia bells and whistles, and they will be highly interactive. People spend more time on AOL in forums than they spend looking up information. The same will be true on the Internet.

4. Know who your site visitors (customers) are so you can attract advertising. Don't be afraid to ask them to sign up as subscribers so you can capture their demographics and determine their usage patterns. If you have a fun site with good information, people won't mind filling out a form to get to it. In some cases, they won't mind paying a subscription fee either. The conventional wisdom that everything on the Net has to be free because it's "always been free" is wrong because the population of the Net is fluid. To the extent that there really is a "Net culture," it is an evolving one.

5. Tie your content into things you can sell, preferably lots of things, all under $50. Take it from me, small transactions will be the biggest business on the Net. The model is France's Minitel. Content that lends itself to selling books, records, theater tickets, T-shirts, etcetera, will be the big winner. Although it will take some time for this business to develop, it will happen eventually in a major way. By the year 2000, this business will grow to $100 billion. Make sure your site gets its share.

6. Develop great technology skills at your company that you aren't afraid to sell to advertisers and outside clients. A "service" component to your business is a great way to augment revenues while you wait for advertising and transactions to build up. All the companies I know that are in the business of providing

Internet design and production services have a lot more work than they can handle.

7. Attract new traffic to your site through "special events" that you can promote through the Internet and through the press. A good site will change every day, and it will always be fresh. A great site will also have events that draw in thousands of new customers. These events can be built around celebrities (today at 3 P.M. PST, Heidi Fleiss answers questions on business management!), or they can be tied to real events (Microsoft's Super Bowl Internet Site is an example).

8. Most importantly, manage your site like the business it is. All businesses, even hip, cool, revolutionary, new-paradigm businesses, live or die on the fundamentals. If you asked Bill Gates the secret of his business success, he would tell you it is to make more money than you spend. A lot of spectacular Internet sites will flame out as they run out of money and their backers get cold feet. No matter how much money you raise, be conservative about spending it. Make your employees fly coach on the cheapest flights available. Make them stay at the Holiday Inn instead of the Four Seasons. Don't let them go out to lunch together and bill it to the company. Treat cash as king because in a digital world cash is still the master.

Remember, many streams make up a river.

Remember, also, that there are issues of greater import than revenues and profits. There is the issue of the ever-widening gap between the haves and the have-nots. The personal computer has penetrated the suburban area. Middle-class and upper middle-class families have computers, and the wealthier school districts have computers. People who live in poor areas don't have computers at home or at school, and unfortunately the computer is so important to so many jobs and pursuits of different kinds that it's creating a doubly disadvantaged class who are living in poverty and, because of their condition, are unable to take advantage of the new computer technologies.

It's very important that we address this issue, simply because it's in the best interest of the country and of businesses that people have access to computers and have the skills to do jobs that require computers and, beyond that, to participate in democracy. A true democracy is a society in which people are well educated and can participate. Without access to computer technology, you're left out.

Another issue is the unequal gender presence on the Web. About 80 percent of the people on the Internet are male. It's been that way for a long time. It goes back to the notion that girls aren't good at math and science and boys are. For whatever reason, technology has been the domain of guys. Men are always working on their cars and gadgets, getting involved with fixing things and making stuff work, and women are expected not to know how to do those kinds of things. This is a problem that will take some time to overcome.

Speaking of democracy, I'm really, really pissed off because the man whom I helped vote into the presidency, spineless Bill Clinton, signed the Telecommunications Giveaway Bill that includes the so-called Communications Decency Act, a draconian assault on the First Amendment that threatens to turn the Internet into a virtual Vietnam. I'm pissed off that any president, Republican or Democrat, would knowingly sign a bill that so blatantly disregards the First Amendment. This president has decided for the sake of political expediency, for the sake of kissing the butts of gun-toting Christian Right meatheads, and for the sake of giving away billions of dollars to media giants to ignore the "first" and most important principle of our democracy. Without freedom of speech, there can be no democracy. None. Zero. Innocent people were at risk of going to jail before this amendment was overturned by a unanimous federal court ruling.

We need a free, unfettered Internet. You can't trust commercial online services to respect your rights. They are too susceptible to commercial pressures, too likely to cave in when their profits are on the line. The Internet is different, and it should stay that way. The future of our democracy depends upon this, because the Internet has the potential to give individuals much more say in government affairs. (Maybe this, not dirty pictures, is what the government is really afraid of?)

The most puzzling thing is that the vast majority of genetically deficient congresspeople who voted for the Telecommunications Bill did so knowing full well that the Communications Decency Act is blatantly unconstitutional and for the most part unenforceable. A friend of mine said the Internet site he found most interesting was one that broadcasts live video from Amsterdam sex clubs! Last time I checked, Amsterdam wasn't subject to U.S. law. If you want to sell dirty pictures on the Internet to the U.S. market in this post–Communications Decency Act era, all you have to do is set up your file server outside the border.

The basic fallacy of this law is that it treats the Internet as if it were a broadcast medium like television, not an interactive, multidirection medium with millions of nodes. Although it was created by the government, the technology of the Internet is now beyond the control of the government. Hackers will always figure out a way to get around laws that attempt to censor the Internet.

To enforce this law, the government would need a way to monitor everything that appears on your computer screen. Luckily, this is not possible, nor is it ever likely to become possible. The only way the government could do this would be to use the old-fashioned Stalinist method of having neighbors spy on neighbors. You might be sitting at your desk looking in on the Amsterdam sex club scene while your neighbor spies on you with his binoculars. Then he might call up the local police department and say, "Hey, my neighbor is looking at dirty pictures on his computer screen."

Oh well, many streams make up a river.

THE SOFTWARE DEVELOPER: <BILL GATES> I worked with David in the very early days of this business, when it wasn't really a business and nobody paid attention. And he did the first computer convention, which was an MITS Altair-based thing. And he did the first interesting magazine, *PC Magazine.* Then *PC World* got involved with encouraging him to do *MacWorld.* You know, it's great to have somebody who's played the role he has. I think it's a real contribution.

THE ORACLE: <PAUL SAFFO> David Bunnell is extraordinary in this business in that he's a pioneer who never lost sight of his roots and seems to follow his heart. At moments he seems to be the only person in Silicon Valley who has any sense of social obligation and takes seriously opportunities to do things with the information-dispossessed. While everybody else has cashed out and decided to hang out around their swimming pools, David is still quietly working away at the things that he thinks matters.

THE CITIZEN: <HOWARD RHEINGOLD> David puts his time and money behind his ideals. He started Computers and You at Glide Memorial Church in San Francisco with his own money, a project that provides computer training to the poorest people in town. If only more Silicon Valley jillionaires would put something back into their communities the way David does.

THE GADFLY: <JOHN C. DVORAK> David Bunnell is a guy who's smarter than even he knows. He's got some sort of a weird visionary thing about him that makes him ahead of the curve to the point where sometimes he fails, because he's too far out front. I admire the guy.

<Doug Carlston>

The Thinker

The Idealist: <Denise Caruso>

Doug Carlston does good things, and does them well, and people like them. He doesn't have to be a jerk about it – it's kind of amazing. He's like that Rodin sculpture. You can feel him thinking.

Doug Carlston cofounded Brøderbund Software after starting a career as an attorney. Today he is its chairman and CEO.

For Doug Carlston, the Internet is a communications medium. "It's an electronic mail and messaging tool, it's for people to move stuff back and forth, it's anarchistic, it's decentralized. There's no there there. There's a million different theres," he says.

We first met at the Brøderbund booth at the West Coast Computer Fair in San Francisco in 1983. The personal computer scene then was dominated by enthusiasts, which was probably the reason the fair was such a high-energy event. I don't recall many people wearing business suits, certainly not around the very lively Brøderbund booth, run as a family affair by Doug, his brother Gary, and his sister, the late Cathy Carlston Brisbois.

It wasn't communications that brought Doug there. He'd been programming computers and creating games since the '60s, throughout his years at Harvard Law School and his five years as an attorney in Chicago and Maine. Doug, who cofounded Brøderbund with Gary in 1980, understood from the beginning the notion of authorship. While a piece of software in the business-applications arena can take huge teams of people years to write, the game business is driven by the efforts of individuals or small teams. In this regard, Doug has always been sensitive to the authors' positions and treated them well. He even extended this courtesy to me when he defended my role and the role of the agent in general before an industry association of software publishers in 1984. This was around the time Mitch Kapor of Lotus was calling me "the Darth Vader of publishing," probably in retaliation for my comment in *PC Magazine.* ("Show me someone who uses a spreadsheet and I'll show you someone I don't have to talk to.")

Doug is steady, levelheaded, and deep. He takes his time. He is patient. He is "The Thinker." I have known him as a friend and in a number of different kinds of business relationships, and he is one of the class acts of the industry. He is a genuine enthusiast about his company, his people, and their products.

In recent years, with the brilliant success of Brøderbund, Doug has been spending a great deal of time playing the mogul, working on mergers, attending to the many corporate matters that require his attention. These are reasonable and expected pursuits at this stage in his career, but I have to believe that his heart is still closely tied to the creation of great software products.

Doug believes that people who come to a Web site do not want to be an audience; they want to interact. "They don't want to spend more than a minute to read something," he says. "They want to do something. They want to click on things and make things happen. They don't want to sit there and be talked to or preached to." He stresses the need to engage people in an interactive process. "Again, that *content* word gets in the way," he says. "This is not the medium for the deliverable. You can deliver stuff to people – technically it's possible. But that's not why people are there. When they're online and engaged, they want to find something and move on."

Brøderbund has become a giant consumer software company because Doug knows what it takes to create a successful product (such as Print Shop, Myst, and Living Books). He thinks like both a programmer and a customer. Current developments on the Internet are only a first phase, he says, "a building block for a much more robust and technically rich environment in which people are going to participate."

The Thinker: <Doug Carlston> Environments like the Net tend to grow organically. They expand not according to any one person's conscious design, but because the Net is by nature a collection of individuals all making contributions to it. The growth is at an exponential rate, though not as much in terms of size as in terms of features and feature sets. Once you get standardization and consistent ways of displaying information, you've suddenly got millions of people with a common set of tools. Today's Web will be unrecognizable in five years. It will essentially be modeled on the real world and involve a three-dimensional prospectus, full-motion video, and avatars.

One of the biggest misperceptions about content is that it's an asset that endures, that has value, like catalogs, libraries, film records, music records, or written archives. However, as Esther Dyson points out, the time value of information on the Net is extremely short. Things degrade instantaneously because you're on the world's largest copying system. Esther suggests that you may not be able to charge for information at all. Not only does information want to be free, as Stewart Brand has said, but information is *going* to be free, whether you want it to be or not. What has value on the Net is the creative ability to unfold, to create new content on the fly.

People are definitely on the Net to find a community and to interact with other people, not just with content. The nature of the interaction is important. There are things that build a sense of community and things that do not. Esther has argued that purely commercial transactions do not foster a sense of community. You can have a marketplace, but you really need noneconomic transactions, what she calls gift transactions, to strengthen the community. You need a free interchange of ideas so that ideas become part of the common glue that holds everybody together and creates value. Online communities like The Well really are communities. Over time, a couple of defining characteristics have emerged from these communities. One is that they weren't too big, so the people involved tended to get to know one another. A second is that there was a lot of sharing, rather than buying and selling. Marketplaces, although socially useful, probably don't create the kind of ties between individuals that you would want to see.

If you want to build a location – a homepage or a community – on the Net, I would argue that you need to have noneconomic as well as economic transactions occurring all the time. Authors might come to Author Night and interact with people, not just to get people to buy their books, but because people want to see the name behind the product and want to interact with the author. That makes the relationship more special. People are probably more likely to buy a book from someone they've interacted with in one way or another. More than that, it makes them value the place they went to engage with the author. Bookstores know this; that's why they have author events. You can do that so much more effectively on the Net.

Providing books to the public electronically or on the Net is not likely to be very successful. The cost of delivery of a printed book to the average user is extremely low now; it's at an impulse-purchase price. The convenience factor is overwhelming. You can take a printed book to the beach; you can pop it in your pocket. I can have five hundred books on a CD that I carry with me but I go on very few trips where I need to read five hundred books. I don't see a CD being a more convenient way to access written text.

The force that drives a book into digital form has little to do with repurposing content and has everything to do with the mechanical process of printing. Publishers are finding that their costs drop dramatically if they can produce digital copy rather than printed copy for typesetters. You introduce fewer errors in the process, you get much quicker turnaround, you get exactly the kind of page layout you want, and you can even come up with standard templates. The mechanical part of publishing, not the sudden access to an electronic book market, is going to drive the digitalization of the printed word for book publishers.

Publishers are trying to redefine themselves by securing the electronic rights to books, because even though opportunities are still limited, the profit margins and overall revenues for digital books will be substantially higher than the typical profit margins for printed books. On average, we can move many more consumer PC products than the average book publisher can move books. Publishers will try to shift their sales forces to give salespeople experience in selling at these much higher price points, at $40 consumer price points instead of a tenth of that. The once-clear division between retail bookstores and retail software stores is starting to erode. Software stores carry books, and a lot of bookstores carry software.

The problem with broadcast businesses is that they fall over into the part of the network currently occupied by broadcast devices, cable into the home to television sets. They've been thinking in terms of set-top boxes, slightly increasing the interactivity, delivering five hundred channels to the home, and so forth, but what's exploding now is the other side of the picture: the PC side, the telephonic side, the communications side. Exponential growth is occurring in this area, regardless of bandwidth. People are going off the curb there on bandwidth, still tapping in at 2400 baud, without being held back. They don't really care about the latency or response time. They want symmetry and real interactivity. People don't want just to be on the receiving end of a whole bunch of content. They'd rather participate. Furthermore, they want to be able to give as good as they get. The telephone companies understand that they're in the communications business.

One business that is going to be enormously affected by the Web is direct sales. Because of postage, printing, and other costs of getting your marketing materials to the customer, you have to get a 2 percent response on your mailing in order to break even. If you want to send your materials to one more person, you still have to pay for printing and postage. On the Web, your costs at the margin are very low. Adding another person to your direct-marketing or sales list isn't going to cost you anything. Instead of requiring a 2 percent return, you can be profitable at a .0001 percent return if you have a large enough base. This is a profound and dramatic change in the world of commerce. If major players in the catalog business can put a catalog in front of fifty thousand people a day and get them to place orders by using a mouse to click on the chosen items, they're in business. They direct-mail the items to the customer using the back office they've already got, and they're infinitely better off. Furthermore, it is possible to target a specific audience in ways that would have been impossible before the Web.

The real question is going to be how to get customers to walk by your homepage on the Web. Suppose Brøderbund puts a button on each of its products that says, "Press this to get customer service for Brøderbund products." When you press it, you connect to a free Web site. While you're there, getting technical support and customer service, you're surrounded by a bunch of stores that sell products related to typical Brøderbund customers, such as parents with young kids. Say we go to Fisher Price, or another company that sells stuff for kids, and we offer to set up a little store on our Web site. "You put your catalog there, and we put a hot button next to every item on the catalog so people can impulse-buy. You handle the fulfillment, and we split the profits with you. Easiest idea in the world, isn't it? We'll have a flow of guaranteed customers; your cost is nothing. You have the same back office you've always had. You don't need to know anything about technology. It's a major business and it can be set up tomorrow. It's not hard, as long as you've got a flow of customers."

Money can be made on the Net by advertising on your homepage in your particular area, though it may not be an efficient use of visual space. People have limited attention spans. Their limit is probably more than one page, but when they go to your site they see only your homepage and you want them to look at other pages. And, your homepage is valuable real estate. You want to do things that will keep people there, within your domain. Can you put a banner in front of them? Sure, but it's a little dangerous unless you have the space right there to convert that into a direct customer relationship such as an order. I'd rather put up three hot buttons selling different kinds of services, products, stores, or catalogs, and get people deeply enmeshed in the process. That homepage real estate is too valuable to me.

The problem with most of the large companies thinking of themselves as content companies is that it doesn't get them anywhere. What Turner Broadcasting really has is customers, and what it has that's marketable to a group of customers is brand identity. More effective is to ask, "What are the natures of the underlying businesses in which I participate?" Turner has a number of good businesses. Probably the best of these is ESPN, which is a brand name to Turner's customers. A lot of people look for ESPN when they want to see sports. That's very powerful. If Turner's assets are redefined as name recognition and a strong customer base, rather than last year's football games or sumo matches stored in its library – content that is not necessarily proprietary – you can start to get a sense of where the company can go.

You have to think of the convergence companies in terms of their multiplicity of functions. For film and television, the locus of control historically has been distribution. They have direct access to theaters in a way that independent producers can't match or onto the airwaves in a way not available to others. That distribution function has been the source of most of the profit in film and television over the years. Most film and television companies have been spinning off productive capability to small independent studios so they can fob off a lot of the risk and then pick and choose the more successful projects. Distribution is a whole new game on the Internet, and it's not clear how controllable it is. If the Net stays as anarchistic as it is now in terms of access, then distribution may not be a good way to control it. A better route may be controlling productive capability. In this case, the people who are going to succeed are the ones who get very good at investing in new products and new ideas, and at being right in a commercial sense.

Another thing that the Net changes about the marketplace is that it now becomes possible to sell narrowly targeted products aimed at a particular niche. The marketplace used to be divided of towns, and every town was a cross-section of America, with different characteristics. On the Net you have a new world divided into affinity groups. Lesbians under the age of thirty go to one area, and parents with children between the ages of nine and twelve with an income over $60,000 go to another area. With that kind of targetable market, you can start narrowcasting your content. You can build software aimed at a much more specific consumer profile, and the Net will help you get to that group of people. That ability will probably change the nature of content. It will probably mean that a lot more will be written for people who hold very strong beliefs (the National Rifle Association, the Mormons), and see themselves very strongly as a group, even if they're geographically dispersed. Diaspora doesn't matter anymore as long as people can hook up with a Web site or through the Net. If I were one of the convergence companies, I'd focus on getting very good at building new content and creative capability. I'd be less sanguine about maintaining the same kind of distribution control that I've had in the past. I'd see myself as a financing engine for new content.

THE CITIZEN: <HOWARD RHEINGOLD> Doug is an example of someone who started doing something he loved, and it swallowed his life. Fifteen years later, Brøderbund is one of the giants. As opposed to your hippie-esque intellectual revolutionaries like Stewart Brand or Steve Jobs, he didn't come from a change-the-world tradition. Doug is your Midwestern, upright, God-fearing, Middle American entrepreneur. He has good values, and he runs a solid ship. In a world of a bunch of crap I believe they call "edutainment," Brøderbund continues to make some very interesting tools for kids.

THE CATALYST: <LINDA STONE> Doug is one of the most stable, steady hands in the computer industry. From the time he started Brøderbund, he's been very conservative, and yet he has an organization that understands how to bring content and technology together. He doesn't take huge risks, he moves step by step, and I think he understands the consumer better than a lot of people in the PC business. He also understands consumer software and tries to make products that are evergreen, products that provide interesting experiences again and again.

THE SAINT: <KEVIN KELLY> Doug has a great heart for the young, new start-up and what they need, and has a very good eye for detecting the kinds of things that people are going to want five years from now. I don't know how he does it.

THE GENIUS: <W. DANIEL HILLIS> Doug proves that nice guys can do well in business. Everybody I know who's worked with him, worked for him, or gone into a business partnership with him has nothing but good things to say. I would be willing to do any type of business deal with Doug without a contract. It's nice that there are successful people in the business who operate on that basis. His company, Brøderbund, has raised the quality level in children's software; it's invented whole new product categories, like Living Books.

The Seer: <David Bunnell> The smartest business people play their cards close to the vest, and Carlston is a great poker player. I suspect that his opponents consistently underestimate him.

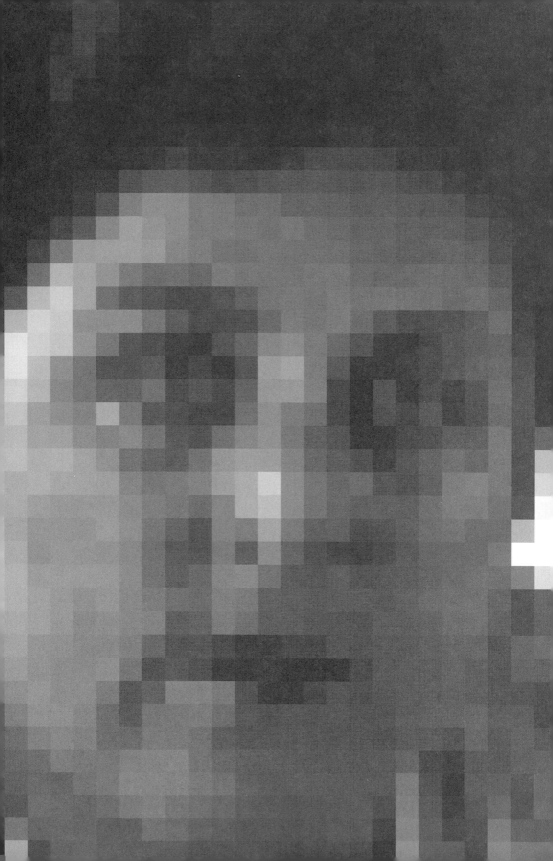

<Denise Caruso>

The Idealist

The Pattern-Recognizer: <Esther Dyson>

Denise is one of the most clear-minded people I know, both in understanding industry dynamics and in understanding people's motivations. But she can be critical of people who aren't as noble-minded as she is.

Denise Caruso runs Spotlight, an annual conference for interactive media industry executives. Her column, "Digital Commerce," appears in *The New York Times.*

"I don't think you should allow people to pick their titles. It's [baloney] that Dvorak isn't 'The Curmudgeon.' [Baloney] that Leonsis isn't 'The Salesman.' [Baloney] that Esther isn't 'The Pundit.' Come on! If I wanted to change mine, I'd be 'The Pragmatist' because taking the high road actually works best in the long run. If more people did the right thing early on, we'd have avoided most of the problems we're dealing with today in the digital world."

Replace "baloney" with the appropriate expletive and you've just read a typical email from Denise Caruso, "The Idealist."

Denise knows everyone. She can get anyone she wants on the phone. When you attend an industry conference and see Denise in one of her "colorful" black outfits, you know you've come to the right place. Her weekly column in *The New York Times,* "Digital Commerce," pulls no punches. She asks direct questions. She keeps people honest. People think she's tough, but the rational ones also know she's fair. The problem, she points out, is that people like the tough part when it concerns someone else and don't like it very much when it concerns them.

A longtime analyst and observer of both the computer business and the emerging interactive media industry, Denise has been writing her *Times* column since March 1995. She is also the executive producer of Spotlight, a conference for interactive media executives, for InfoWorld Publishing Co.

Denise was hired in 1994 by Norman Pearlstine (former executive editor of *The Wall Street Journal* and now editor-in-chief of Time Warner) to launch Technology & Media Group, an information services company that was part of his new media company Friday Holdings. Before launching Technology & Media, Denise was founding editor of *Digital Media,* a monthly industry newsletter that, under Denise's direction, was widely acknowledged as the seminal publication in the emerging new-media industry.

For five years prior to launching *Digital Media* in 1990, Denise wrote the "Inside Technology" column for the Sunday business section of the *San Francisco Examiner,* where she was a prescient advocate of First Amendment rights in cyberspace and one of the first journalists to focus on technology's effects on commerce and culture.

Denise has also contributed to *The Wall Street Journal, Wired, The Utne Reader,* and various other publications on a wide range of technology-related subjects. In addition, she has held editorial positions at several trade publications, including *Electronics* and *InfoWorld* magazines, where she was one of two West Coast editors covering Silicon Valley.

Denise runs an annual industry conference on interactive media: Spotlight, launched in 1995. Spotlight is an interesting conference. First, it focuses only on interactive media – as Denise says, "the dreaded 'C' word, *content*" – rather than on technology or delivery platforms, such as cable modems, PCs, or videogames. It is concerned only with art, commerce, and the software tools required to make the interactive media industry a reality. Though Denise does handpick some hardware to show in the demonstration area at the conference, she keeps these discussions off the stage: she believes they've become irrelevant.

Spotlight is also the first executive-level conference to focus on the interactive media industry. Denise says she "wants to bring together an incredible cross-section of people who actually can make a difference to each other – introducing artists and creative people to those who cut the deals, green light the projects, sign the checks." At the conference, she gets attendees to step back from the daily grind and think about the bigger picture of how to make the industry work better and smarter for everyone. "In an industry this new, it is absolutely true that higher water floats more boats," she says. "The more people there are who do smart things and build smart products that people want, the larger and more successful the industry will become."

Spotlight's début last year was a success according to Denise's criteria: it was a very high-level schmoozefest and the volume level during breaks and meals was amazing. Her bottom line: "virtual, schmirtual – seeing people face-to-face, buying them a drink, and engaging them in meaningful conversation is what makes people happy and is also, not coincidentally, what makes a community. I'm trying very hard to build a community in this industry, even though it's in the middle of a tornado, which is kind of how I see the Web and interactive media in general right now – a lot of hot wind and a high likelihood that when things settle down, the wreckage that's left won't be pretty."

"I refuse to use the word *content,*" says Denise. "It's insulting. Artists create art; writers write ideas. The word will continue to be used, though, because media has become such a huge commercial enterprise. Everything is becoming a commodity – including art, including ideas."

Denise wants her column to make people aware of the incredible amount of hype about the interactive media industry and technology in general. "A lot of the hype is just parroting the public relations departments of Microsoft and TCI and the big media companies," she says. "Somebody needs to give people information that allows them to get to the truth. That's a very difficult thing to do with technology, because it's so difficult to understand."

She says her job is to point out lapses in logic. When everyone was talking about interactive TV in 1994, Denise was the one writing (then in the pages of *Digital Media*), "Excuse me? Do you have *any idea* how long it takes to write the kind of software you're talking about to run these systems? Excuse me! Are you expecting *cable companies* to install all this complex technology and then *service* it? The companies that pin the meter on customer dissatisfaction, and all they have to service is one stupid wire with one-way programming into someone's TV set? I don't think so! And, if we're really talking home shopping and 'interactive *Wheel of Fortune*' here, who cares?"

"These questions don't require a degree in rocket science. They are absolutely logical. Unfortunately, a lot of people get delirious when big media and cable companies start signing billion-dollar deals – whether they ever happen or not – so they don't step back and ask the larger questions. Business reporters are asked only to do the 'he said, she said' story, so they don't get to step back and question the bigger picture about whether anything about these deals is real – the deal itself, the technology, the potential customer base, you name it."

"This is really a dirty little secret inside the industry – everyone in Silicon Valley at least knows that most of what you read about this stuff is utter bullshit. The people who really know what's going on spend a lot of time every day rolling their eyes and saying, 'Puh-leeze, spare me!' So I guess I spend a lot of time pointing out the stuff I believe to be obvious."

"I would hope I make people who work in the industry think twice before making the same mistakes as those who have gone before them, and help them to focus on the long-term view, but that's pretty difficult to accomplish in a business where people's heads are always turned by a pile of cash instead of by what the pile of cash can actually do."

Commerce is becoming important on the Net. "Clearly," she says, "there are going to be financial transactions on the Net, and that's going to drive a lot of the industry. But unless we are also able to address the social and cultural aspects of online commerce – to look at how we are going to make people comfortable with this transition to a culture where so much of the data we receive is in digital form – whether you can sell anything becomes moot."

Denise, who was an English lit major, began writing about the digital scene in 1984, when Stewart Alsop hired her to work at *InfoWorld*. She is highly respected for her ability to talk to people about technology and to get to the essence of what they are trying to accomplish. She steps back and ask the right questions: "Why do we need this? Does it actually work? Does it work now?

What good is it going to do in the future? Has anybody thought this through?"

THE IDEALIST: <DENISE CARUSO> One of the most depressing moments of my life was when I met Timothy Leary for the first time. I was writing in 1984 for *InfoWorld,* and he was getting involved in all this digital stuff. We got into social issues, the haves and the have-nots. I said, "Well, this all sounds great, a very powerful tool, but how are you going to get it into the hands of the people who really need it?" He said, "It's just like evolution: some people make it out of the water and some don't." It was surprising that someone like Tim Leary, who is so high-minded about so many things, could be so cold about this.

Unfortunately, I have the feeling that he was right. I don't see anyone getting a break in our society. Little effort is being made to bring along anyone who's not a white male with access to lots of money. This is a mistake of colossal proportions, because anybody who doesn't think that this is going to cause a revolution at some point is nuts. My fervent desire would be to see the United States and governments around the world turn public libraries into digital learning places with good technology and unfiltered Internet access. We have to help people learn how to use the technology – give them a free place to come and use the new tools of learning. If we don't, the consequences will be disastrous.

Communication is the fundamental activity that people want to engage in. They've always wanted to communicate with other human beings who aren't necessarily standing right in front of them. If the Net enables me to have higher and higher resolution in my communication with people – in the sense that I can feel to an increasing degree that they are "right in front of me" – that's a very interesting business opportunity.

I have always thought that the "killer app" for the cable and phone companies is good, cheap video telephony. Everybody wants to call their mom and let their mom see them, or let their grandmom see them, or show off the kid. As we get more bandwidth and are able to send larger and larger chunks of ourselves across wires, through the air, to each other, that is going to be important.

Content as we think of it today is going to be a mere artifact of our ability to communicate.

Content was a programmer's word. When the technologies of interactive media were born, programmers thought of content as "stuff" you stick on the screen, stuff that merely links you up to more stuff. But just like *multimedia,* the word *content* actually means nothing. A piece of content might be interactive media or simply digital information that you access by using your computer. If the data is a digital news story or novel, you still have to read it the way you would if it were on paper. If it's a digital movie clip, it's still a movie clip. We should call these things what they really are.

Most of the big trends in technology are solutions in search of a problem, gadgets in search of a market. The CD-ROM is a classic example. It has never been particularly good at what it was supposed to do: it is slow, breaks a lot, and CD-ROM titles are mostly incredible inanities. But people believe that CD-ROM is the Next Big Thing because of the enormous sales figures and projections coming from market researchers. They don't tell you those figures include all the CD-ROMs that come bundled with computers and CD-ROM drives – an enormous number. I don't call these sales. A sale is when I get up out of my chair, get into my car, and go down to the store and say, "I'll take that one." That's buying something.

A percentage of people's entertainment lives are migrating onto the computer, but it's a mistake to assume that people want Hollywood entertainment on their computers. Hollywood is doing the same thing, as are virtually all media companies trying to move into new media. They're mapping their former experience onto the Net. Most of it is dumb and boring. There's an imagination drought. I can count on one hand and not very many fingers the people I know who are giving serious creative thought to this new medium. It is sad because there's such an opportunity here and so many people are missing the boat by being unwilling to try the untried idea, the new outrageous concept.

On the other hand, this failure of imagination delights me because as a result the studios and phone companies and cable companies are making enormous investments in communication infrastructure, thinking that the Internet is the Next New Big Thing. They're going to lose a ton of money and lots of them will back off. And when they do, we're going to be left with brand-new infrastructure, and the artists will come along and do something interesting with it. I figure ten years will go by before that happens. All these iterations are absolutely necessary – failure built upon failure built upon failure. I don't think you can speed up that process.

The model for advertising on the Web is going to undergo a complete overhaul within the next few years because studies will finally show us what people want from the Net. Advertising will be increasingly targeted and effective and will no longer be thought of as a default business model for underwriting Web publishers. The key from a cultural standpoint will be our ability to protect our personal privacy while still allowing advertisers to serve our needs as consumers.

Women are very involved in the Net. They are invisible only because women are invisible in this culture. The women I know on the Net conduct their business there and it is a source of great power and freedom for them. You will see more and more women using the Net as a way to command power. The complexion of the Net is going to change as it becomes a useful tool for commerce available to people with a broad range of interests.

What happens when you look at an ad on the Web? When you watch television, you tend to see advertisements because you want to continue watching your program. When you read a magazine, the advertising is right next to the text, in your field of vision, so you can't avoid it. There's a synergy between programming and advertising that you don't have on the Web. The minute I click into an ad on the Web, I am engaged in a new experience – a new kind of editorial content. My attention is no longer focused on the page from whence I came. That fact makes me wonder how – and why – editorial and advertising will stay connected in this medium.

Sponsorship makes sense on the Web. The problem is that you have to find a way to give a sponsor value for money. It's going to have to be significantly different from the kind of sponsorship you see in broadcast media, because one of the things that's really powerful about the network is that you can give the consumers the specific information they want and cultivate personal relationships.

People who say they are making money on the Net are only making money because they're taking money from advertisers, not from customers. That money is going to evaporate when advertisers start realizing they're not getting anything. It's evaporating now. Advertising dollars are in short supply, for all media. Advertisers are looking for an opportunity to have a new relationship with a customer. They are not looking for just another place to put their name, unless they can do so extremely cheaply. Advertising on Web sites is very expensive now, and it isn't worth it unless that new customer relationship is part of the deal. If you're a mass-market vendor, the $1 million that you had for advertising ten years ago isn't going to go as far. Then you had three major networks and CNN. Now you have fifty or one hundred local channels. Sources of information and entertainment are multiplying and multiplying and multiplying. Everybody's saying that advertising will subsidize these new media, but that is just another business-plan buzzword – like in the '80s when everyone said that the early adopters were going to buy every new consumer gadget that came along. Just like everybody else, early adopters had only so much money. They only had so much room on their shelves for personal digital assistants and videogame machines and address-label printers. The model is limited, to say the least.

If I were to talk to the moguls in the media business, I would advise them to stop investing in "the Web" and start investing in ways of using technology to improve their products and serve their customers. My heartfelt belief is that successful interactive media will come from a new generation of artists. The media moguls are, shall we say, pissing in the wind if they think they're going to make money in this interactive medium just by pouring money into it. I would ask them to examine their consciences, to examine what they're really trying to accomplish. The fundamental power of network technology is that it blows apart huge existing infrastructures because just about anyone can put a Web site on the Net and publish for an audience of millions, instantly.

This distributed environment of networking obviates huge media structures. If they don't pay attention, the technology will blow them apart.

This gets to the idea of virtual community, which resonates with me, although the term has become overused. We all slide into and out of many "virtual communities." Regarding the "higher mind," I can experience the consciousness of the world sitting in lotus position; I don't need electronic communication to do that. But it soothes me when I find that kind of consciousness online; it soothes me when I hit a Web site with someone's poetry on it or I can look at digitized photographs showing someone when she was a little girl and the way she looks now. These are things that I find inspiring about the Web – cyberglyphs, the artifacts that people leave around to say, "See, here, this is who I am. Who are you?"

THE PRAGMATIST: <STEWART ALSOP> The "People" column in *InfoWorld* was Denise's column. She hated writing it. She was always pissed off at me. Denise is an idealist.

THE GADFLY: <JOHN C. DVORAK> Denise is a Hollywood reporter, and she's got high energy. High-energy woman.

THE SEER: <DAVID BUNNELL> Denise is passionate about her beliefs, to be sure. This is her strength and her weakness. When she writes about issues that she believes in, she can be very convincing. But when she lets her biases affect the way she judges technology, she is not as convincing. I wish she would focus less on nuts and bolts and more on issues because that is where she can really contribute.

THE CITIZEN: <HOWARD RHEINGOLD> Denise has the greatest combination of soft heart, tough, battle-hardened exterior, and wicked sense of humor. She seems to have her antennae out in a lot of places.

THE SCRIBE: <JOHN MARKOFF> Denise came into the computer industry with zero knowledge and has worked herself up by studying, and being in the right places, and knowing a remarkable number of people. This is a woman who's connected, who works the crowds, gets the dirt, and knows where the bodies lie.

THE JUDGE: <DAVID R. JOHNSON> Denise is a staunch defender of the rights of the denizens of cyberspace, extremely outspoken, and very effective in communicating her strongly held positions.

THE IMPRESARIO: <RICHARD SAUL WURMAN> Tough. She's won a tough fight to gain the across-the-board respect she now garners from the industry.

<Steve Case>

The Statesman

The Competitor: <Scott McNealy>

AOL has the big challenge we all have: it's right in the middle of the vortex of the change. One of the things it has been able to do is adapt and deal with the new and different competitive threats and regulatory environments and technology changes driving the business. This is one business where you want to spend very little time in internal strategizing and a ton of time with your head outside the window, or on an airplane, flying around, trying to figure out what's really going on. Technology in AOL's space is moving way faster than it does in the hardware space or the operating system space or the product space. Steve Case has done a good job of keeping his head in an environment that is swirling like crazy.

Steve Case is the founder and CEO of America Online.

Steve Case has been at it a long time, which means he's tried more things and failed at more things. I met him in my office in 1985. He had just started Quantum, an online service, and wanted to see if we could do some business together. He was an earnest, bright, engaging twenty-six-year-old man, but I was not keen on the business prospects. First, I didn't see a way to make money. Second, the idea of sitting in front of a computer screen and "communicating" left me cold. I told him so, perhaps too brusquely. Twelve years later, his company, renamed America Online, is the dominant online service in the United States, with more subscribers than the combined readership of the country's five largest newspapers. Part of my charm is that I am always wrong.

The convergence of different ideas, technologies, and cultures is driving the new online medium. Companies like Microsoft have a software-centric perspective. Companies like AT&T are communications-centric. Companies like Time Warner are media-centric. One of Steve's strengths is that he's not an expert in any one area but knows enough about each to be dangerous. He also knows more about how these perspectives intersect than anyone else. His goal is to position AOL at the center of that convergence, with an eye more toward what consumers want and how they want it than toward what software might allow, what communications might enable, or what content might be possible.

Steve Case is "The Statesman." He excels in building strategic relationships, partnerships, and alliances. In the space of two weeks in February 1996, he dazzled the business world by announcing major deals with Netscape, Microsoft, Sun, and AT&T, companies viewed as AOL's major competitors. The day-to-day drama of the unfolding events was more compelling than any novel I have read in years. He could probably retire on the sale of the movie rights to his story.

Steve explains this significant turnaround by saying that these deals are "a recognition that this business is mostly about consumers and mostly about building audiences. If you have millions of people using your service, you have some credibility and momentum that is of terrific benefit to many companies, whether they are technology providers or content providers. People want to reach the widest possible audience, and AOL is that audience. A lot of companies want to work with us – as opposed to competing with us."

Steve envisions an engaging interactive experience that cuts across not only the diverse categories of entertainment, information, transactions, communication, and education, but also cuts across various technologies, access devices, and communications networks. "Lots of technologies are stirred together to create an interesting base-level platform," he says, "and then lots of interactive experiences are placed on top of that, mostly through entrepreneurial efforts. There's a thirst to participate in this industry. It's very similar to what I felt in the early '80s, when personal computer software emerged as an entrepreneurial opportunity, a magnet for creative minds. The same thing is happening in this interactive space."

Steve plans to take all the parts and assemble them in a way that can excite the imaginations of tens of millions of people on a global basis. He has little use for people who view the industry through the prism of the past, wishing and hoping that their own perspective and business model will prevail. In Steve's new world, the wants and needs of consumers will prevail.

THE STATESMAN: <STEVE CASE> The concept of interactive services on the Internet is starting to move to the mainstream. Millions of people are connected, and more are joining every year. It will be as important as the telephone or television some day, but we are still very early in its development. Only 11 percent of households in the United States subscribe to online services. The question is, How do you reach that mass market? Things that AOL is focused on, such as ease of use, useful services, fun, affordability, and creating an engaging experience, are what it's all about. There's too much focus on technology in the industry, an obsession with bandwidth and the latest browsers. What's much more important is creating a magical interactive experience, for which the technology is certainly an enabler. Human creativity is really going to drive us.

AOL went public in 1992. We had 187,000 subscribers, and a market value of $70 million dollars. Four years later, we have nearly 6 million subscribers, and a market value of nearly $7 billion. The value has gone up a hundredfold in four years, which shows the power and possibilities of this new medium. AOL's circulation is larger than the combined circulation of *The New York Times, USA Today, The Wall Street Journal, The Washington Post,* and the *Los Angeles Times,* the top five newspapers in the United States. Consumers are voting to participate in interactive services, and the majority, we're pleased to say, are voting to join AOL.

There are probably many reasons for this, but fundamentally our company has been about people who believe in the possibilities of this medium. They eat, drink, and sleep it. They are not just on a career path. They are building an industry. Look at other companies, Netscape, for example, which came out of nowhere in the last couple of years. Why? The quality of the people. The credibility that Jim Clark provided, the technical insight that Marc Andreessen provided, and the management leadership that Jim Barksdale provided have taken Netscape from nothing to a major leader in this market – overnight. That's the power of people. In such an important new industry, it's gratifying to see that the key criterion is the people. It's true in most industries, but I think it's particularly true in something that is so new and is evolving so rapidly.

AOL has always been open-minded about partnering with companies. One of the things we've done better than most in the last ten years is establish a tapestry of alliances with many companies from many different industries. In the case of some of the core Internet technologies around the Web, we realized that although we could continue to build these ourselves, the pace of innovation was accelerating, and several companies, including Microsoft, Netscape, and Sun, were pouring in significant resources. It made sense for us to partner with one or more of these companies, as opposed to competing with or trying to replicate what they were doing. We ended up establishing alliances with all of them, because we wanted to have access to all the technologies and also to have some influence over the evolution of those technologies. We decided to work primarily with Microsoft for the built-in browser for AOL, and primarily with Netscape for the built-in browser for GNN (Global Network Navigator), while offering our consumers their preferred choice.

The Microsoft alliance was the one that surprised people the most, because we have been fairly public critics of The Microsoft Network's business strategy, particularly bundling it with Windows 95. We had to take a step back and understand their technology strategy and their willingness to pursue new business models, including bundling us with Windows. The more we looked at the situation, a partnership with Microsoft to provide a wider consumer base with access to AOL through Windows 95 struck us as the right business decision. Competing with companies at one level while partnering with them at another level is an increasingly typical strategy, though it requires subtlety and finesse.

We are partnering with the Microsoft group responsible for Internet technologies, and we have no responsibility for The Microsoft Network or for content. Our day-to-day interaction is primarily with a group that views us as an important partner. The people in the group are bending over backward to try to meet our needs, because they believe that AOL embracing their technology substantially increases the momentum for Internet Explorer in this Web market. We're just another customer. Obviously, when all the dust settles, it is one company, and Bill Gates is in charge of that company. Part of his job is to balance the different factions and constituencies and do what's best for the industry and what's best for the stockholders. At Microsoft there's a real pragmatism that might not have existed before; it is concerned with recognizing the new realities of the market and what's happening with the Internet.

There is an almost mindless debate about the Internet versus online services, the Web versus AOL, as if there's some inherent tension between them. Over time people will realize that AOL is the leading on-ramp to the Internet. We provide full Internet access and a whole lot more, not just content but also context and community. In this world of virtually infinite choices and no barriers to entry to create content, the battlefield will be context and community, and the ability to build large audiences and commerce and revenue streams, to the overall growth. The perception that content is king is naïve. Content will be king if it's got an audience, and in order to get an audience, you need distribution muscle, which means plugging into services like AOL to make sure that your brand gets out there. There's a sense that if you create a Web site, tens of millions of people will knock on your door, because tens of millions of people have access to the Web. But nobody would be so naïve to think that if you started a new business tomorrow and had the phone company install a phone line, a hundred million people would call you the next day.

There are terrific benefits and wonderful opportunities that accrue to this medium as it moves mainstream. The way we'll get information, communicate with others, buy products, and learn new things will fundamentally change and improve. Some negatives also come with that growth. There is a tendency to have knee-jerk reactions to issues without fully understanding the dynamics. In new industries and new technologies with subtleties that aren't really appreciated, this tendency is particularly dangerous.

The debate over the Communications Decency Act is a perfect case study. A well-meaning legislator inserted this act into the 1996 Telecommunications Bill. The CDA is based on keeping pornography away from children, on making access to pornography difficult for children. If you're a typical politician in an election year, it's particularly easy to vote in favor of protecting the children. That's essentially what happened. A lot of companies, including AOL, immediately filed suit to challenge the CDA. The intent of the bill is fine, but the way it deals with the issue is seriously problematic.

Legislators have not understood what distinguishes this medium from newspapers and television networks. It's more interactive. It's more participatory. It's more like having a conversation in a restaurant than like having stuff flying off printing presses. The interaction and fluidity of conversation are what make these services so interesting. The soul of this medium is people talking to each other. To try to regulate and censor that is problematic, and to try to do that given the global nature of the Internet is naïve. The community standards boards in the United States would probably not agree with the community standards boards in China or Singapore.

We advocate fairly vigorously that you can't put your head in the sand and say, Well, it's a new medium, and since there is freedom of expression, anything goes, then wind up with a seedy Times Square that everybody is scared to wander into. The right answer is to use technology to address the problem by creating tools, like those enabling parental control, so members can customize the service to meet their own particular needs. That's what we're trying to do at AOL. The global aspect makes our business more complicated, because you need to be sensitive to global customs and local laws while remaining focused on trying to build a medium on a global scale. My sense is that there will be some more bumps in the road, but when the dust settles, say five years from now, we'll have in place a reasonable public policy structure that balances the different interests, that recognizes the uniqueness of the medium while also recognizing the legitimate concerns some people have about its potential negative aspects. As long as the approach is disciplined, deliberate, and balanced, we'll be OK.

The penetration of online services in 1996 is not deep enough to have a societal impact, but it will be in four years, when politicians start realizing the number of people who are connected to these services and the influence they have, the way information is discussed and disseminated, and the way polls are taken and so forth. Politicians will say, We'd better make the Internet our friend if we want to get reelected. The pivotal decision point in the presidential election of 2000 may be what happens on interactive services, just as the pivotal point in 1960 was the television debates between Kennedy and Nixon. That was the birth of television as an influential part of society. The same thing will happen in the next presidential election.

Another aspect of interactive online services that we are sorting out has to do with privacy. We have what we call terms of service, which articulate our rules of the road. There are federal statutes that force all email to be private. The situation gets a little more complicated when you get into things like junk mail, which is not necessarily a privacy issue per se, but is a keep-these-people-from-bothering-me issue. That's going to be a tough one. To block people from sending email to other people is a form of censorship. Yet there is a significant nuisance factor if people get a lot of unwarranted, unwanted, irrelevant junk mail when they sign on to a service like AOL. But one of the natures of this medium is communication. If people want to know who you are and you're posting information publicly, they will know who you are, and if they then want to annoy you, they have the ability to annoy you.

We do think you should not be able to use this communications medium to break the laws of the land. The levels of cooperation required by court orders issued to Federal Express or to the U.S. Postal Service, and viewed by society as appropriate, will also be deemed appropriate for the online medium.

The wall you have to climb before you get our cooperation is pretty high. One requirement is a subpoena from a court with a specific information request that is reasonable. Because email is private, we will not know if somebody is using email to send information or pictures that are illegal until it is brought to our attention. If an individual receives information or files that are suspected to be illegal and voluntarily brings them to our attention, and if in our judgment they are illegal – child pornography, for example – then we would turn the material over. Often what isn't appropriate is less clear.

AOL has seen significant growth over the last couple of years because we have struck a chord with mainstream America in the kinds of service desired. For example, AOL works pretty well on 14.4-kpbs modems. To handle new areas, we download the graphics to you once and then store them on your hard drive. This may be a little annoying the first time you go in, but the next time you go in, the graphics pop up instantly. The Web doesn't work that way. Every time you go to any area, all the graphics are retransmitted, which makes the Web a terribly unsatisfying experience for people with 14.4-kpbs modems, who make up two-thirds of the consumers today. A growing number of consumers have 28.8-kpbs modems, but even at 28.8, the Web is only marginally satisfying, because it was originally designed for people who had direct connections – high-speed Ethernet connections on college campuses, and almost unlimited bandwidth. That's Marc Andreessen's original target market, but that's not the way the real world works when you're trying to reach consumers. There's a lot of tension between what technology enables versus what consumers want. Part of what they want is an experience that's satisfying given the hardware and networks they have in place today. This has also been the source of the perception that there's a tension between a service like AOL and the Web. However, AOL emerged quite quickly to provide an easy, useful, fun way to get into and around the Web, as well as to offer a whole sea of content and context and community not available on the Web. It's a more satisfying experience, and it's ten bucks a month. You stick in a disk and click on a few things, and you're up and running.

What's the disconnect? It is the presumption by people in the industry that the mass consumer audience is like them. In the industry we all have high-speed PCs, and most of us have high-speed connections. We are tolerant of complexity, so downloading the latest Netscape alpha browser and installing programs such as Shockwave and Java applets is fun. But all this is out of step with what most consumers want. They're curious about the world of interactive services. They've read a little bit, or their friends use a service, and they want to try it, but they're a little nervous. They want to make sure there's a brand they can trust, a brand that'll make the experience easy and useful and fun and affordable. For millions of people, that brand has been AOL. We hope it will continue to be.

There are lots of reasons why more people aren't using online services, and we're trying to do a better job of addressing each of them. One is that it's too hard. We're trying to make it easier. Another is that people don't think that being online has sufficient value. We're trying to create a more engaging interactive experience with more original content, improved context, navigation, and personalization, so AOL becomes *your* AOL, not *our* AOL. By building a sense of community, we can help people feel like members of the service, like participants. At this stage in the industry, and particularly in AOL, we're able to reach out to entrepreneurs and encourage them to join us in the creation of the content technology that can take this to the next step. Our AOL Greenhouse program is an example. We've funded several dozen entrepreneurs and, more importantly, have provided distribution to help build their brands.

In the past year, we've built new brands, like Motley Fool, a community of interest area on AOL that focuses on personal investments. Motley Fool, run by Tom and Dave Gardner, two brothers in their twenties, is a raging hit and one of AOL's most popular areas. We have been able to create a new brand by leveraging the audience reach of AOL in concert with creativity of bright young entrepreneurs. We made a deal with Simon & Schuster for a Motley Fool book that has now been published and is selling quite well, and we'll probably negotiate now for a TV show and other media forms. In a couple of years, the whole development of new media has turned upside down, because up until quite recently, online services were the last stop on the media value chain, and people said, Well, let's repurpose our media a little bit, we'll get a few incremental dollars by licensing our content to one of these guys like AOL, we'll throw it up there and they'll send us checks every once in a while. Suddenly the new media ideas are being nested in the online world, like Motley Fool, which will lead to spinoffs such as books, movies, and TV shows. Almost all the major media brands created in the next decade will be initially nested on services like AOL and then taken more broadly to the Web, and then taken more broadly outside of the interactive world to more traditional forms of media and distribution.

THE PRAGMATIST: <STEWART ALSOP> "The Statesman?" He's a street fighter. He loves to win. He's floating on cloud nine because he got Bill Gates to do a deal with him.

THE MARKETER: <TED LEONSIS> I think Steve is a historical figure and I'm not saying that because he's my boss. He will go down as the William Paley of this business. Paley didn't invent television, Sarnoff did, but Paley was the one who figured out how to build a business model and bring it to the masses and then kept up the quality of programming in the golden days of television. That's what Steve's role here is, to be the voice of the member. Steve focuses on what works for consumers and how people will extract value.

THE CATALYST: <LINDA STONE> The spirit of AOL reflects Steve Case in many ways. To look at the service is to look at Steve. Wish I'd get flowers as often as I get AOL disks in the mail.

<John C. Dvorak>

The Gadfly

The Scribe: <John Markoff>

John C. Dvorak is definitely an industry gadfly, but he's worked at being one. Everything with John is incredibly calculated. If you talk to John much you'll realize that he thinks about things like cross-marketing himself. What an absolutely bizarre concept. But he's really the funniest person in the personal computer industry, he's one of the most irreverent, and he doesn't tolerate all the bullshit that goes down, which is my favorite quality about him. He doesn't buy into this vision shit and he's a useful antidote to the mass delirium that goes on around technology.

John C. Dvorak is a columnist for *PC Magazine, PC/Computing,* and *Boardwatch;* the host of *Real Computing,* a radio program broadcast on one hundred public stations; and the software reviewer for *C-Net Central,* a nationwide cable TV show.

"What we're dealing with is not really a content revolution," says John C. Dvorak. "In fact, the computer revolution is not even supplanting the Industrial Revolution. These computers that do things we couldn't do before with our brains, with our bodies, are just another new extension to man." Pretty good, I think to myself. Lip-synching Marshall McLuhan! He's got the words down. Even the rhythm's right. Marshall, whom I got to know when he spent a year at Fordham University in 1967, is probably up there somewhere, delighted that thirty-three years after the publication of *Understanding Media,* his words reverberate in the deep recesses of John's skull.

"The revolution is in the increased communication capability," John explains. "This is a continuation of what started well before the Industrial Revolution. Genghis Khan was one of the first to grasp the concept of the necessity of quick transmittal of information. He had horses positioned every twenty miles, and when guys wore out a horse, they jumped on the next one and the next one. They made two hundred miles a day, which was a big deal back in the year 1200. Now we can do everything instantly, worldwide. It's frightening."

John is "The Gadfly." He has been a major industry columnist for fifteen years. First he wrote the "Inside Track" column for *InfoWorld,* before he jumped in 1986 to *PC.* Today he's a one-man column factory, and he's on radio and television as well. People read him for his biting wit, his inside intelligence, and his sense of humor – unparalleled in an industry not known for laughter. If I were pitching his story to a Hollywood studio, I would describe him as "Don Imus meets David Letterman."

I met John in the early '80s on the floor of Comdex in Las Vegas, where he must have learned the secrets of success that have served him well over the years. First, there was Dvorak's daily walk, a party in motion, through the miles of exhibits, during which he was trailed by media people, various cognoscenti, and me. He always had an endless supply of insights and wisecracks. Second, there was "Dvorak's Unofficial Party List," on which he kept a tight rein, and which, if you were lucky, might provide you with the necessary information to crash the big events of Commodore, Osborne, Visicorp, Digital Research, and other dominant industry players. Third, there was his uncanny ability to go through life without paying for anything. Who needs credit cards, who needs cash, when people are throwing gourmet food and cases of wine, champagne, computers, and software at you simply for walking by their booth and insulting them in person and in print?

After a decade and a half, I can personally confirm that John has not lost his touch.

THE GADFLY: <JOHN C. DVORAK> Content is anything that contains information; it's a shortened form of the term *information content.* It could be art, it could be a picture, it could be a video, it could be an essay, it could be an old magazine, it could be a live TV feed from the freeway showing you that the road is clear and you can now get in your car and go someplace.

Audience is always delivered by some form of content. People want to find something out when they visit a Web site, whether it's how to pick up a prostitute in Las Vegas or where to get the best coffee in the world, which incidentally comes from some obscure farm in Mexico at $15 a pound. Ultimately, content is the realm of personalities and writers and auteurs who can create it. I think people want new content more than they want old content.

We're seeing a couple different kinds of interactivity. The first is online interactivity, people talking to each other about different topics that interest them, but at a low bandwidth and a slow speed. It's a group thing, and it has a sense of anonymity that people like. They can spew out their thoughts without having to worry about somebody ridiculing them for being an idiot. People like to interact, and anonymous interactivity has an appeal. But it's an entertainment vehicle. I don't think any substance is involved. It's just fun.

In the other kind of interactivity, people interact with, for example, a television program. This is something they've been trying to do for decades, and nobody's really interested. David Letterman said he went to one of those movies where the audience got to pick the ending, and he joked that he went to *see* the movie, not to write it. People don't want to interact with everything; sometimes they want to sit back and relax. I don't want to interact with the book I'm reading. I just want to read it!

Community is an issue here. Are we really little network clubs that allow somebody in Ohio and somebody in Pennsylvania and somebody in Florida to get together and talk about canaries? These communities are false because a community requires close person-to-person contact over a period of time within a certain region. Genuine communities are not separated and fragmented. I've seen too many instances where an online community appears to be solid, like a little town, and then it deteriorates. It turns out that one member is a complete phoney, and another just got arrested, and one guy is really a woman. Too much lying goes on for the online community to exist except in this very shallow, weak form; it is unable to withstand the pressures that would be put on a real community. These are fake institutions.

The Well is an interesting phenomenon because it pretends to be a community, but is getting slick now and is going to start falling by the wayside. One member committed suicide. Before he died, he somehow hacked The Well and erased all evidence of his existence. This got The Well all atitter for a very short period. Ultimately, though, it was just one of those head scratchers that occurred in an isolated moment in time, like watching a weird news report.

Intellectual property issues are where the lawyers are going to make all their money. Over the last decade, publishers have been trying to wrest control of authors' rights to such an extent that it's hard for authors to retain electronic rights to their work. If you're writing for magazines, publishers usually want you to work under a work-for-hire contract, where you give away your copyright. Publishers see a bonanza down the road in terms of electronic rights and electronic distribution. They have no model that proves they can make a nickel on this stuff, but there's a greed factor. They've decided to try and get all the rights from the writers up front. Writers have to resist. Too many writers say, "I'd just as soon write for free if my ideas can get out there." These guys with all that idealistic crap are hurting everyone else.

We've got all this information, and someone is going to have to decide if it's good information or bad information. Unfortunately it's the end-user who too often makes that decision. Eventually it will all be done through clearinghouses, and we'll have the same situation we do with magazines or newspapers. You have to trust editors to look at the information, have their meetings, and say, "This is good information. This is what you should know about." Reliability is going to be a big issue in the next century.

People seem to lose all sense of reality about the computer scene. It's not as radical as everyone would like to believe. We like to think of ourselves as being in the middle of a revolution. It makes us feel a lot better at the beginning of this massive societal upheaval. Anyone who thinks that DOS is going to be around in a thousand years is nuts, because even within recent memory we've lost a number of operating systems. The old Commodore machines have been put aside, and the CP/M world is all but dead. These things are changing quickly because of the inadequacy of the software available today. Most of the stuff won't be with us ten years from now.

One of the reasons we're having these weird conversations about computer technology is that we're basically an agricultural society too easily wowed by technology. The World Wide Web is pretty boring if you look at it objectively. Compare the six-channel Dolby movie, which is a spectacular piece of technology and amazing to watch, with the sluggish World Wide Web, which has a few graphics here and there. It's ridiculous to be too giddy over the Web and these other computer-based technologies.

I don't think the Web is going to make money for anybody until things smooth out a bit. Right now it's a rough go. People aren't going to pay a lot to go on the Web and wait forever for a site to be accessed. Nicholas Negroponte got this one right when he said that we're going to nickel-and-dime people to death with small transactions. It's all going to have to be done with ecash. People will end up subscribing to some system or other, and when they want to use a service it's going to cost them a nickel. People are going to say, "Oh, it's only a nickel," so they'll go along with it.

Many people have opened up archives on the Web, and there's an I-can-do-better-than-you attitude among Web sites. Someone says, "Well, I'm going to see if I can post the entire library of our university on the Web." What's the value of that to the average guy? It's valuable to me because I can find an old book that somebody wrote in 1890, download a copy on my computer, and search the downloaded text for a particular reference, instead of having to read the whole damn thing. This is terrific if you're a researcher or a writer or you're in the arts. But what is the guy who drives a taxi going to get out of the Web? Maybe he'll learn something; maybe he'll get a different job; maybe he likes being a taxi driver. I'm not absolutely sure that the Web is universally valuable. The Web, the Internet, the entire computer scene, may be stratifying society in ways that aren't particularly healthy.

Privacy is dead and there's nothing you can do about it. Instead of Big Brother, we have Little Brother, and he's watching all the time with his camcorder. It's going to become very difficult to maintain privacy over the long haul. There's just too much intrusion. We're going to have to live with the fact that our lives are now subject to public scrutiny. That's why these fringe groups lock themselves away in Montana or Idaho. They sense that this is happening and they can't stand it.

A couple of institutions will be affected adversely by the changes in communications. One is the newspaper business. If I want news, I can go online. I can get all of today's stories. I can get in-depth stories. I can go to the *Los Angeles Times* and to *Time,* which has a daily service. The newspapers have got a real problem on their hands. The numbers show it, and it's getting worse. It's not just the news. If I want to buy a Nikon camera, I can go to the *Chicago Tribune,* the *San Jose Mercury News,* and a bunch of other places around the country and search the want ads from all these newspapers at once online. I don't see how newspapers in print form, especially with the rising cost of paper, are going to survive. Magazines have a better chance of surviving because they have a higher bandwidth: hi-res color. Even they are probably doomed at some point, when special-interest Web publishing becomes more common.

Newspapers are specifically protected under the Bill of Rights but other media are not protected adequately for my taste. Worse still, I am concerned that NBC is owned by General Electric, CBS by Westinghouse, ABC by Disney. GE and Westinghouse are companies that had price-fixing scandals in the '50s. Now they own two of the three major networks. The fact that the government allowed this to happen is astonishing to me. You have to question what kind of investigative reporting these networks would ever do about Westinghouse and GE. Do you think anyone could run a negative story about the company that owns it? That's not likely to happen. The potential for losing control of our press freedoms is quite high and disturbs me more than anything.

THE PRAGMATIST: <STEWART ALSOP> Dvorak is the David Letterman of the PC industry. He once told me that you have to make a third of the people happy and a third of the people unhappy at any one time. I've used that often.

THE PUBLISHER: <JANE METCALFE> My Dvorak story: I was at Comdex and one of our investors introduced me to Dvorak: "This is the founder of *Wired.* All this exciting stuff's going to happen. You really ought to know these people and follow what they do." Dvorak wouldn't even speak to me. The next day I see him in the airport. I'm wearing an extremely curvy suit, and I am kind of dolled up. He comes up and says, "Hi! John Dvorak! Nice to meet you." I'm thinking, "Yeah, I'm the same person you blew off last night."

THE IDEALIST: <DENISE CARUSO> Every industry needs a contrarian, and John Dvorak's a damn good one. That said... better him than me.

THE CITIZEN: <HOWARD RHEINGOLD> Dvorak demonstrates that a small amount of knowledge, a large amount of attitude, and a good organization can bring in the bucks.

THE SCOUT: <STEWART BRAND> Widely read indeed. Widely respected?

THE SOFTWARE DEVELOPER: <BILL GATES> He's even funnier in person than he is in print. He's a very funny guy.

<Esther Dyson>

The Pattern-Recognizer

The Coyote: <John Perry Barlow>

Esther is the smartest woman I know. She would rather have me say she is one of the five smartest humans I know, which I could also say. But I'll stick with calling her the smartest woman I know because there is something about the combination of that kind of intelligence and femininity which is still too rare in the computer field. There is a quality to her insight that is not masculine and is incredibly powerful as a result.

Esther Dyson is president of EDventure Holdings and editor of *Release 1.0.* Her PC Forum conference is an annual industry event.

In Esther Dyson's vision of the Internet, people will do the same things they've always done, with some major differences. There will be a new structure of communication: today we talk one-on-one on the telephone or passively receive television and radio. Tomorrow, on the Internet, we will operate more like a radio station and broadcast to the world, and people will talk back as yet more listen – more like talk radio than newspaper or magazine publishing. We will use our new ability to shift time. With email, we can copy messages to more people. We will all have extenders to our fingers that can manipulate communications much more easily. Esther cautions against developing businesses based on selling copies of intellectual property. You need to create intellectual property and then figure out creative ways to exploit it – as a service, as a performance, as a process. She favors, instead, approaches that emphasize the talents of people who can deal with process. The future on the Internet belongs to those who can conceive of, and act upon, the idea of the Internet as a performance art space.

Esther has published the monthly *Release 1.0* since 1982. It is the computer industry's most intellectual newsletter and deals with the future of the information and communications industries. Esther and Jerry Michalski, *Release*'s managing editor, attempt to be the first to discover and explain the new companies, new technologies, new ideas, and new business models that are changing the direction of these industries. They are the people to read for expert and timely pattern recognition, to find how people will use new technology and how companies can make a profit from it.

Esther runs her own venture capital firm, chairs the Electronic Frontier Foundation (EFF), and occasionally writes for other magazines and newspapers. She also runs PC Forum, one of the industry conferences of consequence. Through these activities, and her interactions with industry bigwigs, she sees many demos and business plans at an early stage and has a comprehensive understanding of what's going on in digital technology. She also has a sense of social responsibility and an awareness of social consequence, which make her a powerful force for positive change. Yet she is light and she is playful.

Esther and the electronic digital computer shared a few years of childhood in the early 1950s at the Institute for Advanced Study in Princeton, New Jersey, where Esther's parents met in 1948. John von Neumann and Julian Bigelow occupied an outbuilding at the edge of the institute's woods, cooking up a 40-bit parallel-arithmetic processor, with one thousand words of high-speed memory. From these beginnings, the computer industry soon sprang. Esther's father, Freeman Dyson, a mathematical physicist and one of the principal architects of quantum electrodynamics, and her mother, Verena Huber-Dyson, a mathematical logician, represented the two fields whose intersection brought the computer revolution to life. At the time, both were working in group theory – the study of transformations, relations, and invariances, whether in mathematical physics, number theory, or social institutions – which is exactly what Esther excels at, with keenness and discipline that allow no pattern, however subtle, to escape. Esther Dyson is "The Pattern-Recognizer."

One evening in 1990, I gave a dinner for Freeman Dyson; his daughter Mia, who is a nurse living in Maine; and his son George, who for many years lived in a tree house perched ninety-five feet off the ground in a Douglas fir in the British Columbia rain forest. The occasion was George's talk before the Reality Club, to be held later in the evening at the Metropolitan Club, hosted by Hugh Downs. The fascinating relationship between Freeman and George, a Baidarka builder who is redeveloping the Aleut kayak, was portrayed in 1978 by Kenneth Brower in his classic book, *The Starship and the Canoe.* What an evening it was! The conversation, the ideas, seemingly moved through the air across the table like invisible electrical circuits instantaneously connecting three brilliant lightbulbs.

And where was Esther? She was out of town. George pointed out that the family hadn't had dinner together since 1965, except for rare distracting affairs at Esther's conferences and an occasional large social event. "What is so remarkable," he said, "is that with essentially no personal or even intellectual contact, our paths are still somehow cohered."

I don't see Esther as often as I used to or would like to. In the last five or six years, she's spent a lot of time in Russia and Eastern Europe. Fluent in Russian, she is a regular keynote speaker at conferences such as Comtek, International Computer Forum, Windows Expo, and CERF in Bucharest. In 1990 she organized the annual East-West High-Tech Forum, which has played a key role in defining and developing the commercial computer markets of Central and Eastern Europe. Modeled on the PC Forum and designed to encourage long-term business relationships, the forum is not another conference about the market; it *is* the market. Meetings have been held in Budapest; Prague; Warsaw; Bratislava, Slovakia; and Bled, Slovenia.

These activities in Russia and Eastern Europe have great meaning for her. "Look," Esther said to me recently, "if I were a maid, I would prefer a messy room to a tidy room. Eastern Europe is a great mess, especially Russia." As George Dyson explains, "She believes that the decentralization of personal computers, and computer-mediated communications, could undo some of the damage done by the attempt to centralize the economy over seventy years."

Unique Esther is, living without a telephone at home, refusing to drive a car, spending much of her life in transit, on airplanes, in hotels, and in swimming pools, carrying around her world in canvas tote bags. During the '80s I attended a number of conferences where Esther could be seen before sunrise in the pool, swimming back and forth, back and forth, hour after hour, still a daily regimen. Sometimes up early, I would sit and watch her swim, wondering to myself, What is she thinking about? What is she swimming toward, or away from?

The Pattern-Recognizer: <Esther Dyson>

The Net is becoming less and less a thing and more and more an environment. It's going to be all over the place. People are going to do things in it, instead of keeping it in boxes, like packaged software. Imagine that suddenly water showed up in a world where we had drinking water – but before we had rivers, oceans, swimming pools, etcetera – and suddenly water changed from being this little thing in a glass or in a bottle, and suddenly it started being all over the world, and you could travel on it, you could fly over it, you could fish out of it, and you could grow things in it.

The key to thinking about the Internet is this: the Internet changes the economies of scale in favor of the little guy. It used to be only big guys could send stuff, only big guys could advertise, only big guys could have newspapers. Suddenly everybody can reach the audience they deserve, more or less for free. They won't necessarily get a mass audience, because they may not be good enough, or they may not be worth listening to, but everybody can distribute their information pretty much as widely as they want, almost without cost.

But people can get overexcited. We're still not talking about telepathy. We're talking about the traditional boundary between me and you. I still need to put things into words. I can show you pictures, but there's still a distinction between me and somebody else. However, the channel between us has changed: it has become much more efficient, broader, and cheaper. What's happened also concerns the whole notion of interactivity.

The fact that you can send as easily as you can receive makes a huge difference.

If you're the head of a telephone company, a cable company, or an entertainment conglomerate, and you don't make a billion dollars, doing business on the Internet is not interesting. But if you're five guys, you can make enough money for ten guys. If you're twenty guys, you can make enough money for forty guys. The economies of scale don't favor the big guys. They favor the small guys. You get a return for your effort, not for your huge investment capital. That's why it's such a decentralized, fragmented business. The individuals, instead of the big corporate owners, get what's coming to them. That's why it's a very moral culture.

TV people no longer have it so easy – they've got a lot more competition. They're still in the business of either buying or developing content that's supposed to attract audiences. There's going to be so much more content out there, some of it really crappy, some of it not. It's going to be a lot harder to get people's attention, and there will no longer be a premium on their distribution mechanism, which was based on the shortage of channels. Suddenly there are millions and millions of channels, just the way there are millions and millions of phone lines.

On the other hand, people are cynical and sensitive to quality. There's going to be a lot of junk, so the brand name, for example, of *The New York Times* is still going to be valuable, if *The New York Times* does it right. People still don't want everything tailored for them; they want to watch what everyone else watches. They want to watch Jay Leno and David Letterman and laugh at their jokes. They want to be part of that broad community.

The "convergence" companies are all trying to vertically integrate. They think they should be in every part of the business. That doesn't make a whole lot of sense. The reason is that good content wants to and will go everywhere. Because every channel wants it, good content doesn't need to be stuck to one distribution mechanism. In the same way, any carrier, any distribution system, wants to be free to get all the content, the best content; it doesn't want to be tied to one source of content. Consumers are not going to want to be restricted in the content they can receive. If I had a telephone that could call only France or Germany and not Russia or the western United States, I'd get rid of it pretty fast.

I've been cast as some fanatic, radical, anticopyright crackpot. What I'm really saying is that this is not an issue of law, and it's not an issue of morality. Copyright is entirely justified; I should have the right to control what I produce. There is going to be a strong movement toward proper attribution and maintenance of the integrity of one's work. There will be a profusion of content, because it's easy to produce and almost costless to distribute on the Internet. The price of content, not necessarily the intrinsic "value" of content, will go down. The people who produce content are going to have to think of new models for getting paid. It may be charging for a performance or for consulting, or it may be paying Stephen King to read one of his books. There are different kinds of models, and people have to understand that simply putting content into a box and selling it will probably be the least effective way of exploiting it.

Electronic commerce is exciting, but people are overexcited about what it's going to do. Digital cash is going to make the world vastly more efficient, but what the Net does to social and interpersonal relationships and the balance of power is much more important than what it's going to do to commerce. What's magical is how it's going to affect people and relationships.

A new kind of community, not a culture, is coming. The difference between a culture and a community is that a culture is one-way – you can absorb it by reading it, by watching it – but you have to invest back in a community. Absent this return investment, it's not really a community. People will be investing in sharing content and sending messages to each other, in spending time together, and, in part, that's what builds these communities.

People talk a lot about the expansion of democratic government with the fall of the Soviet Bloc. The real issue isn't democracy versus tyranny. It's individual choice versus control imposed by big forces, whether it's big government or mass media. Quite simply, democracy is the tyranny of the majority over the minority. In more and more spheres of life, ranging from your choice of breakfast cereal to the school where you send your children, to the books you read or what you see on your screen, we're moving to a fragmented individual-choice world. It's not between democracy and tyranny. It's decentralization. More and more things are chosen individually. It's the primacy of the small unit. You can now be as efficient in a small unit as you are in a big unit.

People think that being rich means having power. If you sell a million copies of Windows, you get a lot of money, but you don't control what people see through Windows, and that's the fundamental difference. There are lots of large companies, and they're going to make a lot of money, but they won't control as much of consumers' lives as they used to. Consumers will be able to move from one supplier to another. The balance of power between the large employer and the individual employee is also going to change. Employees are going to be more visible; they're going to have more ability to move; they're going to be more aware of their rights.

The real issue regarding the Net is going to be people's ability to use it, their education, and their literacy. The world will definitely favor the educated. It was easy enough to take the land and redistribute it to the peasants if you wanted to. It was easy enough to take the money and the capital and redistribute them to the workers of the world, as the Soviets showed, even though it wasn't terribly successful. But you can't take knowledge and just give it to people. They have to *take* the knowledge. They have to learn. We're becoming a society in which people who don't contribute really don't get anything, and you can't redress that imbalance. Individually, people have to learn that they must contribute.

It's not strange to me that some people don't understand these new ideas concerning the Internet and the communications revolution. When Copernicus was around, people thought he was a crackpot. Most ideas go through a cycle. The first time people hear an idea, they don't even pay enough attention to disagree. The idea just slips by. The second time, they say, "That's really stupid. If that were true, we'd know it already." The third time, they seem to get it vaguely and say, "Hmm, you know...." The fourth time, they say, "Oh yeah, well, everybody knows that. That's boring."

THE SCRIBE: <JOHN MARKOFF> Esther is the First Lady of Cyberspace. She has also earned the right to be called the First Lady of Personal Computing, and before that the First Lady of the Semiconductor Industry. There's a homeless quality about her that I've never been able to define; she can't really find her niche. She's had the ability to stay outside the groove of the industry. She's always been one standard deviation off, which is foresighted.

THE SAINT: <KEVIN KELLY> I am in awe of Esther. Her brilliance is almost intimidating, and she has the unusual and enviable knack of being able to absorb very complex, complicated technical information and cut right through it. I rely on Esther to tell me what's real and what's hype. She's the best B.S. filter I know, because she undersands it. Unlike most of us, she actually knows what's going on.

THE STATESMAN: <STEVE CASE> Very insightful. Some of the topics she's spent a lot of time exploring in the last decade have been over my head in terms of the possibilities of technology in an increasingly global society. I've always been struck by her ability to move across very different worlds. One day she's in Poland, creating online services and hosting conferences, and the next day she's attending Comdex in Las Vegas. Maybe it's a genetic thing, given the intellectual curiosity of her family.

THE THINKER: <DOUG CARLSTON> Esther is the smartest person in the computer industry and the most cogent observer of the whole technology area. Often her writing looks too far out into the future for people to fully understand its value. An interesting exercise is to read what she wrote two or three years ago and see how utterly germane it seems today.

THE IDEALIST: <DENISE CARUSO> Esther has persisted and persisted and pushed into new areas, and her intellectual curiosity is just amazing to me. I disagree with her at least 50 percent of the time, and it's completely OK. I can't say that about very many people I disagree with.

The Lover: <Dave Winer> Esther swims, Esther's a dreamer. She's cool. In many ways, she's superficial. I'm not sure she really gets the stuff that she writes about. But on the whole I'm delighted that she's been as influential as she has been. I read a thing by Max Frankel in *The New York Times* recently that was entirely about Esther. I would love to talk to Frankel about that and tell him why he shouldn't be scared.

The Marketer: <Ted Leonsis> Esther Dyson is truly an amazing woman. I thought at the TED Conference there was a new Esther. She had become a fully realized human being. She was talking about love, about relationships, about quality of life issues. Here's a person who's dealt with the industry and her life on her own terms. Most of the people who have had the opportunity to travel with her as I have, and spend time with her, have come to admire her. She's onto causes all the time; now it's privacy and Eastern Europe. She's very spiritually deep.

The Judge: <David R. Johnson> Esther is the embodiment of the optimal way to construct your network of communication in the world. She personally bridges the cultures of East and West, or the cultures of business and digital. She has always been a very significant voice in support of the need to think through policies in the context in which they're occurring, and to develop creative and thoughtful decisions, in addition to standing firm to protect basic rights.

The Software Developer: <Bill Gates> Esther has been kind of a high-IQ intellectual observer of our business for a long time. She's written a lot of smart things.

The Cyberanalyst: <Sherry Turkle> Esther Dyson's great strength is that she approaches her work not only with energy and passion but with discipline and perseverance. She learns by immersion – her knowledge is concrete and can be trusted.

THE IMPRESARIO: <RICHARD SAUL WURMAN> Somewhat without ready humor and always intimidating. As she speaks, I never think "Why didn't I say *that?*" because I never would have thought of *that.* Great genes, great intellect. I want a blood transfusion, or, perhaps better, a brain transplant.

THE GENIUS: <W. DANIEL HILLIS> Esther's invented herself from whole cloth. The wonderful thing about Esther is that she's not just in the computer business for the business; she cares about the people that she works with. She has been a catalyst for the industry, because she's always hooking people up, connecting people that ought to know each other and be connected. She's fantastic at that, because she has a deep understanding of what's going on.

<Bill Gates>

The Software Developer

The Saint: <Kevin Kelly> *Gates is incredibly sharp. He's simply fantastic with numbers and things stored in his head. It's like he has the ultimate RAM in his brain. That's his inner nerd. But I was surprised by how much I liked him as a person, given how much I disliked DOS. Although he is extremely cagey — he is always playing a game with how much he says or doesn't say because he is involved in so many embryonic deals — he is also witty and accessible. He's curious about things. He likes to think big and wide — he looks globally, in long terms, and across many disciplines. It would be impossible to be bored around him. Most importantly, he "gets it." He groks the current reality. I found he has a razor-sharp intuition of exactly how things are. He may have to fudge what he says because he represents a large corporation, but you can tell that he grasps what's really happening underneath, even at a cultural level. But the thing that most impressed me about Gates was his ritual of taking a couple weeks off every semester to read and think. I can't imagine anything more important to do in a world accelerating as fast as the one we are traveling in is.*

Bill Gates is CEO of Microsoft Corporation and author of *The Road Ahead* (1995).

"Jim Clark and Marc Andreessen better watch out. Bill's comin' after them. He'll get 'em. You just wait." David Bunnell lapses into his Nebraska twang to make a Cassandra-like prediction on the fate of Netscape and its two founders. He is driving me up Interstate 280, from Silicon Valley to the San Francisco airport. "Hell, just look at what he did to Lotus and Borland," he continues.

"Microsoft was just getting on the map in applications in the mid-'80s. Now it owns the desktop." David was talking about his friend Bill Gates's successful move into the spreadsheet market with Microsoft Excel, a product that dislodged Lotus 1-2-3 from the Number One slot in the market and effectively fought off a worthy competitor in Borland's Quattro Pro. Neither company exists today as an independent entity.

David likes to reminisce. When he gets all warm and fuzzy, his favorite word is *Bill.* I have to confess, I probably hear more about Bill than I need to or want to. But I have to listen to David: we're partners in a business venture. I have no idea, however, why I listen to our mutual friend Dr. Eddie Currie, who – along with David, Bill, and Paul Allen, the cofounder of Microsoft – was in Albuquerque working at MITS in 1975, when the personal computer revolution began.

What would you like to know? How Bill and Paul became friends as kids in Seattle? The positive effect of Bill's parents on his character? I bet you don't know the story of Bill's first and most important victory, the arbitration with MITS over the ownership of Basic. Well, I do.

"Why," I ask myself, "do I have to know all this stuff? Why must my head be the databank of David and Eddie's memories of Bill Gates as a teenage phenom? What are they doing to me? Enough already!"

Tom Wolfe, where are you? What these guys began twenty years ago was nothing less than the beginning of the most important revolution of the century. Who is going to do for Bill Gates and friends what Wolfe did for the astronauts in *The Right Stuff?* Spielberg, Geffen, Katzenberg, where are you? This is the epic movie America is waiting for, one the whole family can enjoy. No violence, most certainly no sex, not even aliens (well, not really): just a story of a bunch of young men who changed the world.

When it comes to Bill Gates, David pales next to Dr. Currie, who now runs a C^{++} tool company. The last time we got together, he braved a blizzard to drive into Manhattan for a dinner party, during which he spent an hour trying to convince my fifteen-year-old son, Max, to donate his brand-new Macintosh 7500 PowerPC to the Computers and You program at San Francisco's

Glide Memorial Church and switch to a Pentium machine running Windows 95. I waited for an exegesis on the technological issues, but to my astonishment Eddie based his pitch on patriotism: what is good for Microsoft and Windows is good for America. "Ask not what Microsoft can do for you," Eddie said, "ask what you can do for Microsoft." Or something original like that. "But I don't want a Pentium machine," Max replied. "I like my Mac."

"Don't be a selfish teenager, Max. We need standardization," Eddie pronounced. "How many different kinds of operating systems do we have for automobiles? Cars all work the same way, and you don't have to know what's under the hood. Just turn the key and you're off and running. Standardization will strengthen us as a nation. That's what Bill can do for America, not to say what he's already doing for our balance of payments." With that, Eddie opened the door, looked back at Max, and said, "Everybody loves to hate Microsoft and Bill simply because they're Number One, but when the history of twentieth-century business is written, you'll have Henry Ford, Bill Gates, and then the rest. Remember that." He went off to brave the storm, leaving us with visions of crashes dotting the highways.

"David's bonkers, but Dr. Currie is really nutty if he thinks I'm giving up my Mac for Windows," Max said. "Well," I replied, "maybe there was something in the water in Albuquerque. But remember what Dvorak told you last year? 'There's a Windows machine in your future. Get used to the idea.' Anyway, why do you have attitude about Microsoft? What has Bill Gates ever done to you? So you found out that he has two friends. Big deal. Don't let it ruin your day."

A month later, in February 1996, David called to say he was flying into New York for an Internet conference at the Jacob K. Javitz Center. Did I want to meet up with him to hear Bill speak first thing the next morning? So there I was at 8 A.M., in line with about two thousand other people eager to hear Bill's pronouncements about Microsoft and the Internet.

Bill's talk was a masterful presentation aimed at illustrating how Microsoft planned to embrace and extend all the new open technologies and allow its customers to interact with the Web in exciting ways through the integration of new versions of

Microsoft desktop applications with Microsoft Explorer, a proprietary Web browser. The demonstration was convincing and well executed. "Pretty impressive," I said in a whisper to David, who sat beside me. "Can you do this now on your IBM ThinkPad?" "Are you kidding?" he replied. "This is pure Bill. It's known as FUD: fear, uncertainty, and doubt. Two thousand people in this hall, many of whom make key hardware and software buying decisions for the big corporations, are not going to risk going all the way with Netscape or Sun and find themselves locked out of Bill's vision in a few months. He's already having a formidable impact on the marketplace. That's why he's a genius."

In a blink, the lights went up. Bill Gates was gone. I closed my eyes for a moment and had a flashback. I was sitting next to Abbie Hoffman in Madison Square Garden in the early '70s, staring at a brightly lit, empty stage as an announcer intoned, "Elvis has left the building. The King has left the building." I opened my eyes. No Abbie. No Elvis. No Bill. The King had left the building, but David was still there beside me. "John," he said, "what you just witnessed was the end of the beginning of the personal computer revolution. Bill's a digerati now. You gotta put him in your book."

Bill Gates is "The Software Developer."

THE SOFTWARE DEVELOPER: <BILL GATES> The vision that really got Microsoft going – a computer on every desk and in every home – was always dependent on low-cost communications coming along. There was the notion that eventually you would get to a critical mass, where you would have enough people connected up so that it made sense to start publishing lots of information in electronic form.

We didn't know exactly when critical mass would happen or exactly what protocols or standards it would coalesce around. We weren't certain when lightning would strike, although it became clear that corporations were building up more and more connectivity, that communications was the killer application for PCs, and that multimedia would be a key part of the experience.

We were investing in all of this through our research and product development work. We talked about how CD-ROM was a transitional technology, and that eventually high-bandwidth networks would eliminate the need for the physical disk. CD-ROM was a great bootstrap because of its capacity to show how an encyclopedia, different types of learning experiences, and catalogues of information could be put together in electronic form. That had a positive effect. It turned into a good business and certainly did a lot to get people moving along with tools.

In terms of the hardware, there was always the question: will PCs or TV sets be at the center? A lot of phone companies and cable companies talked about interactive TV as the defining application. Most people would say that a more evolutionary approach clearly starts with a PC but moves to incorporate new devices that are more like TV sets. In a sense, you can say these devices are just the result of the PC getting better and better and moving into more forms. These devices – PCs or information appliances – all connected at high bandwidths, will allow the user to do many powerful things. As a result, the Internet is getting richer and richer.

In '93, we began to see universities using the Internet as more than just a phenomenon in the engineering or computer science departments. Cornell and other schools started to create intranets, putting out class schedules and lots of other useful information. University students got tied in with electronic mail. This was great, because we were always evangelizing about electronic mail and information sharing as a big productivity gain. Then in '94 you got people doing hypertext through the Web protocols. There was more commercial involvement, more than just using the Web for FTP or telnet or electronic mail. That's when we started up our first big projects and shipped our first Internet-based products.

By early '95, it was clear that you had critical mass. It was the starting point for the Internet in the same way that the IBM PC became the seed corn for the PC revolution, despite all the arbitrary and weak elements in the IBM PC. In that case, once the phenomenon got going the weaknesses of the PC almost became a strength as new companies were founded to eliminate those weaknesses.

Of course, there are similar weaknesses with the Internet. For example, is it bad that the Web doesn't have security? Sure, but

Microsoft and Netscape are just two of many companies coming in to fix that problem. Is it a problem that things are hard to find on the Web? Sure, but there are lots of start-ups in the business of helping with that problem.

What has developed is a gold rush atmosphere: any company in any business is thinking about the Internet. This phenomenon is now the center of gravity of the computing world. The question now is: How are we going to tie into this, for information inside businesses, for business at large, for education, and, as the bandwidth moves up, even for entertainment?

Right now, much of the content on the Web is created by people who have a product to sell you, like a General Motors, or a Fidelity, or a Schwab. They are publishing with the goal of building a customer relationship. We're seeing a tremendous amount of interest from the media. *The New York Times, The Wall Street Journal,* and others are looking at the Internet, trying to sort out how to bring new value to the medium, and how to protect their readership.

The people who are investing a lot of money in doing unique material for the Web base their approach on a view that the number of users will grow substantially, and so advertising and subscription revenues will also grow. Microsoft is doing a lot of things predicated on that optimism, and thousands of other companies are jumping in. Time Warner's Pathfinder is a good example; they have been trying to add value in a more significant way than just taking material from other media.

There will continue to be high levels of investment over the next two or three years. But there will come a point when companies will ask, "If the revenue's not there, is this a great way to be spending money and tying up our people?"

Eventually, we'll look back on this era and say there were a lot of people who went way overboard – and wasn't it silly what they did – but we'll certainly see a few people who got the combination right, invested in the right areas, and built an asset of great enduring value. That's what makes it so exciting right now. You're dealing with a lot of optimists and people who don't want to be left out. That makes this a fun time.

In terms of the Web experience, right now it comes across as a bit isolating. But the Internet is evolving so rapidly that the majority of sites eventually will be 3-D worlds where you will explore an environment more like a physical world. You'll talk with people and share experiences with them in entirely new ways, and things will be very active, with animation, sound, and video. The pages won't be flat 2-D pages, and they certainly won't be static like a lot of pages are now.

Another thing that will happen is that people using the Internet will start to develop their own profiles, so the information they receive will be based on their unique interests and location. When you connect up to Microsoft, for example, we'd like to show you different material if you're a Mac user working from home than if you're the CIO of a corporation with one thousand personal computers. Already, you can get localized news, localized weather, and highly targeted information sent to you automatically on the Internet.

While the issue of content on the Internet sorts itself out, there are a lot of other dynamic changes happening in the computer industry. The hardware industry, for example, is a very competitive world. Companies like Compaq have managed to do very well with their brand and engineering. That's great. The miracle of the microprocessor is being passed through at very low cost to end-users. As the microprocessor is getting faster and faster, it is taking on more and more applications and is not too far from being able to take even the most demanding applications. For people in the computer world who have been protected from the very fast-moving parts of the PC world, and the low prices, certainly there's a big threat. There's a threat to IBM, DEC, certainly Sun, and even the Unix crowd.

Similarly, things are very dynamic in the software industry. If someone makes a browser that's very popular, we'll make sure our browser has the same features. If our browser, Internet Explorer, has good features and is popular, Netscape and others will do the same thing. This is a complete repeat of what happened in spreadsheets, what happened in word processing, what happened in network operating systems.

Essentially, Netscape wants to take a browser and turn it into an operating system. We want to take an operating system and have enough Internet capability built in so that people continue to view Windows as the best way to use the Internet. That is what our customers expect us to do. Unless we're doing a better operating system and keeping the prices low, somebody else is going to come in. Nobody has a guaranteed situation as you look ahead a couple of years. Companies are moving as fast as they can, and the marketplace is the judge of who gets these things right. This competition is great for the end-user, because all the companies involved have very low prices and there is a lot of free software being made available.

The Internet certainly is changing how people look at the world. It's a revolution in communications that rivals the invention of the printing press, the phone, the TV. The difference with the Internet is that it has such incredible potential for interactivity, for letting you find people with common interests, for letting you go in your own direction. You can reach out and be put in contact with people who share what you care about.

With this new communications revolution we'll be less constrained in terms of living in cities and in terms of only viewing ourselves as being part of a geographic community. We're still not at the point where all of the world's knowledge is available electronically and all of the world's commerce can be done electronically. There's probably another decade to go before all that happens. Then there may be another decade or more before people are so used to the Internet that it redefines how they go about their everyday activities.

Most revolutions take forty or fifty years to complete, but this new communications revolution is moving at an accelerated pace. Although it's still hard to get connected to the Internet – it's still kind of expensive and the user interfaces aren't right – that you can talk about it as a place where people are getting together, where lots of information is becoming available, and where commerce is beginning to be transacted, shows that it's dramatically beyond what it was even two or three years ago.

One of the best examples is electronic mail. More and more people will be drawn to email as part of their regular daily activities. I'll expect my doctor, my lawyer, anybody I work with on a professional basis to be accessible on electronic mail and to be able to answer questions, organize meetings, etcetera. People like me who are enthusiastic about all of this tend to draw in more and more people. I've got all my relatives hooked up. It's great.

Intranets are also becoming very important. The beauty of them is you don't have to go buy any new hardware, just some simple software that allows you to use the tools that you know and take corporate information and make it easily available. At Microsoft, for example, you can call up the internal web and find out about any activity happening on campus, about HR policies and benefits, you can read the latest internal newsletter or join a social group.

Right now, activity around the Internet is still largely U.S.-centric. This is surprising for a country that five or six years ago was thought of as falling behind Japan. As you look at this new revolution, it's interesting to me how the companies of interest at all levels are largely U.S. companies. But now there are whole cities in Europe that are getting connected, and in the next couple of years the Internet phenomenon is going to explode throughout much of the developed and developing world, just as it has in the United States.

THE COMPETITOR: <SCOTT MCNEALY> Bill Gates and his company get a lot of people at Sun Microsystems up in the morning. The world needs an alternative. The world needs competition. I believe in choices, and I don't believe there's much choice in a Microsoft environment. The world needs open, multivendor, clone, competitive, well-priced, innovative product. This is Sun's opportunity, and we certainly have a worthy challenger to that goal in Bill and Microsoft.

THE PRODIGY: <JARON LANIER> I am not against Bill Gates the man, but he's playing a historical role that demands a harsh critique. Within his lifetime, Bill will have probably acquired, by accident, a kind of power that has been rarely sought and never before achieved. The medieval popes sought to be the intermediaries for all thought and communication, even as they were the patrons of the elite intellectuals of their day. They serve as the best precedent we have for what is truly an unprecedented situation. In twenty or fifty years, when most human affairs, intimate and grand, are conducted via computer operating systems, Microsoft could become the universal gatekeeper of thought. Microsoft has so far not been malevolent when it has exercised editorial power. But absolute power corrupts absolutely, and Microsoft could well end up with a new type of absolute power.

THE MARKETER: <TED LEONSIS> The man is brilliant. While people think he's a great software person, he's the world's best marketing person. The Windows 95 announcement was unbelievable. It wasn't a cure for AIDS, it was a software upgrade. Yet it commanded the attention of the entire county. His prowess is as a business thinker, a marketer, combined with being a great software thinker. Bill Gates knows he's in the media business.

THE LOVER: <DAVE WINER> Bill Gates gets a bad rap; I don't know why that is, why he specifically provokes so much negativity from people. He is successful because of his confidence, partially, but also because of everybody else's gross incompetence.

THE PRAGMATIST: <STEWART ALSOP> The Henry Ford of computing. Part of being friends with Bill is that he's allowed to make obnoxious comments about you. Bill is uncompromising. It doesn't matter who you are. His fundamental integrity requires that you always be perfect. If you don't measure up, you have to suffer the consequences.

THE STATESMAN: <STEVE CASE> I don't always agree with what Bill does or how he does it. I think Microsoft suffers a bit because it's still too Bill-centric. But you can't argue with the results. He still has that edge, and this whole battle over the Internet has awakened him and reignited those passions. It's really something quite remarkable to watch.

THE CONSERVATIVE: <DAVID GELERNTER> I have a feeling that Bill Gates is unsatisfied by who he is. When I read his book, *The Road Ahead,* I was reminded of Marilyn Monroe and her need to marry intellectuals; she felt she needed to switch identities in order to get the respect she deserved, but she didn't, or at any rate shouldn't have. I wish Gates had written a book about business instead of the future of technology. We would all have learned a lot. As a businessman, Gates is a phenomenon and an original. What's wrong with that? That's a remarkable thing to be. As a technology visionary, he does nothing for me.

> **THE GADFLY: <JOHN C. DVORAK>** The most underrated business executive of the twentieth century. Bill turns his charm on and off like a water faucet.

THE CATALYST: <LINDA STONE> Bill is one of the most driven, most intellectually curious people one could ever encounter. I have no doubt that he is one of the greatest business leaders of this century. To be at Microsoft when Bill initiated the strategy shift to embrace the Internet was to experience something as awesome as an abrupt change in seasons. What may be less well known is that this guy has a terrific sense of humor.

> **THE IDEALIST: <DENISE CARUSO>** Bill is probably the most driven person I know in this business. The guy owns something like 85 or 90 percent of the PC desktops in the world, right? If there's anything we know today, it's that Microsoft has a lock on the market for operating systems. But during an interview, when someone made mention of that fact, he interrupted the guy. "Oh, do we have a lock on it?" he says, all sardonic. "Should I take a vacation?" Yes, Bill. We think you should.

THE GENIUS: <W. DANIEL HILLIS> Bill Gates is a prime example of the power of a smart person being focused on exactly what he wants. He accomplishes his goals while the rest of us are just muddling around. Watching Bill operate makes me realize, for better or worse, how unfocused I am.

<David Gelernter>

The Conservative

The Skeptic: <Cliff Stoll> *There are lots of clever computer scientists; David Gelernter is one of the few who is wise. He understands the need to interact with people rather than computers. He understands the limitations of computer science. He speaks to the problems of technologists, namely, how come there are so few women online. He addresses serious questions — why there is so little useful stuff on the Net? He realizes that there is much more to context and content than merely bits of information here and hypertext jumps over there. He is a historian, social commentator, and sage with a snicker. In* Mirror Worlds, *Gelernter predicted the power of computer models. His book on the 1939 World's Fair is a joy, showing how we've gained the future but lost our way. Despite, or because of, his deep experience in computing, he questions the maniacal adoption of computers and hypertext in schools and society.*

David Gelernter, a Yale University computer scientist, is the author of *Mirror Worlds* (1991), *The Muse in the Machine* (1994), and *1939: The Lost World of the Fair* (1995).

David Gelernter, a leading figure in the third generation of artificial intelligence (AI) scientists, is highly regarded for his parallel programming language Linda, which allows you to distribute a computer program across a multitude of processors and thus break down problems into a multitude of parts in order to solve them more quickly.

The day I met him, he walked into my office and began to lecture me on the problems with current theories of consciousness.

"The discussion of consciousness is dominated by two opposite positions," he said, starting to pace back and forth in front of my desk. "On one side you have your friend the philosopher Daniel C. Dennett, who, in *Consciousness Explained,* presents his reductionist agenda for thinking about the mind. On the other, there are the holistic ideas of the mathematical physicist Roger Penrose in *The Emperor's New Mind.*" He stopped, turned, and faced me. He looked me in the eye and in a very measured and direct tone said, "They're both full of crap!"

I loved it. A new generation arrives with new ideas that do not answer the old questions, but subsume them in a new paradigm. In David's case, he was presenting a new theory of consciousness, incorporating the full spectrum of cognition, from "high focus" logical thinking to the dreamlike "low focus" thought that characterizes so much of our daily thinking patterns. He believes that bringing emotions, the body, and aesthetics into the discussion about the mind enables him to arrive at the intellectual center of our era.

David is "The Conservative." He's a contributing editor at the *City Journal* and *National Review,* a contributor to *Commentary,* and an art critic at the *Weekly Standard.* He has also put in appearances as token conservative or technology pundit at *The New Republic, The New York Times, The Washington Post,* and *Feed,* a Web magazine.

THE CONSERVATIVE: <DAVID GELERNTER> The Net is a fad. The Web is a fad, an interesting fad. The Net has been a serious communications medium for only ten or fifteen years. What we're seeing is prehistory; the history of the Net per se hasn't yet begun. This fun-and-games period will come to an end when someone comes up with an application that matters, which won't be the sort of stuff we're seeing now. George Orwell's *The Road to Wigan Pier* makes it clear that the '30s was a more technologically intensive time than today. During that period, technology had revolutionized everyday life in ways that really mattered to people. The technologies that matter are those that make daily life less obnoxious and more pleasant, applications that you can leverage all the time, not the glitzy fun and games that are going on now. When the Net really matters to American culture and society, people won't recognize it. It is going to happen with software a lot different from what we see today.

The Net is going to start mattering in a significant way when it relieves people of the burden of dealing with the garbage inherent in the information flow of everyday life. The Net is going to matter when I can rely on it to store the information I now keep on disk, and the computer is a completely transparent object. I plug in one computer, I see through it to the object that matters to me, and I have my entire information life online, in chronological order, searchable from my electronic birth certificate onward. All the documents and pieces of information important to me are maintained by the Net with sufficient reliability so that I can unplug my computer and smash it with a hammer without affecting anything. I can walk up to any computer anywhere and focus it on my own life stream, my own information object. A laptop begins to look like a Winnebago, something that is a little eccentric to carry around with you.

The Net is going to matter when all of my information transactions with the outside world go through it. I buy an object of some sort and can find the owner's manual on it, all my bills and correspondence go through it, I can save snapshots and videos on it, and it serves as my appointment calendar and electronic diary. At that point the Net is not going to look glitzy. It's not going to be virtual reality. It's not going to be splashy graphics. It is going to be something transparent that you can easily forget but it will be hard to picture life without it, like central heating.

The most important way people are going to make money on the Net is on the model of the electric power utilities or cable TV companies, by providing a service that you are going to pay for monthly. I am going to hire a server to manage all my documents, I am going to throw out my desk and file cabinets, I am not going to care what computer I use, and I will be happy to pay $12.50 a month for an absolutely reliable storage facility. This company stores my documents, supports all sorts of fancy searches, and makes my documents available anywhere. However, we aren't moving in that direction. A big transition has to happen: people need to get over their boyish excitement, stop playing games, and get serious.

A lot of work has been done on electronic newspapers. They have failed because they have not given the public anything that's worth money compared with paper newspapers. The developers haven't grasped why an old-fashioned paper newspaper is a great technology. An electronic newspaper could offer something that I would pay for, but first of all, it has to be designed by someone who grasps why a paper newspaper is a great technology: it's cheap, it's portable, and it fits in my briefcase. I can spread it out on a table and read it while I drink coffee and eat a doughnut. I can browse it. If I have an electronic newspaper, I am going to give up a lot of those things. A company that is going to make money on electronic newspapers will have to come up with something different. A page that looks like *The New York Times* will not do it.

I would like to see an electronic newspaper that has multiple translucent layers, with each layer evolving at a different rate. The top layer is late-breaking stuff, and as I delve down as deeply as I want into the layers, I get more detailed information. It's got good features. I don't have to read it for a few days or a few weeks and I can rewind and essentially fast-forward through the time I've missed. A good feature for me is that I can read it with my eyes closed. If I've had a hard day in the office, I can lie down on the couch, close my eyes, and read this electronic newspaper by plugging in headphones, pointing to a story with a mouse, and having it read to me. Maybe these features are not the ones that will make a billion dollars for a new company, but whatever it is, someone is going to have to have an idea different from the product out there now.

The standard question that people in computing and information management are discussing is how to organize information in new ways. At Yale, where the concentration is on history, we are looking at a different kind of interface that we call a fuzzy space-time interface. The way this interface works is that you see a map of the world on the computer and you designate the part of the world you care about. If I am interested in Basque sheep shearing in the fourteenth century, I draw a circle around the Basque country and steer the thing back in time by pulling on a joy-stick to go back to the fourteenth century. Then I type what I care about, essentially key words. The interface has a heuristic kind of database, and based on the piece of space-time

I focus on and the key words I type, it shows me some points, each having to do with a document, and it uses colors to tell me whether the document is warmer or colder relative to what I am describing. What's interesting is that I can use the interface to organize not only documents but people. If there is someone in Tokyo who is an expert in Basque sheep farming, he can be in there too, and I can find his business card and send him mail. Is the fuzzy space-time interface going to make a billion dollars? It could. It's something new and different, and there's an idea behind it.

We see lots of image databases on the Net today, and the images are usually lousy quality. Why are people excited about art museums and fine art online? Why is Microsoft, among other companies, making this huge investment? Why all these companies are turning to CDs of fine art is beyond me, because the image quality is pathetic. You can get better, more nuanced colors from a $2 box of Crayola crayons than you can from a $5,000 monitor. On the Net we are seeing old ideas that aren't well suited to the technology. There is an idea void: too many people, too excited, who spend too much time playing and not enough time thinking.

What kind of people use the Net and the Web? What kind of community are they and what are their activities doing to the country, the world, the culture? It may sound like a parochial issue that women don't like computers that much, but they don't, and the issue is a tremendously important one. It is a fact that there are not many girls majoring in computer science, and there are not many women in the field. People have been doing handstands to get more women to enter the field. An article in *Time* magazine fifteen years ago about the first wave of videogames in penny arcades observed that boys played them and girls didn't. It stated in a serious, sanctimonious way that experts were asking how can we get girls to play videogames. My response is, Why should they want to? They are not attracted to this world, certainly not to the extent that men are, and that's one of the reasons why it is such a spiritually impoverished world. Most men with a reasonable degree of sophistication are happier in an environment that includes women. One of the problems with the computer society is that not only is it an almost all-male society, but it is a little-boy society, part of an ongoing infantilization of the society over the last half century.

The worrisome thing about computers from my point of view is the extent to which they play off our worst tendencies. There's a feedback loop whereby computers make it easy for us to do certain bad things that, unfortunately, we tend to do anyway. Look at education. Schools have been lousy for two decades, teachers have been unwilling to teach what students don't like to learn, and basic skills have been suffering. With computers you can say, "Don't worry about the basic stuff, because a spellchecker can check your spelling and a grammar checker can check your grammar, a drawing program can make your pictures come out right, and a smart database program can do your research." We wind up with uneducated morons.

Within the computer community, we defensively believe that 80 percent of the people are too dumb to use software properly and that our friends or colleagues who aren't up-to-date on the latest software are manifesting stupidity and a lack of technological or scientific intelligence. A vivid example is that pathetic piece of software Microsoft released called Bob, to tell people how to use an earlier version of Windows. It uses cartoon characters and its message is that if you don't understand how to use Windows 3.1, you are stupid and deserve to be treated like a child.

Society has temperamentally conservative people in it. They don't like machines and they never will. These may be very bright people for whom the computer world is never going to be a completely satisfactory world. In addition to this 35 percent, there's another 35 percent who might be great computer users but who realize that computer software stinks and both hardware and software are poorly designed. They realize that the whole computer world is set up on a primitive basis: that they should not have to worry about compatibility, that they should not have to worry about backing up their disk or about the format of my floppy disk. Consumers wouldn't put up with any of this if they were serious.

Some people who use the Web as a community, who turn to the Web for friendship and fellowship and companionship, are sufficiently inept at dealing with their fellow creatures face-to-face that they have no recourse but to deal at arm's length, by remote control. A community is not a community of disembodied spoken statements, in part because the most important aspect of the communication that people have is emotional, and one often communicates emotion not in terms of text but as subtext. The physical body is not irrelevant to a human community. The emotional subtext of human communication is crucial to human thought. It isn't a footnote. Too many computer scientists don't understand this. They conceive of cognition as something in a box over here and emotion in a box over there. In fact, there is no thought without emotion, and there is no real communication without emotion – subtle emotions that allow us to recognize another human being and understand the nuances of what is being communicated. This doesn't happen online.

THE SCRIBE: <JOHN MARKOFF> Gelernter prophesied the rise of the World Wide Web. He understood the idea half a decade before it happened.

THE GENIUS: <W. DANIEL HILLIS> David is one of the pioneers in getting many computers to work together and cooperate on solving a single problem, which is the future of computing.

THE PRODIGY: <JARON LANIER> David Gelernter is a unique and profoundly important presence in the information technology community. He's a full-out visionary, able to present ideas as wild and on the edge as anyone (see *Mirror Worlds*). But at the same time he remains grounded in the simple basis of human life, in the family, in the values of love and regeneration. He is also, obviously, a rare example of someone from our community who has had to face real danger, and he's done so with courage and without falling into bitterness. Mostly I value him as a clear thinker, able to get to the bottom of technical and moral issues with equal grace.

THE DEFENDER: <MIKE GODWIN> David Gelernter demands that human beings refuse to let technologies or extraneous circumstances define themselves and their society. Instead, we have to make value-driven choices and do the defining ourselves. Even when I disagree with him, which is often, I think he is a valuable contributor to the debates about the technologies we increasingly rely on and the unquestioned visions of the future that we've predicated on those technologies.

The Impresario: <Richard Saul Wurman>

In this tome you call Gelernter "The Conservative." I think I'd lump him with Danny Hillis and call David "The Genius II" or, since he's older, call Danny "The Genius II." His book *1939: The Lost World of the Fair* is worth a detour.

<Mike Godwin>

The Defender

The Judge: <David R. Johnson> *Mike is a tenacious defender of First Amendment rights, and he knows the constitutional issues involved better than almost anybody. His online discussion style is such that everybody who tangles with him is careful before they dive in. He takes every aspect of every sentence that somebody has written and provides the refutation in detail.*

Mike Godwin, an attorney, is counsel for the Electronic Frontier Foundation, the San Francisco–based cyber-liberties organization, and author of *Cyber Rights: Free Speech in the Digital Age* (forthcoming).

Any new communications technology brings with it the fear and loathing of the ruling classes. Inevitably their agenda is to gain control. In the case of the Internet, they will say that new laws are needed to save our children from the purveyors of pornography. Nonsense. We already have laws on the books that will do this. The goal is always power and control.

Mike Godwin understands this. "It is difficult to overstate what it means to take the power of the First Amendment – which many people thought was a sort of special pleading for big media like Time Warner or CBS News – and tell them that the promise of this constitutional guarantee is one that belongs to the individual citizen, and that now you have the chance to use it. In the *ACLU* v. *Reno* decision, which I was lucky enough to contribute to, we're finally seeing the fulfillment of a promise that was made more than two centuries ago."

Mike Godwin is "The Defender." He wants to protect your right to publish on the Internet any content that would be legal in a newspaper or a book.

Mike has been the counsel for the Electronic Frontier Foundation (EFF), a public-interest civil-liberties group, since its founding by John Perry Barlow and Mitch Kapor in October 1990. Mike was the first person hired by the EFF, which focuses on (a) assistance and advice to individuals with legal problems and questions about cyberspace, (b) education of policy makers, law enforcement personnel, and the general public about these issues, and (c) where appropriate, attempting to influence public policy. The group's role is to ensure that the principles embodied in the Constitution and the Bill of Rights are protected as new communication technologies emerge. Mike says, "I started as an (a) and (b) kind of guy, but lately I've been doing a lot more (c)."

When I interviewed Mike in San Francisco, he walked into my hotel suite while I was packing to leave and said, "Don't stop what you are doing. Turn on the videocamera." What proceeded was a nonstop sixty-minute monologue that would please any sane person. Mike is ready to go to bat for us against a government that would curb our right to free speech the moment we attach our computers to a modem.

THE DEFENDER: <MIKE GODWIN> As a civil-liberties lawyer, I am interested in how the Internet functions socially and legally. What you have is something that looks like the fullest flower of First Amendment values the country has ever seen. Looking worldwide doesn't detract from that a bit. Even though, when you talk about the global legal structure, there is no First Amendment elsewhere, people across the globe are immensely hungry for freedom of speech and the ability to talk to those who share their interests, without intermediation – whether the private intermediation of editors or the public intermediation of governments.

One of the difficulties we face now, and the cause of a backlash of fear of the medium, is the problem of pluralism. Most of us don't have to deal with the full range of opinions and ideas – from the inspiring to the obnoxious – that exist in the American landscape because the mainstream mass media filter them out. When you spend time on the Net, you discover that people are hungry to read and talk and that the political landscape is a lot richer than you ever thought it was. People hold beliefs that are orthogonal to the usual Democrat versus Republican scale.

For the first time in the history of mass media, you don't have to be a highly capitalized individual to reach a mass audience. Normally, mass media could be understood by C. Wright Mills's discussion of the power elite: people are powerful because they have access to powerful institutions. Either you're rich or you know somebody who's rich. Now it takes minimal capital investment for people in America to participate in the great public colloquy about life, culture and the arts, politics, and science. This is revolutionary.

Something that started as the subject of great optimistic hype, and has become the subject of a great amount of fear and trepidation, is that the Internet turns everyone into a publisher. I find it exciting. The framers of the Constitution did not draft the First Amendment only for the printers and publishers of Colonial America. They were acting on the assumption that potentially anyone could become a printer or a publisher. That implied proposition of the First Amendment is becoming expressed in the reality of the Internet. The question is how we cope with it.

In the past, the American legal and social systems have reacted negatively to new media. It took a long time before motion pictures were protected expression under the First Amendment. Broadcast TV and radio are still not understood to partake of the same protections of freedom of speech and freedom of the press that print media in the United States can claim. The American public believes, rightly or wrongly, that there is something special about TV or radio that requires special regulation. Nowadays people have no trouble with Federal Communications Commission control of television content. They are ready to see the medium regulated – never mind that they are entirely comfortable watching TV themselves, certain that they are not going to be subject to any kind of brainwashing. We built, incorrectly, a social consensus that TV and radio are unusually threatening. The last thing we want to see is this same kind of consensus constructed around the Internet. We need a consensus that the Internet is an institution of First Amendment expression, that it partakes of all the protections of the First Amendment, and that it deserves the same kind of legal and constitutional protections that any newspaper on any newsstand receives.

Some of the backlash against the Internet and online communications has to do with the way mainstream media tend to construct issues. The fact that there is a computer dimension to a case seems to be a plus when it comes to getting national headlines or coverage on national news broadcasts. Some of this is a function of news reporters looking for sexy stories, and a lot of it is the result of particular forces in American public life trying to shape an agenda about American cultural life, particularly the cultural Right, or the religious Right, which is trying to build a new consensus that new media belong in a more restrictive regime for speech than exists for the traditional press.

For many of us, especially civil libertarians, there are problems with the Supreme Court's definition of obscenity. It is not fully defined. It varies according to community standards, and it is hard to know what your community standards are until you've been prosecuted. This puts people in the position of proving that speech has serious literary, artistic, or social merit in order to survive obscenity prosecutions. Civil libertarians regard that as too restrictive. The Right regards that as too liberal and too loose. Those on the Right do not want to see any kind of escape clause in terms of publicly acceptable speech that has to do with serious literary, artistic, or social value. They would like to say there are some things you cannot say in public, even if they have serious literary, artistic, or social value. The Right plays on our fears in order to advance that agenda.

Various organizations associated with the religious Right have constructed a fiction that pornographic content is rife on the Net; that it is pervasive, out of control, and getting worse; that when you log on, the stuff will flood over your monitor; that somehow pedophiles will be able to reach through your monitor and grab your child. Those are potent buttons to push for people unfamiliar with the medium. In reality, while it is true that pornographic content exists on the Net, almost none of the other propositions about pervasiveness seem to be true. It is very hard to encounter material without actively looking for it. In the public debate about children, someone will tell a possibly apocryphal story about a child who had been online for only two or three minutes, when some pornographic image or obscene phrase or profane language suddenly flooded over the Net at the child. You point out that this is the most programmable technology we have ever had. It is relatively easy to filter out that stuff from the beginning so that a child never sees it and is never the passive recipient of it. Then comes the response that children are very smart about computers and can figure out a way around those tools. The debate has suddenly shifted from whether the child was a passive victim to the concern that the child's curiosity is too great, a fundamentally different problem of parenting.

My short answer is, if you're concerned about your child being a passive recipient of inappropriate content, it is relatively easy to prevent that from happening, and it is more effective to do it from home than to implement it through a federal statute or through standards set by the FCC. If you are concerned about your child having a bad thought or being curious about inappropriate content, there is no software tool or law that prevents your child from acting on that impulse. What you do is to teach your child values. If you want your child not to look for pornography, teach your child that pornography is bad. That will be more effective and more preemptive than anything the federal government, whose inefficiency is legendary, can ever implement.

It is ironic that in an era of suspicion about the role of government, people are ready to have the government decide what's appropriate when it comes to the Net and to give the government more power to make those decisions than it has on the newsstand. I have no issue with the government having the same power that it has at the newsstand, but more power over the medium is inappropriate. When we allow people to speak to a mass audience, some are going to use that prerogative badly and say things that offend me. But I'm going to tolerate that, because I'm committed to a free society in which that person's right to say something that offends me is equal to my right to say something that offends him. We believe we live in a world that can tolerate full and vigorous expression of conflicting ideas in every medium, some of which many might find offensive, including so-called hate speech or Nazi propaganda. In this country, you can say what you like, but you can't use speech to commit a crime – like fraud or blackmail or threatening the president.

Once we narrow the issue to what writers and editors can say, it's worth pointing out that the traditional way we have reached audiences has involved a lot of intermediaries. This can be a burden on creative people. On the Net that all changes. You have a much better chance of reaching an audience of hundreds or perhaps thousands who will appreciate your poetry on the Net than through traditional book-publishing channels, because the mass market for poetry is almost nonexistent. A poem can stay on the Net indefinitely and be read again and again. It can be put in an archive on your own system where people can download it. The countless things you can do to reach an audience are incredibly empowering. This frees us of the traditional process that comes from having to deal with institutions that, rightly or wrongly, act as filters between us and the audience we want to reach.

Another exciting aspect of the Net is that it's leading to a revival of written culture. People who are not professional writers are now participating socially in virtual communities and public debates in which the power of what you say is a function not of who you are or which newspaper you appeared in, but simply of the quality of your prose and the quality of your ideas. That is incredibly democratic and liberating.

If we allow the free market to work, we will have a range of online providers, including some that will act as conduits to sources of content on the Net with little editorial control and others that will market themselves, for example, as the Disney Channel of online services. If we trust freedom of speech and the free market to let providers decide what kind of services they're going to offer, we will have the maximum ability to protect ourselves and our children from material that we don't want to see or we think is inappropriate, because every service will offer something unique. We don't need the FCC to dictate standards. It skews the market and it skews freedom of speech in ways that are disturbing in an open society.

THE CITIZEN: <HOWARD RHEINGOLD> Someone once said, "Never try to out-asshole Mike Godwin. He's the most ferocious and tenacious debater I've ever encountered." I called him a bulldog and he corrected me: he regards himself as a terrier. I'm sure glad we have one well-read terrier on the side of civil rights in cyberspace. If you are going to argue with Mike, be prepared.

> **THE SCOUT: <STEWART BRAND>** A lucid and focused legal mind. Mike has had an enormous effect on public computer policy at both the grassroots and the general levels. I've been delighted by his insights such as his proof that online communication is "more" intimate than face-to-face contact. Don't get in an argument with him, though. He fights to the death.

THE IDEALIST: <DENISE CARUSO> Mike Godwin could be pulling down a quarter-million dollars a year at some highfalutin' law firm in Washington, D.C., or Silicon Valley. But he is absolutely steadfast about public service. And I've never seen anyone so competently and systematically decimate the opposition, in real time, under almost any circumstances.

<W. Daniel Hillis>

The Genius

The Thinker: <Doug Carlston> *Danny is one of the great spirits of the computer industry. He's the one fellow every techie I know would give his right arm to work for. Although his last company didn't survive, Danny is the sort of guy to place your bets on.*

Danny Hillis is vice president of research and development at the Walt Disney Company and a Disney Fellow. He was cofounder and chief scientist of Thinking Machines Corporation.

There's nothing odd about Danny Hillis's working for Disney. The founder of Thinking Machines Corporation and the innovative designer of the massively parallel "connection machine," Danny used to drive to work in a fire engine and was once a toy designer for Milton Bradley. In college, he became interested in building a computer out of anything. As a demonstration, he and some friends built the Tinkertoy computer, which was composed of ten thousand Tinkertoys and could play tic-tac-toe. His interest in building gadgets and games was, to some degree, influenced by his friend, the late physicist Richard Feynman, who would leave Caltech in the summer to go to Cambridge, Massachusetts, to work for Danny at Thinking Machines.

Part of Danny's charm is his childlike curiosity and demeanor. The first time we talked was on the telephone one Sunday morning in 1988 when he was at his home in Cambridge. We got into a serious discussion about the relationship of physics to computation. "This is interesting," he said. "I'd like to come to New York and continue the conversation face-to-face." Three hours later, my doorbell rang, and there stood a young man, looking like a clean-cut hippie. He had long hair, wore a plain white T-shirt and jeans, and carried nothing. We talked for hours.

I later returned the visit. This was a different side of Danny, the chief scientist and cofounder of Thinking Machines, at the time one of the hottest companies in America. He lived with his family in a huge old house off Brattle Street. The domestic scene I entered included a bunch of babies, two au pairs (a blonde from France and a brunette from Argentina), a dog, and a houseful of interesting guests – all presided over by Danny and his wife, Patty. I sat in the living room with Danny and evolutionary biologist Stephen Jay Gould as they discussed the effect of massively parallel computers on evolutionary theory; meanwhile, Danny's mentor, computer scientist Marvin Minsky, played Mozart sonatas on the grand piano in the adjacent room.

Danny's energies have concentrated on getting processors to work together so that computation takes place with communicating processors, as happens with the Internet. The Net's potential to become an organism of intelligent agents interacting with each other, with an intelligence of its own that goes beyond the intelligence of the individual agents fires Danny up. "In a sense," he says, "the Net can become smarter than any of the individual people on the Net or sites on the Net. Parallel processing is the way that kind of emergent phenomenon can happen. The Net right now is only a glimmer of that."

Danny describes the Internet of today simply as a huge document that is stored in a lot of different places and that can be modified by many people at once, but essentially a document in the old sense of the word. In principle, the Internet could be done on paper, but the logistics are much better handled with the computer. "I am interested in the step beyond that," he says, "where what is going on is not just a passive document, but an active computation, where people are using the Net to think of new things that they couldn't think of as individuals, where the Net thinks of new things that the individuals on the Net couldn't think of."

Danny asks questions like What are the limits to what computers can do? Can they think? Do they learn? His intellectual range is startling. Unlike many other people engaged in the world of computing, he does not limit himself to any particular group of colleagues. Some of his biggest fans are among the brightest people on the planet. Marvin Minsky says, "Danny Hillis is one of the most inventive people I've ever met, and one of the deepest thinkers." Philosopher Daniel C. Dennett says, "What Danny did was to create if not the first then one of the first really practical, really massive, parallel computers. It precipitated a gold rush." Physicist and Nobel laureate Murray Gell-Mann notes that "he's not only a daring person, which we know, but also a deep thinker – and a very effective one." Danny Hillis is "The Genius."

THE GENIUS: <W. DANIEL HILLIS> People are so tuned in to the near term that they aren't thinking in terms of decades. Yet, over the long run, we have a chance of fundamentally changing humanity. Many people sense this, but don't want to think about it because the change is too profound. Today, on the Internet the main event is the Web. A lot of people think that the Web *is* the Internet, and they're missing something. The Internet is a brand-new fertile ground where things can grow, and the Web is the first thing that grew there. But the stuff growing there is in a very primitive form. The Web is the old media incorporated into the new medium. It both adds something to the Internet and takes something away.

The Web provides a large set of people with a new kind of accessibility. There is more equality in the Web's ratio of mouths to ears than in the mass media. In fact, unlike the broadcast media, you can even have more mouths than ears on the Internet, as you often do. It is enabling because it lowers the threshold of publishing, the threshold for getting information out. People distrust institutions. They don't like having their voice limited by institutions. The idea that they can take the power into their own hands and put something out on the Net fits very well with this mood of the times, which calls for self-reliance. The energy from the Web is not coming from people who are seeking information. It's coming from people who have information that they want to send out or who are providing a mechanism for giving that information to others.

The old idea of information concerns something that is of value to the receiver, but that kind of information is not what causes people to go online. If you look at what's driving the Web, it's clear that the act of communication is often of as much value to the transmitter as to the receiver, and perhaps more so. The people who are doing exciting things on the Web are the people who are publishing Web sites, not the people who are reading them. The real business opportunity on the Net right now is giving people who have something to say a way to say it and a place to say it. A great example is Industry.Net, a company that charges people to list their products on a product-finding service on the Web. It doesn't charge the people who are searching; it charges the people who want to be found by the searchers.

Part of the energy stems from the idea that the Web is a frontier, where people can stake a claim, strike it rich, and make a name for themselves. Just like the gold rush, the primary consequence will not be how a few people can make a lot of money. Most of the consequences of the gold rush were cultural and societal: the change of community, the habitation of a new area, and different relationships for people. There are going to be a lot of ghost towns on the Web.

When people look at the interaction between the content and the person, or the computer and the person, the first thing they see is that the Internet offers a new mode of interaction. People with something useful to say that is of interest to other people don't have to go through the process of convincing the bureaucracy, the Powers That Be, in order to connect with their customers. It can happen very quickly; on the Web, two guys working in a basement who have a computer and a good idea can become a multinational corporation overnight.

Both good news and bad news accompany that capability. The good news is the opportunity story, the gold rush story. The bad news is that there are perhaps too many stories of "two guys in a basement" who want to establish contact with you. In some sense, they are making the channel noisier. The impact of the Internet on human communications has the potential of leading you to increasingly superficial interactions with more and more people. Attention is the scarce commodity on the Internet because individuals have only a finite attention span. Mechanisms that manage attention become increasingly important.

One consequence is that brands become much more important on the Internet. Brand identity has been diluted in some products because brands have diversified so much that a lot of them don't mean anything anymore. Disney is one of the few studios, perhaps the only studio, whose brand means anything, which is important. If you, the consumer, are not locked into your relationships by physical mechanisms – the truck route, the guy that delivers the products onto the grocery shelf, and so on – if you are free to form any relationship with any supplier, the importance of knowing who is making the product is increased. The brand becomes important.

The funny thing about selling information is that I can't show you what I have to sell you without giving it to you. When you pay for information, you're always paying for the last information you received, not the next information you're going to get. The only thing of value in that transaction, then, is the relationship with the party from whom you got the information last time. That's the value you expect from the channel. If you got the information through the Internet, the only valuable thing is the brand, because that's the name of the channel. In this regard, a person can be a brand name. A book author is the perfect example.

Disney is a brand because if the label on the box says "Disney" you have certain expectations. MCA/Universal is a corporation. Maybe Universal has economy of scale because it can do things like negotiate with unions, but consumers have no particular expectation of what they are going to get with that brand name. Bill Paley used to talk to me about the old days of radio, when the name CBS meant something, as distinguished from NBC. What Bill did was make CBS mean something special. Today it doesn't mean anything; you expect to see the same things on CBS that you see on NBC.

Take a company like Encyclopaedia Britannica, Inc. Its greatest assets used to be its sales force. In this new world they've become a liability. But what is of incredible value is the brand, and if the company can work out a new way of exploiting the brand on the Web, completely divorced from the physical books, the brand can become a much more valuable asset.

There's a lot of confusion about what interactivity means. Being told a story has value, but interacting with a set of characters is not always better than being told a story. Being given a complete kit of parts to design your own automobile, or to design your own clothes, is not as useful as having somebody do it for you. I don't go to a restaurant to cook my own meal. In the same sense, being able to throw together your own magazine or newspaper with all the bits and pieces of information you can find on the Web is not as useful as having somebody put together a magazine or newspaper for you.

Looking down the road, the Internet promises something even more exciting than people interacting: computers interacting with computers in nontrivial ways. It's popular now to view the computer as a multimedia engine. In other words, it's an engine that absorbs all the other media, like pictures and sounds, manipulates them, and plays them for people and makes them dance on the screen. That's interesting because of the human interaction it causes, but it misses a lot of what's fundamentally possible with computers – computers don't have to manipulate the human representations of ideas; they can actually manipulate the ideas themselves.

This comes back to the view of the Web as the first form of life to grow on the Internet. It's the slime mold of the Internet. I don't want to disparage it, but it's primitive. When computers pass around Web pages, they don't know what they're talking about. They're just passing around bits, and they can be meaningless bits as far as they're concerned. They're just acting like a big telephone system. It's much more interesting when computers actually understand what they're talking about. Java is one of the first beginnings of this happening on the network. Java represents one computer saying to another computer something that's meaningful to the two computers. Java is perhaps a bad example, because the meaning I refer to could be just a command to paint a line on the screen. The meaning is usually trivial, but it's not fundamentally trivial because it means that computers are beginning to understand themselves.

In the long run, the Internet will arrive at a much richer infrastructure, in which ideas can potentially evolve outside of human minds. You can imagine something happening on the Internet along evolutionary lines, as in the simulations I run on my parallel computers. It already happens in trivial ways, with viruses, but that's just the beginning. I can imagine nontrivial forms of organization evolving on the Internet. Ideas could evolve on the Internet that are much too complicated to hold in any human mind.

In *The Moon is a Harsh Mistress,* Robert A. Heinlein writes about a network of computers becoming sentient. That's an extreme example, but we can certainly detect forms of organization that we didn't design. We do that in biology all the time. We watch, and observe a pattern of organization we can identify, and we can even make sense out of it, but that doesn't mean we engineered it. As the Internet gets more complicated and computers start interacting – not just carrying messages for humans but actually transmitting content meaningful to the computer – we may see patterns that we can appreciate, just as we appreciate the patterns of living organisms. We won't necessarily understand all the details, just as we don't really understand all the details of living organisms. Over the long term, this could be extremely important. Some new forms of organization that go beyond humans may be evolving. In the short term, forms of human organization are enabled.

The Seer: <David Bunnell> Danny has somehow become an adult without giving up the best qualities of childhood. There are many geniuses who act like children. Danny is not one of those. He acts like a grown-up who knows how to play.

> **The Cyberanalyst: <Sherry Turkle>** Danny Hillis is able to translate complicated matters into simple, direct, and vivid explanations. Among his many gifts, he is a great teacher.

The Searcher: <Brewster Kahle> Danny has the rare combination of technical insight and a good personal nature. I call him a mentor, and so would many others. In terms of understanding technologies, Danny was always able to see the trends and come up with the right answers despite too little information. When people talked about CPUs, Danny was talking about the network – I am amazed to see the vision of a massively parallel computer being currently incarnated on the global scale of the Internet.

THE SCRIBE: <JOHN MARKOFF> Danny is someone who's seriously committed to the idea of building machines that think. He's been engaged in a decade-long quest and he's still trying to figure his way there. He's gotten sidetracked for the moment, but I'm hoping he'll come back to that.

THE IMPRESARIO: <RICHARD SAUL WURMAN> Already a legend, even if he just plays marbles for the rest of his life. Even his sidebars are worth saving.

THE CATALYST: <LINDA STONE> Intelligence is a combination of common sense, sense of humor, and point of view. Danny has all three in such great quantity that he is amazing to be around. There's nobody quite like him. He simultaneously moves straight forward and comes out of left field.

<David R. Johnson>

The Judge

The Idealist: <Denise Caruso>

David was the voice of reason when I was on the board of the Electronic Frontier Foundation – sometimes too reasonable, in fact, when what was required was to be uncompromising. But one of the most memorable experiences I had during my time on the board was watching and listening while David and John Gilmore debated the issue of absolute anonymity on the Internet. Begrudgingly, they came to an agreement they both could live with. I learned a ton – not just about anonymity, but about how compromise can sometimes be the best solution for everyone.

David R. Johnson serves as chairman of Counsel Connect, the online meeting place for the legal profession, and is codirector of the Cyberspace Law Institute.

I got to know Washington attorney David R. Johnson in 1995, after I received a letter from Network Solutions, Inc., the company that administers the InterNIC, the body authorized to administer the domain-name system. The letter demanded that Edge Foundation, Inc., a nonprofit foundation I formed in the '80s, relinquish or change its domain name – edge.org – in fourteen days or be banished from the Internet.

I immediately called David, who I had met when he was chairman of the EFF. He also helped draft the Electronic Communications Privacy Act and has counseled major online system providers. David explained that while Edge had a trademark that would have precedence under trademark law in court (the foundation had published books and newsletters, run conferences, etc., for nearly ten years), that didn't matter under the new InterNIC policy. David went to bat, advising me, making calls to leading trademark lawyers, and going directly to the managers and attorneys who framed this policy.

The main function of Edge Foundation, Inc., is to serve as the organizational umbrella for the Reality Club, a group which has, over the years, been compared with the Lunar Society of Birmingham, the Bloomsbury group, and the Algonquin circle. Notice I did not write the Lunar Society of Birmingham™, Bloomsbury™, or Algonquin™. Anyone with a sense of cultural history would recognize the absurdity of doing so. The Reality Club is about ideas, not commerce.

The conventional wisdom is that the big development in this communications revolution is that each of us can be a publisher, and has the same power to communicate as the giant conglomerates. Not so. Through a policy, which seems to be designed primarily to cover potential liability for Network Solutions and the InterNIC, we are headed back to business as usual, much to the delight of the major corporations that want to own the Internet. Our politicians are more than happy to sell it to them.

David Johnson thinks about such weighty matters. He also acts judiciously. He is "The Judge."

THE JUDGE: <DAVID R. JOHNSON> About five years ago I gave a speech urging the creation of what I called the Electronic Guild Hall for the Legal Profession. Steven Brill of American Lawyer Media and its affiliate, Court TV, understood the potential of an online community of lawyers, and launched the service called Counsel Connect, which has grown to be a 35,000-member online service for the legal community.

At an early stage in the Counsel Connect experiment, there was great debate about several things: whether or not members should own the copyright on their postings, whether or not people posting there would inadvertently form lawyer-client relationships or expose themselves to conflicts, whether or not their words would come back to haunt them. We found that the more people got involved in the online discussions, the more they relaxed about those things and understood that the terms and conditions of this new medium are different from those applicable to traditional media. In fact, the law has typically been treating online services by using old analogies – to a printing press, or a broadcast television network, or some other thing. But the Internet is a new interactive medium all its own.

We're going to see more difficulties arise as people new to the Net take the time to learn the special characteristics of the medium. There are not yet as many good cues as to when you're in a public place and when you're in a private place as there need to be in order to make people comfortable with what happens to the messages they send online. So we're going through a gradual acculturation process. With regard to the use of copyrighted materials, there's still a great deal of uncertainty as to how somebody who has traditionally created content embodied in tangible objects can contribute to the Net in a way that rewards this production of value. The answers may well be found by establishing ground rules that are specially tailored to the Net community and are not the same as traditional copyright law.

On Counsel Connect, our very first decision was to establish a different "copyright" regime. We couldn't allow everybody who uploaded a comment to the public forums to enforce their copyright. Nor could we prevent those who read it from making a copy by sending it to a friend or printing it out for the benefit of a client. So we required everyone who entered this space to grant an irrevocable license to make copies of their public postings. The effect was to open up the flow of discussion. That's a specific example of why the copyright laws as they traditionally have applied to tangible market-based materials, like books and movies and so forth, may not be the right default rule for online communities, where the incentives to create new works come from the need for people to participate in the community, and where the value created is not inherently tied to the ability to tell someone else they can't make a copy of what you've just said.

One of the major topics of discussion on Counsel Connect has been the Clinton administration's White Paper, which proposes some changes to the current copyright law that seem to be both too much and not radical enough. For example, the proposed bill would cover as an infringing copy every transmission of copyrighted material over the Net. The problem is that, on the Net, reading and browsing inherently involve making a copy.

The Net is a global copying machine. In the real world, it's fairly easy to know when you're making a copy, so putting the burden on you to get permission in order to make a copy is reasonable. On the Net, anytime you take any action, you're making a copy. There may be an argument, at least for materials that originate on the Net, for establishing a difficult rule that allows you to engage in the normal processes of communicating across the Net, even if it does involve "copying," without getting permission.

In other words, the burden would be on the person who wants to restrict access. A good example of this is the "caching" of Web pages. It might be reasonable to think that everyone who puts a Web page up on the Net is giving an implied license to everybody who can access that Web page anywhere in the world to make a copy and download it. In order to speed up the delivery of Web pages, some of the large online services have created host computers that make what's called a "cached" copy of that Web page in order to allow the second person who comes along to get it more rapidly. Under existing copyright law, making that copy is infringing, and a Web page owner could revoke the implied license to do so. But if you post an English-language disclaimer on the front of your Web page saying this may not be cached in the computers of the XYZ Company, the computers of the XYZ Company don't have a way to read that and therefore can't obey the order.

The real question is what the default rule should be. Should it be that if you put something in your store window on the Web, someone should be able to look at it unless you cover it up by some technical means? Or should it be the traditional copyright rule that says everyone has to get permission every time they make a copy? It's pretty clear the Web couldn't function if you didn't make the default rule that the information can flow freely.

What impact the new telecommunications law will have remains an open question. One of the keys will be what role the Federal Communications Commission takes in implementing regulations. The instinct behind the Communications Decency Act is understandable because the Net appears on a screen and that, to some people, makes it similar to a television screen. It is true that children can access the Net without effective parental supervision, particularly because they're more facile with the technology than many parents are. On the other hand, it's very different from the broadcast models that have traditionally allowed some form of government regulation of otherwise permissible First Amendment–protected speech. In particular, on the Net you have to seek materials that are offensive; they don't come in to you unbidden. So we have an example of the failure of the lawmaking apparatus to understand the technology fully, and to take into account the ability of new technologies to provide filters that would allow parents to control what's accessible to their children and solve the problems of concern to legislators in a much less intrusive way. But we can take heart from the three-judge federal court that overturned the CDA as unconstitutional. The best thing about the court's opinion is that it explains the decentralized, chaotic character of the Net.

The court's opinion also recognizes that the Net is a global phenomenon. That's a plus in the sense that it's impossible for any one national government to control the content available on the Net. Some governments are trying, but it's clearly a losing battle. On the other hand, as John Perry Barlow says, the First Amendment is a local ordinance, and for many governments across the world, there is not as strong a commitment to legally protecting free speech as there is in this country. If we want to preserve the free flow of information over the Net, it may well be that we will have to begin to speak in terms of a global doctrine of free speech, a global free flow of information principle, that enables the new global commerce to take place without undue local regulation.

One of the difficulties posed for the Internet has been the collision between traditional law relating to trademark and the new needs of this new medium. The engineers who built the Internet created a registration scheme which worked on a first come, first served basis. Anyone could create a domain name as an easy-to-remember mnemonic address that links into the Internet protocol number through which a machine is located. That worked very well in a small community, but at some point the large corporate entities with a lot invested in trademarks started to notice that domain names closely corresponding to their trademarks or company names had been reserved. As everybody anticipated the growth of commerce on the Net, it became a matter of great interest to McDonald's whether or not it owned mcdonalds.com, for example. The engineering group that focused on making the Internet work and tying everyone together has no desire to become involved in legal questions about who ultimately owns a trademark to the word *mcdonalds*, so they tended not to focus on the policy questions raised by that conflict.

On the other hand, trademark law as it has traditionally developed is geographically based. There are different rights in different countries and different rules as to who can have a right in different countries. The Net allows the same name to be accessed from anyplace in the world. So you face the question whether the use of a given domain name on the Net is simultaneously a trademark use in every country – in which case you are required either to register or at least to avoid infringing other people's rights – or whether it's not a use in any country but a use only on the Net.

There are lots of other respects in which the traditional trademark doctrine doesn't deal with the particular phenomena that the Net gives rise to. All these policy questions have to be addressed by somebody.

Will the Net develop a self-regulatory organization that takes on these policy questions and resolves them in a thoughtful way – allowing, for example, nonprofit organizations, which don't have registered trademarks, to gain some priority in the use of names on the Net if they have used them for a substantial period of time? Reasonable accommodation has to be made between the engineering and social needs of the Net, on the one hand, and local regulation and traditional law, on the other. If the Net policy makers are wise, they will take steps to accommodate the claims of the owners of strong global marks who have invested millions of dollars in promoting those marks. If they are wise, they will also reserve to themselves the ultimate decision on how to develop an architecture of names on the Net.

The Internet, because it is an emergent technology, raises a very interesting set of issues about who ultimately owns the policy questions and the right to set rules that apply to the Net. On the one hand, a small group of engineers and others have focused on this communications technology and have dominated the decision making for a long time. On the other hand, a large number of people increasingly feel that they've been around long enough to have a say in what the rules are. Because the United States government originally financed some of the development of the Net, some representatives have suggested that it owns the right ultimately to determine, for example, the policies for the domain-name space. But it's hard in the end to see how you can justify the control over all the global policy questions raised by the Net solely on the ground that one particular government used to own the computer on which the phenomenon grew in its infancy. It's still an open question, though, whether some essentially internal political community voice will emerge from the Net to assert the right to make the ultimate policy decisions or whether, if that doesn't develop quickly enough, external legal authorities will impose their will by virtue of having the power to control the actions of particular individuals and companies.

I came on the board of the Electronic Frontier Foundation in 1993. I had worked with EFF for a long time and with various members of the staff on the Electronic Communications Privacy Act and various other early efforts to assure electronic privacy. One of the unusual things that happened in Washington with regard to new technology and privacy was a realization that the new technology was so complex that you could never get a sound bill if you took all the different parties and put them in a confrontational mode in a hearing room. Some of the people who ended up being staff members of the EFF created an off-the-hearing-room-floor process to talk through the complex issues, with the goal of getting legislation that would be endorsed by everyone, from the ACLU to the Justice Department. That consulting process has been going on for ten years or more. When I came on the board, I tried to help the EFF go from being a Washington-based political group to being an educational group with regard to the Net as an ecosystem, which I think is a great metaphor for this complex animal we're dealing with.

The EFF brought together people with a wide range of perspectives, but with a shared enthusiasm for the potential of the Net to create a new, more open social space, in effect to aspire to a new form of democracy. One of the great joys of the EFF has been creative discussion at board meetings of how to help the Net develop more freely and fully. There's always been a tension in EFF between, on the one hand, the civil rights origins focused on the First Amendment and the need to strike a strong pose against government censorship and regulation of the Net, and, on the other hand, the desire to take the Net seriously as its own phenomenon, view it in all its complexity, help people understand it, and help convey that the most important rules with regard to the Net are not likely to be made in Washington, but by those who participate in the Net itself.

What's happening on the Net is that the combined decisions made by a systems operator setting rules and the users who vote with their modems, by deciding which areas to frequent and how often, are creating competing environments where different rules and different laws obtain. It's the first time that I know of in the history of the world in which we've had Darwinian selection pressure on the law. People engaged in online activities can reward those kinds of rules that are empowering and penalize those that interfere with what they want to do online. We have moved collectively from an understanding of this new phenomenon in terms of the application of traditional law to an understanding that it will, in effect, remake the law, as much as it will remake the way people engage in social dialogue and formation of operational groups.

Unfortunately, the government has created uncertainty that has a disproportionate adverse effect on small players. For a long time, the forty thousand or so people who are engaged in bulletin board systems have been at risk of unfair impacts from the law. They can't afford lawyers; they die on contact with the legal system. The government has missed an opportunity to create a workable set of rules that will enhance the overall flow of online trade. But everyone is beginning to realize the potential importance of electronic trade for our posture in the global economy, so I haven't given up hope.

When there have been disputes online regarding whether or not something infringes a copyright, or is defamatory, or is otherwise wrongful, systems operators have felt that they were at risk if they didn't take down the file every time. If we rely on a dominant system operator, or place too strict liability on all system operators for a copyright infringement or a wrongful posting by an individual, anything that's controversial or raises a question might be taken down right away. The alternative is to provide a dispute resolution mechanism inside the Net itself that would take a complaint and get it discussed and assessed by a neutral online arbitration system. A new experiment, the Virtual Magistrate Project, is designed to do just that. It was set up with seed money from the National Center for Automated Information Research, with the cooperation of American Arbitration Association, and its Web site is at the Villanova Law School. If the Net is going to develop its own self-regulatory mechanisms, it's going to need a lot more such experiments, run by lots of people who care deeply about the Net.

John Perry Barlow's idea that the Net should be thought of as a complex ecosystem has stimulated thinking about why this environment might need to develop its own internal structures different from those governing activity in the real world, and why in many cases the best response to troubles or wildfires might be to do nothing. Barlow has shown incredible leadership in helping us think through the way in which we should respect the complexity of the new environment.

Watch for the development of a new global legal order applicable to the formation of organizations and transaction of all forms of interaction on the Net. First of all, because the local territorial governments cannot effectively regulate the Net and will give deference to a self-regulatory structure of some kind. Secondly, because the legal questions raised by the Net are going to be special and new. We're dealing with people who may appear only as screen names. We're dealing with places defined not by geographical boundaries but by whether you have to go through a password or a particular screen to get there. We're dealing with things that differ from material objects like books and may be more like a large database from which a particular paragraph can be extracted. When you change people, places, and things, you're going to get a different law, one that will have the benefit of being capable of being very diverse, where the people who do business on the Net, or interact in communities on the Net, will be able to choose from lots of different sets of rules to govern their life online.

THE COYOTE: <JOHN PERRY BARLOW> There may be no one who has a better intuition of how law will develop in cyberspace than David Johnson. He has a deep instinct for clarifying the unusual legal conditions of the virtual world and exposing the error of trying to adapt existing legal regimes to them. I believe his Cyberspace Law Institute will become one of the central repositories for clear thought on this subject.

THE PATTERN-RECOGNIZER: <ESTHER DYSON>
He has an affable, friendly approach that belies a razor-sharp mind. He's a brilliant, unconventional thinker in lawyer's clothing.

THE DEFENDER: <MIKE GODWIN> Some lawyers want only to build a good track record, but David Johnson saw cyberspace as a new chance to build a society.

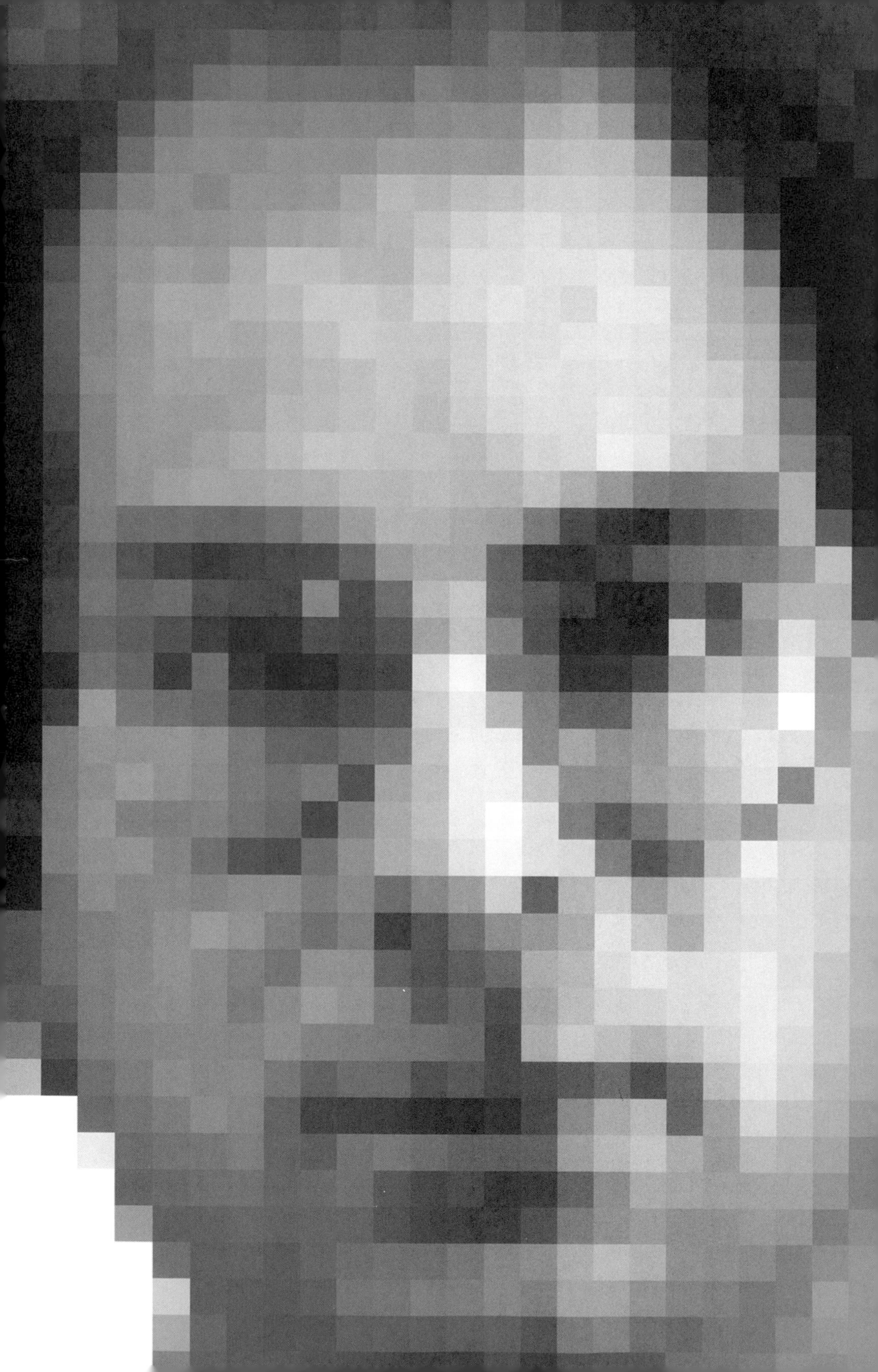

<Brewster Kahle>

The Searcher

The Webmaster: <Kip Parent> *Brewster is one of those guys who has been successful in spite of the fact that he has never been after that kind of success. He's been pushing protocols for the benefit of humanity in order to make things run better. What he's done with Wais and protocols has been instrumental in bringing about the success of the Internet.*

Brewster Kahle is inventor and founder of Wide Area Information Servers Inc., which was recently acquired by America Online, and founder of the Internet Archive.

"The Web is a lonely place," says Brewster Kahle. Brewster and I, meeting for the first time, are splashing around in a pool at a vineyard in St. Helena, California, trying to beat the 110-degree heat. We have both arrived that morning to visit our mutual friend Danny Hillis, who is spending the summer in the vineyard's mansion (home for the TV series *Falcon Crest*). "It is not a community-building technology as it currently stands," he continues.

We are discussing the commercial possibilities of "publishing" or "broadcasting" on the World Wide Web. Brewster is dubious. "The Web was designed as a hypertext system and has been pushed in the direction of a user interface for simple services," he continues. "What is missing is discussion, hobnobbing, flirting. We get these things through email and bulletin boards, but they are stuck in ASCII-only mode. I hope that we move the community services forward in an open environment rather than having separate 3-D worlds that segment users into different proprietary systems. The Web is great in that it is a free-for-all based on open standards. Now we have to move community tools into the graphical and animated world."

Schooled at MIT, Brewster designed supercomputers in the 1980s at Thinking Machines Corporation. In 1989, he formed the Wais (Wide Area Information Servers) project to take commercial advantage of the growing Internet. He wanted to figure out if executives would turn to their computers to answer questions, rather than call someone on the phone or ask their assistant or research librarian. Would they use an online system to find the answers? What he found in 1990 was that they would. The key factor was the networks. That was when the Internet started becoming big.

So he founded a corporation in 1992, out of a joint project between Thinking Machines, Apple Computer, KPMG Peat Marwick, and Dow Jones. Wais was an Internet publishing company that created tools and services to help publishers make money by publishing on the Internet. The company made "surf" software and software for those sophisticated enough to self-publish. It also worked with publishers to create an Internet presence, through the World Wide Web and, before that, gopher. Customers included the *The Wall Street Journal, The New York Times,* the Government Printing Office, the House of Representatives, the Senate, and the White House, all of which were interested in making their information available on the Internet.

Brewster sold his company to America Online and then worked with AOL for a while as an Internet strategist, helping the company understand how to take advantage of the change from vertical, centralized, online services to a more horizontal Internet market.

Brewster is "The Searcher." He has started the Internet Archive. He wants to create the next great library. "We are indeed trying to archive as much public material as possible," he says. "The estimated space needed to archive the World Wide Web, NetNews, and gopher is between 1 and 10 terabytes. Some technically interesting complexities in this project seem to stem from the different systems we'd need to crawl."

"There are a bunch of legal and social issues as well. Most institutions cannot touch this because it hits every privacy, copyright, and export controversy. I feel like we've touched a raw nerve in attempting this project, since it can change the Net forever – from an ephemeral medium to an enduring one."

The Searcher: <Brewster Kahle> The Internet is causing different companies to sprout up in many different niches. America Online is a vertical-market company. It creates the publishing tools, the network, the user interface. The customer support is all in one company. There is a real need for the competencies of America Online. What America Online fundamentally does is large-scale operations, computer operations, customer service, and packaging of information for consumers, as well as being a marketing machine. It has the momentum to build an extremely large customer base. In core competencies, it is far ahead of other Internet-based services. A current idea is that AOL and the like are dinosaurs and will die off. I don't see this happening if they are smart.

America Online is not going to be able to keep up with all the technology improvements. What it must learn to do is leverage the other companies that are creating great content for the Internet. I see the Internet having a great technology stream and no revenue stream, and AOL as having a great revenue stream and no technology stream. How to get these two together is what companies are trying to figure out.

At America Online, I was helping to bring the Internet culture into a company that did not see the Internet as a big part of its operation years ago. Today, AOL sees the Internet as a major influence in what it is doing. It sees that half the email messages on AOL go over the Internet gateway. AOL is the biggest gateway to the Internet in terms of mail. Its members are demanding more and more Internet activity. AOL engineers are continually improving the capability of its Web gateway so it can handle more users.

America Online is focused on consumers, on its customers, on its "members" – what it thinks of as its company. AOL has not concentrated as much on the information providers, and, in fact, a lot of providers are not that happy with America Online. AOL is trying to remedy that by doing things like acquiring Wais and by gatewaying into the Internet, where information providers can have their own way and use their own tools, without having to make specific deals with America Online.

The successful Internet sites are not repurposing data from other sources. They are new breeds of services. The Yahoo!s, the directories of the Internet, are a completely new kind of content. These areas are ones that are really going to grow. How long will text be the dominant form of information on the Internet? I would say it is not the dominant form now. Most people are not using the Internet and the Web for what they were designed for, which was the hypertext linking of documents to documents. They're using it as an interface toolkit for doing actual services, for interacting with customer service, finding things, doing searches. This shows that the interactive nature is really what's important to the Internet, and we are starting to see new capabilities, through Java, to make it more programmatic.

The new exciting areas are the agenting technologies and the movement toward audio and video. The network-news stations put a big dent in the newspaper business, and the same will happen to network news. The CNN site, *CNN Interactive,* already has textural descriptions of the hot news of the day, and you can click on short video clips. They are slow, but they show where things are heading.

If I look at the classic magazine publishing model, there are three different sources of revenue: advertising, subscriptions, and mailing list sales. All three revenue streams are necessary to make most magazines go. What do we have currently on the Internet? We have a start at advertising-based revenue, but we don't have sales of subscriptions or mailing lists. The subscription-based revenue stops at services like PSINet, America Online, and UUNet, where people pay for their Internet access. None of that money is paid to the people creating the content, or the Web sites, or whatever software that's making it interesting. A model that took some of the revenue from subscription payments and had a royalty structure paying money back to the content creators who made the Internet interesting would make for a more robust Internet. It would also enable providers with only a small niche to have an easy mechanism to make a little bit of money. We're getting there so far on the advertising model. We have to get the subscription model going.

Mailing-list sales seem Big Brotherish to most people, because they give other people lots of information about what you want and what you do in your spare time. This kind of information in the computer world will get even more dangerous as more and more of our interactions can be watched online. For some people, dangerous is another word for opportunity, so this area has to be watched carefully and crafted well with appropriate protective laws. Mailing-list sales will also be used to help find the information that you do want, so there will be good aspects, as well as bad, to having this information out there.

My current project is to launch an Internet Archive that gathers, stores, and allows access to all public information on the Net. The Internet Archive has a project going with the Smithsonian Institution to archive the 1996 presidential election on the Internet, to see how the medium affects the political landscape. In addition, we're collecting Web sites over time and have acquired several that have already gone dark. We are contributing those to the Smithsonian, where they will be put into an exhibition that will be on view between the election and the inauguration.

That project is a starting point for something much broader: archiving the whole Internet in order to understand this Internet phenomenon in the future. The interesting thing about the Internet is how fast it's evolving, and the goal of a running archive is to track the changes in the Internet over time. It's important for historians and scholars to be able to look back and understand the Web at different times.

The Internet Archive is not just for historians. It can be an active component of the Internet infrastructure itself by becoming, over time, as critical to the workings of the Internet as the domain-name service or directories. The archive can be a backup for dead sites when Webmasters graduate or when Web sites just go away.

The size of the Internet currently could be somewhere between 1 and 10 terabytes. In fact, no one really knows how large the system is. In ten years, systems of that size will be commonplace and we'll have the old source material. If you have a full copy of the Internet in one place, you can do clustering studies to understand the evolution of communities and their overlaps, as we move from being a global village where everybody is chanting the same theme song from a popular sitcom to having lots and lots of different communities out there. We can track demographic shifts and even experiment with new indexing technologies. A centralized resource may not be the correct long-term solution, but it's a way to get started quickly.

The idea is to do the archive as a commercial-nonprofit combination. That has some precedent, but we will be creating a new model. The commercial entity is extremely important in fueling the technology for the archive, but the nonprofit entity will actually hold the bits. A nonprofit entity garners a certain amount of trust because it's going to be there for the public good and over a long period of time. I am endowing the Internet Archive with enough funding so that any bits donated will be kept alive forever.

I see this in a broader context than just making a time capsule. I'm not proposing that I know how we can build the ultimate digital library, but at least we can start the collection for those libraries that in a few years will become an integral part of our information ecology.

Marshall McLuhan had it wrong when he talked about a global village. With the Internet we're not constructing a global village. We're constructing a globe of villages where every group has its own separate culture. The villages are overlapping and geographically distributed; people can be part of several different villages that span the globe. We've moved beyond the brain-dead nature of the mass media.

THE GENIUS: <W. DANIEL HILLIS> Brewster is one of those people who saw the potential of the Net very early. He realized that the hard thing was going to be making connections between people with content and people looking for it. So he invented the idea of Wais, which is the first Net-searching engine that I was aware of.

THE SCOUT: <STEWART BRAND> When Brewster shows up, I feel an elf has just arrived. A shockingly effective elf.

THE STATESMAN: <STEVE CASE> One of the early pioneers in the Internet. I first met Brewster when he was still at Thinking Machines and coming up with the Wais protocol, pursuing a better way to search through a growing sea of information.

THE EVANGELIST: <LEW TUCKER> Brewster always thinks about the big picture, and both he and I seem to think best when walking. At Thinking Machines in Cambridge, Massachusetts, we always found our best and often craziest ideas came while strolling along the Charles River discussing the Internet and its potential to change everything we do.

THE CATALYST: <LINDA STONE> Brewster is one of those very persistent people who had an idea and kept digging and digging and drilling and drilling until he started to get somewhere with it.

THE IDEALIST: <DENISE CARUSO> Brewster is one of the nicest and smartest people I've met in this business. I remember that during one of his many cross-country driving trips – it might have been when he moved from Cambridge to Menlo Park – we exchanged quotable quotes all along the way. He also has vision galore. Not only did he foresee the importance of search engines for the Internet years before anyone else, now he's taking on the equally important task of archiving the Net.

THE MARKETER: <TED LEONSIS> Brewster's a great guy who's off on his next journey, trying to catalog the entire Web. He's a deep thinker, someone who firmly believes in the merits of Web technology and packaging. Brewster will always be a generation ahead of where the commercial application is. If you listen to Brewster and you have patience, you'll eventually get to the right spot with him. Brewster founded Wais, the first company that understood that publishers would want access to the Web and would need databases and services to post and bring up their content. We needed that kind of expertise and personnel. We are very happy with the acquisition. We bundled it into AOL's operations. Now Brewster's off doing his next big thing on the Web.

THE SEER: <DAVID BUNNELL> Brewster is brilliant. He might have the best ideas of anyone I've talked to. However, he is also very introspective and somewhat unsure of himself. If he had Bill Gates's confidence, he would change the world.

<Kevin Kelly>

The Saint

The Publisher: <Jane Metcalfe>

Kevin's on the road to Buddhahood. He's a deeply spiritual man. He has an intellectual curiosity that is infinite. His Socratic method of inquiry and development is wonderful. It used to annoy me. I used to think, This guy's an editor. He's a futurist — that's fine — but I've got to do some business. Why is he bothering me with these questions? But the more time I spend with Kevin, the more I realize that the way his mind wanders across things keeps us all on the edge.

Kevin Kelly is the executive editor of *Wired* magazine. He is the author of *Out of Control* (1994).

Kevin Kelly believes that computers are over. "They're history," he says. "All the changes that computation is going to cause in our society have already happened. Computers primarily sped up society by automating a lot of processes, which was a sufficient change, but that is all it was." Kevin believes we are in the initial stages of a communications revolution, which he finds more exciting because communication is the basis of culture.

Kevin is executive editor of *Wired.* According to *The New York Times,* he is "*Wired*'s 'Big Think' guy." He brings depth and fresh ideas to a publication that can otherwise get carried away with "attitude." He's a mature influence for a group of creative young people who work at a place characterized by Jaron Lanier as "a dormitory for the hormonally challenged." I have known Kevin since the early '80s when he was a contributor to the *Whole Earth Software Catalog.* He has also served as editor of the *Whole Earth Catalog* and the *Whole Earth Review.*

Kevin thinks and writes about the new biology of machines, economics, and social systems. His book, *Out of Control,* a '90s classic and a bible for the business and technological communities, describes a new universe in which the economy and all that soars around it take on the attributes of an ecological, or living, organism. That may sound poetic, but enough is known about the new economy and new kinds of technology being created for the digital world that we can take new approaches that are useful to businesspeople as well as to scientists, and try to understand how these systems work.

Kevin points out that we are about to live in an era governed by the law of increasing returns. "Bigness is not going to go away in this new economy," he says, "it's going to be made and composed in a different way. Rather than being monolithic and vertical, it's going to be flatter, horizontal, with nested hierarchies, rather than hierarchies by rank (i.e., differences of control are nested within each other as concentric circles rather than stacked on top of each other as they are in a pyramid). It is going to have lots of blurred edges. It's going to be a decentralized being. Robots or other large systems can't operate in a fast-changing environment unless they're decentralized. In the new digital economy, things are changing hourly, and you have to be very adaptable, very flexible. The cost and the price of that kind of adaptivity is to have decentralized control."

In May 1996, Kevin sent me an email in which he announced that his own Web page would provide an interactive version of *Out of Control.* What was of interest was the site's URL: *absolutvodka.* "That's the other half of what is going to be on the site," he wrote. "Besides being a different kind of book – one in which you can tweak the ideas – it is also a new type of advertising on the Web." Kevin went on to explain that "magazine-like ads, even great ones, don't work on the Web. The Absolut Company has been hip enough to realize this, and so they have initiated a new theme. They are encouraging 'visionaries' – instead of their trademark visual artists – to create some wild 'thinking spaces' on the Web. These endeavors are located within their general home space of absolutvodka.com."

Oh, by the way, the name of Kevin's Web page... Absolut Kelly. Is he trying to give us a better idea of what he means by *Out of Control*?

Kevin is "The Saint." I have an image of him walking barefoot on the road to Damascus, questioning everything. His questions question themselves.

THE SAINT: <KEVIN KELLY> *Wired* is a cultural magazine. It's about the culture of technology. It's not a technology magazine. It rocketed out of nonexistence into a circulation of three hundred thousand in the United States in two and a half years because it hit the right place at the right time – by recognizing that a new culture is emerging from technology. This technology culture was, in some curious way, invisible, even in 1991, when *Wired* was conceptualized. The concept for the magazine came from Louis Rossetto and Jane Metcalfe, who were publishing in Amsterdam an odd and interesting English-language computer magazine, *Electric Word,* that very few people saw. I had been reviewing it and raving about it because it talked about computers in a very broad way. They were interested in the consequences of the technology. That magazine closed down because it grew too far from its original premise, which was machine translation and word processors.

Louis and Jane came to California because that's where digital technology was happening. They got in touch with me because I also was trying to cultivate the culture of technology – with my experiences at The Well and the *Whole Earth Software Catalog,* as well as *Signal,* a catalog of personal communications. It was evident that they were interested in communicating about this same culture, so they started *Wired* to talk about technology in a cultural way – the visionaries who were making this revolution happen, the personalities, some of the common devices and instruments that we all saw but didn't know who made, and the future.

All these things rolled in with a design that by its mandate felt like it was coming from the future, dropped in from the year 2020, were all the right ingredients. It was a very optimistic magazine: it was saying the future is friendly and a place where we want to go to.

We watched, in about a year or less, as Al Gore and the National Information Infrastructure and the superhighway became common terms. By that time *Wired* was there. After writing about this mass migration onto the Net, *Wired* now has a lot of imitators, not so much in any particular magazine, but every single publication now has a *Wired*-like cyberbeat to report all these things.

While *Wired* embodies an optimistic view of the future, it is not a noncritical view. It suggests that the future increases our options and possibilities. Although many of these possibilities will be negative or harmful, the positive possibilities will be increased. The best way to prepare for the future is to have some optimism about it. Doomsayers don't prepare for the future well.

From the very beginning, *Wired* was seen as a male magazine. That was a demographic we understood, primarily because as editors we knew that the best way to make a magazine is to write about things you want to read about. The advertisers have to have a clear idea of what works. We wanted a young audience. What is interesting about youth magazines is that they're all to one side or the other. *Rolling Stone* is predominantly male, not as male as *Wired*, but it's male. We were going after a core audience of people who were very tech-oriented, and our demographics reflect that audience: 85 percent male, 15 percent female, about the same as the population on the Net in 1993.

We broaden the content in each issue. And, as *Wired* gets broader, the curious thing is that the entire culture is shifting toward *Wired*. Our pool is expanding tremendously because mainstream culture became nerd culture or, rather, nerd culture became mainstream culture. It won't be civilized until it has gender equality, until it has just as many women as men. That is the definition of civilization. First you have this frontier: cowboys, male hormones, wild, rough. That has been the Net, but the Net cannot become more civilized unless women play a greater role.

The old hoary have/have-not question in the digital realm concerns many people. The premise is that digital technology is somehow widening the gulf between those who have or know and those who have not and know not. The evidence for this is flimsy. The concern is really between the haves and have-lates. People are going to get this technology. The questions are, When are they going to get it and Can we speed it up? In fact, this technology is penetrating as fast or faster than most technologies – like washing machines, air conditioners, cars, telephones, TVs – have penetrated in the past. Globally, TVs have been one of the fastest penetrating technologies, while telephones have actually been penetrating very slowly.

Alan Kay says that technology is anything invented after you were born. In a sense I agree with Jaron Lanier that for the older generation, content is something that is fixed, while for the younger generation, content is interaction. Something else will have to come down the line to wow them. Content is the new technology for us.

Jaron asks how we would know if we were wrong about the future, if we were wrong about our optimism. First of all, if you know you were wrong, you would know too late. We'd go ten years into the future and find fewer options than there are now. If I want to create art, I would have fewer choices about where I can make art. If I want to think something, I'd have less of a space in which to think. It would be a pretty dire future, if that were to happen.

There is a utopian dream that the coming of the Net will bring positive social changes. I have my doubts about that. It is going to bring great social changes, but they won't all be positive. At the same time, if I have a positive feeling about what's happening with digital technology and the revolution that it brings, it is because netification, computerization, and digitalization all increase choices. That is about all that technology gives, but that is a very large thing. For example, a person born now who is interested in the arts can paint, sculpt, make films, and make music in many different spheres. Two centuries ago, there were fewer choices. Each time the media reinvent themselves, they expand the number of choices without excluding any of the previous ones. On this simple level, the Net and the literary space – the thinking space that it creates – will allow a whole new space for the arts. It is also a space that will allow new kinds of political and social structures, and it will allow them as a net gain.

What we are talking about now is a communications revolution. That is exciting, because communication is the basis of culture. Culture is a process of communication among individuals and groups. We are amplifying and enhancing the foundations of culture and society with this communications revolution. All the dynamic and revolutionary effects we are going to see will come from these tiny chips being used in a communications mode.

With the Net, we're going to see ideas of a type that were almost impossible to think about earlier. Technology shapes our thought, just as our thought shapes technology. We're in a period where technology is going to re-engineer and redesign the space in which we can have thoughts.

One of the effects of this new-coming thinking and literary space, due to the Web and the Net, is a continual shift into a new sphere of thinking, which is ecological, relativistic, postmodern, full of uncertainty. Philosophically, this creates and further promotes the kinds of things we've seen happening in the culture in the last two decades. Compare the idea of the book, which is fixed, to the postmodern idea in a space in which truth is assembled and not fixed (e.g., a hypertext novel, slippage of authority, a sense of interconnectedness, rejection of prime causes of things, the dogma of relativity). Moral certitude becomes more and more difficult to find. Agreement on some basic societal values becomes more and more difficult. Socially, we are going to see an even more difficult period ahead.

THE THINKER: <DOUG CARLSTON> Kevin is deceptively perceptive. He sees things for what they are, but more importantly he finds things that other people haven't considered yet or haven't thought about.

THE GADFLY: <JOHN C. DVORAK> Kevin is a guy who is stuck in a rut, and he can't perceive that he is in a rut, and he can't extricate himself and go on to something important. It's just a rut; you can see it.

THE COYOTE: <JOHN PERRY BARLOW> Kevin and I have become so joined in our intellectual enterprise that he can finish my sentences accurately and I can finish his sentences accurately. Kevin contributes a great part of what I would otherwise regard as my thinking. It's our thinking to a large extent. He's right when he says computers are over. This is not about computers. Computers are in the way. Computers are most valuable when their users don't know they are there.

THE SEER: <DAVID BUNNELL> Kevin's view is that the personal computer is dead because it's built into networking, and what's important is the ability to communicate and network and interrelate with people. Well, I've got news for Kevin. The first application we thought of with the Altair was looking at the modem in a phone, creating information links, and using it as a communications tool. That's not something that came along recently; it was in the works and in the plans from the go. The personal computer has facilitated that transformation, and to say that it's dead is silly.

THE BUCCANEER: <LOUIS ROSSETTO> Kevin is a saint, the progressive priest in a small Irish village in the middle of the nineteenth century. Everybody comes to hear his far-out ideas, and at the same time gets the most down-to-earth wisdom out of the man.

THE IMPRESARIO: <RICHARD SAUL WURMAN> The branch of inquiry that is represented by *Out of Control*, like its subject matter, will reproduce by dividing and infesting our fundamental thoughts about progress and change. A disarmingly great presenter of his ideas.

THE CYBERANALYST: <SHERRY TURKLE> Kevin Kelly combines an open mind, intellectual generosity, and good taste in ideas. This is a winning combination.

<Jaron Lanier>

The Prodigy

The Oracle: <Paul Saffo> *When we get a century or so into this revolution, Jaron Lanier is going to prove to be one of the most prominent deep thinkers. As brilliant as Jaron is, we only have a vague glimpse that there's somebody very special in our midst. This is an intelligence that comes once in a generation. It's not an exaggeration to say it's a little bit like meeting a Mozart.*

Jaron Lanier, a computer scientist and musician, is a pioneer of virtual reality, and the founder and former CEO of VPL.

Jaron Lanier leads a curious, double life. First, he is a member of the computer-science community and computer industry. He is the best-known pioneer of virtual reality and the founder and former CEO of VPL, one of the first companies to develop this technology. Second, he is a composer, performer, and recording artist. In addition to playing the piano and other Western instruments, he plays ancient instruments from around the world. Jaron is "The Prodigy."

"There is something extraordinarily similar between doing science and playing music," he says, "but this is true only for playing music on noncomputerized instruments. When you play music on an acoustic instrument, there is a fundamental sense in which you are directly contacting the physical universe as a source of mystery. You can play the piano for twenty or thirty years and still learn new things about it. You become more and more sensitive to it. It is a bottomless source, not containable by any set of ideas. Every time you think you have completely contained it, something new is revealed." But science, Jaron feels, is an extraordinarily humble activity in the sense that you can never believe anything. The scientist builds up a very fragile and temporary island in the middle of the sea of mystery of the physical world, creating theories that are all temporary and subject to being disproved. "Both the scientist and the musician are in contact with this fundamental mysteriousness," he notes, "which I find very spiritual in its humility."

He asks us not to consider computers as things that exist in their own right, but to look at them as artifacts that allow us to understand the way in which we are all connected. "Computers make our abstractions real," he says. "The danger is that they can limit our interaction with the fundamental mysteriousness of the world, which is the source. A nice expression for this is drinking your own whiskey. You can't simply be recycling your own ideas. You can't make music forever out of what you call notes or the notes cease to have any meaning." Jaron asks us in all interactions with computers to continuously go back to the source of the mysterious part of the universe. "We can't simply be reshuffling a deck of cards of ideas that we have already programmed into the computers," he says. "That's exactly the source of blandness and shallowness that you can see in computer content."

Blandness and shallowness are not words people use to describe Jaron. In fact, *Ebony* magazine once named him "Black Artist of the Month." (Jaron is white.) I saw him recently on stage in an avant-garde theater in the SOMA district of San Francisco. He was performing with The Perks, a multimedia dance company, which is led by one of his close collaborators, the dancer Rebecca Stenn. Jaron, standing in the shadows, seemed to be a modern-day Minotaur, swaying to and fro, as the semi-nude Rebecca swirled around him. It was dazzling.

THE PRODIGY: <JARON LANIER> The new media are different from the old media, of course, but one of the primary ways is not just in content, but in the solidification of our method of thinking. What we see with interactive media like the Web is not only the end result of the creative process, but the creative process itself, set down for all people to see and to share. This is extraordinarily exciting. It is also scary, because software has an unfortunate quality sometimes called brittleness. Pieces of software work together only if they're compatible, and once a piece of software has become pervasive, it tends to persist eternally because other pieces of software have been built on top of it and rely on it. Therefore we might now be depositing a codification of our method of thinking, our method of doing culture, that could persist for many generations.

The main thing that computer-based media do that's entirely new to the world is to make abstractions real. Take music: if you play an acoustic instrument, you are essentially growing more and more sensitive to this piece of the mysterious physical world. It's the same mysterious physical world that scientists study without ever fully knowing, and approach with successively better theories but ultimately can never touch. Musicians approach a physical instrument in the same way, striving to learn it but ultimately never knowing it. In particular, the abstractions we associate with music, such as the existence of notes, don't have any objective reality; they are just interpretations. But when you use computers in music, for the first time notes actually exist. In a computer, the program must be built out of ideas. All of a sudden, instead of ideas being your interpretation of reality, they *become* reality. This can be very exciting; it can also be very scary.

One of the processes that concerns me is what I call the "Karma Vertigo Effect." We have an extraordinary amount of what you could call karma in this generation, because this generation is creating the computer network and the infrastructure of computer software that will be running for a thousand years. I call it the Karma Vertigo Effect because when you realize how much karma we have in this generation, you get vertigo!

Can this solidification of abstractions affect us in ways that might be even more important to us than the nature of musical notes? Can they affect the future politics of commerce? Yes, they can. A good example is the recent controversy over the Clipper Chip and related issues, in which privacy would be determined by the layer of technology created for future layers to be built on top of. The Clipper Chip was a proposal from the intelligence communities for a chip that would be used essentially universally for digital communications, to provide a reasonable degree of encryption security between civilians communicating with each other. You could send a confidential message, a cash transaction, or something of that sort to another person, but a back door would give the government universal access to the information for itself. The argument in favor of the chip is that it would help with the capturing and prosecution of child pornographers, terrorists, and other bogeymen. The argument against it is that the whole idea in American government is never to trust the government that much. The proposal has been defeated, although the idea behind it has certainly not been defeated.

Perhaps the area in which this process of abstractions being made permanent by computer technology could have the most profound effect lies in our definition of who we are, our definition of personhood. This is where computer science intersects with spirituality and politics, in a curious way. I hold an opinion that is not in the majority in the computer community. Many people active with computers believe that the world simulated inside the computer eventually could have the same status as the physical world, once computers get good enough. Many people would think that I was one of the originators of that idea because of virtual reality, which might at first pass seem to suggest that kind of equivalence. That is not at all what virtual reality suggests.

What I love about virtual reality is the notion that computers could provide a way for people to share their imaginations with each other in new ways. I am not interested in replacing the physical world or creating a substitute for it. I am excited about the notion that you could get beyond this dilemma that we all live with; namely, that we have infinite imaginations and are completely free so long as we retreat into our heads, into our dreams, into our daydreams, and make everyone else disappear, but as soon as we want to share this with other people, we become very much not free. I would like virtual reality to provide a way out of that dilemma, where you have a world that's fully objective like the physical world, but also completely fluid like the imagination.

The strongest statement of that idea is artificial intelligence, the idea that a computer and a person are essentially the same thing, except that a person is better, and once computers get better, once they get faster and the software is worked out, they can essentially be the same. It is profoundly important to get to the core of this idea, because one's whole aesthetic in using computer media flows from where you stand on this issue. The notion of artificial intelligence was first conceived in 1936 by the English mathematician Alan Turing, who in 1950 wrote a paper, known as the "Turing Test," in which he proposed that if a computer and a person are both trying to convince you that they're the same, and you can't tell the difference, then you have no basis for believing they're different, and you have to decide that people and computers are the same. The flaw in the idea is that even though it is true – that if a computer and a person become indistinguishable, it might mean that the computer has become very smart and humanlike – another equally good interpretation is that the person has become stupid and computerlike. That's what I see as the danger. If people believe in computers too much, if they believe in computer simulation, if they believe in the ideas and abstractions of the computer as being fully real, then people will have a tendency to reduce themselves to support that illusion.

Do we think of computers as things that exist in their own right, or do we think of them as conduits between us? We should treat computers as fancy telephones, whose purpose is to connect people. Information is alienated experience. Information is not something that exists. Indeed, computers don't really exist, exactly; they're only subject to human interpretation. This is a strong primary humanism I am promoting. As long as we remember that we ourselves are the source of our value, our creativity, our sense of reality, then all of our work with computers will be worthwhile and beautiful.

The key to the Web is that the market itself built it. It wasn't created by studio moguls somewhere who said it was what everyone wanted. The Web was created by the users. This is a hard thing for traditional media businesses to get used to. But if they do accept it, the benefit is going to be a huge business.

The Web has taught us some amazing things about what content is going to be like in the next century. Before the Web arose so suddenly, people were promoting the idea of online content, but America Online, CompuServe, and other online services were doing it completely the wrong way. They thought that you should package a bunch of services with practical value, "entertainment value," and people would pay for them just like they pay for cable TV. A few people did. But all of a sudden, after the enormous amount of money spent promoting these online services, the Web arose and instantly surpassed the online services, without any planning, without any capital, without any marketing, without any advertising. Why did the Web succeed so quickly? What created this explosion? The answer is simple: the Web allowed people to be creative. This is what people want. People derive an existential pleasure from being their own guides, from being their own stars.

One of the metaphors I use when talking about this is Californians and cars. If you give Californians the option to take a bus between locations, which would be faster, cheaper, easier, they'll still take the car. Why? Well, because there's an existential pleasure to the car. It's your car. You chose it to express yourself, it has your stuff in it, and you feel free and in control in it even if you're not. It's a powerful force that is hard to give up once you've tasted it. The Web gives people that same pleasure for the first time in computer media, and now they can't give it up. The key to the Web's success is that people can go where they want, when they want, and they can even put their own stuff up. Equally important is that there is a freedom about the Web that is created by the mystery or lack of knowledge about what's there. The Web has a very erotic quality. You know that just around the corner, just around the next link, there might be something amazing, and so you're driven to explore, to keep on tracking that next link. That self-sufficiency makes the Web so intoxicating.

The worst thing in the world would be to try to turn computer networks into movies-on-demand, to say that cable TV is what people want. We can view the Web as a market test that already proves that this is not what content means in the future. It is the first true anarchy in history; there's never been one before. This comes as shocking information. It turns out that, free from the constraints of real estate, people actually can live in an environment of anarchy and mysteriousness and lack of known boundaries – and thrive. It's quite wonderful.

One of the ways to make money on the Web is by helping people connect with each other in an easy-flowing way. The world is so large, so diverse, that merely providing a connection over a network is not enough. You also have to provide community. It is also a bit like real-estate development. A good piece of real estate, developed well, has a kind of magic that attracts people, businesses, and the right kind of traffic. Good developers have a touch that not-so-good developers don't have. Cyberspace is similar. If you can create meeting points, where people of like mind and like spirit want to connect with each other, they'll pay to be there. You are like the MC. The crowd makes the party, but without the MC the party doesn't get started. People are willing to pay at the door to go to a party with a great MC, even though they themselves are making the party. They are the co-creators. It is exactly the same principle.

Web site creators are going to become the talent on which new media empires are created. They are analogous to the "tummeler" from the old borscht belt, the people planted in the audience to rile folks up and get them happy. People will be paid to be out in the interactive world as moderators or entertainers, or to serve some other spontaneous, live, real-time, and very human function. That is a step removed from where we are now because it assumes a higher bandwidth network than we currently have. Even the old content is going to be mediated by the live communities that I have been talking about. The community becomes everything; it becomes all important.

Another aspect to content, which is harder to talk about because it is unfolding before us, is what we call interactivity. We don't entirely know what interactivity is yet. We know that the experience of playing with interactive machines brings an unexpected pleasure. We know that when people are, for instance, surfing the Web, they are experiencing an existential pleasure. We have traditionally thought of content as being things like text and pictures, which are somewhat solidified in form and might be accessed interactively. But people who had the opportunity to grow up with computers have a much deeper understanding of what interactivity means.

Interactivity is a style of concrete conversation with the media. It is a way that you dance with the computer. For instance, the fact that the Macintosh is visual is not important. What is important is the rhythm of interaction; there is a feeling to it that ultimately is quite hard to articulate. The creation of that feeling is not easy. Certain people can do it, rather like artists. There are no textbooks that explain how to do it. It is a new art form. I'm convinced that the next generation of folks, the generation that grew up with computers, is going to be more sensitive to the flow of interactivity.

As the channels for getting information increase, another issue is the critical need for confidence in the information that you get. The current notion of how you get that confidence is by branding: this information is from a well-known consultant or analyst and therefore is reliable. That will not be sufficient in the future: there will also be a desire to get other kinds of information – factual information about the world, statistics, and so forth. There will be so many channels to get it from that some channels will have false information. Being able to provide people with a basis for believing in what they get over the network will become important. The challenge of providing information reliably and with confidence is not going to be easy to meet. A news or information-gathering organization will face the same problems that an individual will. People will pay to know what is real.

THE COYOTE: <JOHN PERRY BARLOW> Jaron is a case of childlike genius. He's incredibly good at stating the previously unconceived obvious in simple, elegant terminology. Jaron is the person who said to me what is probably the most important thing anybody ever said to me in defining my digital mission – "information is alienated experience." Suddenly a lot of things became clear to me.

> **THE STATESMAN: <STEVE CASE>** It was 1982 or '83 when I met Jaron at a consumer electronics show. He had licensed his [VR] glove to a small software company. I can't remember the company name. They were going to sell this thing for around $49, and, of course, the product never got beyond the price point. But I remember him. Once you meet him you'll never forget him.

THE SCRIBE: <JOHN MARKOFF> Jaron Lanier is one of the oddest people I've ever met. Really interesting ideas. It seems that he's unable to translate them into business practices.

THE SCOUT: <STEWART BRAND> Jaron's mind is omnivorous. He seems the utter brilliant dilettante, and then he bears down and makes fine music or a whole genre (virtual reality).

THE SEER: <DAVID BUNNELL> Jaron is right about so many things, but who's listening? The problem is that he's not just a little bit ahead of the curve; he's created his own curve.

THE CONSERVATIVE: <DAVID GELERNTER> Jaron Lanier is a fascinating guy. The virtual reality he pioneered is a lovely technology, but the people who designed and built it better get out into the real world and start learning what people actually do with computers. The technology is beautiful, but it's going to be dead and buried fairly soon unless they come up with interesting applications. The most exciting ones have to do with visualizing the internals of software itself, and they've barely been touched.

THE PATTERN-RECOGNIZER: <ESTHER DYSON> I often think Jaron is too far out, but I don't argue with people I don't respect. I love arguing with Jaron, because he's worth fighting with.

THE GADFLY: <JOHN C. DVORAK> Jaron Lanier? He's a wacky guy. What can I say?

THE CITIZEN: <HOWARD RHEINGOLD> The most interesting things Jaron Lanier does haven't been done yet. He created the virtual reality industry as we see it, by recognizing very early what its potential was and by bringing his unique kind of entrepreneurial business spirit and his deep technical knowledge. He got sucked into the celebrity of being "Mr. VR" and it spun him around like a whirlpool and spit him out. Somewhere down the line, five years from now, my wish is that he's going to do something very interesting that has nothing to do with virtual reality.

THE EVANGELIST: <LEW TUCKER> I have always been intrigued by Jaron's view that technology changes the way people relate to each other. Even in virtual reality, it is the interaction between participants that brings life to an artificial world.

The Impresario: <Richard Saul Wurman>

I still remember the first time I saw Jaron; I couldn't believe it. I remember the last time I saw Jaron – I still can't believe it. My memory is caught up with what seems like the innocent and poetic truth of what he says, covered like a sesame bagel with bits of twinkle, humor, and creativity.

<Ted Leonsis>

The Marketer

The Gadfly: <John C. Dvorak> *One of the most high-energy guys in the business. Always attracted good-looking women. Tells a good joke, maybe that's the key.*

Ted Leonsis is president of the America Online Services Company.

"Several people suggested that I meet Ted Leonsis a few years ago, but I didn't know too much about him or his company, Redgate," says Steve Case. "I had breakfast with him in Boston in October of 1993. By the end of breakfast I offered to buy his company, which focused on new media marketing, database management, interactive shopping, and private networks. It was quite clear to me, even in a couple of hours, that he had insights into this medium which would be terribly valuable to us. He was able to absorb a lot of ideas and inputs and perspectives and see the future."

At the time, AOL had 1 million members. Now it has 6 million members, is the first billion-dollar franchise in the online business, and has a market cap of $6 billion. Much of that growth came from Ted's vision and his ability to turn AOL into a media company, instead of a utility. That's probably why Steve paid him $40 million for Redgate.

"AOL saw Redgate," Ted says, "as being first and foremost a broadband and midband kind of programming company, with a lot of relationships with content companies. AOL looked at our intellectual capital. We had about a hundred people that 'got it,' and at the time AOL had four hundred people. It was a big acquisition. Redgate was generating $20 million; AOL was generating $100 million in revenue per year. Now we're looking at a combined billion-dollar business. That was just two years ago, so the velocity has been terrific. We've had to execute well. There's no manifest destiny for any company in this market, America Online included. If you don't block and tackle, if you don't deliver the product and service well, at an affordable price, you're going to get your butt kicked."

Steve and Ted seem to get along very well and to complement each other's talents. "Steve's Bill Paley, and I'm Brandon Tartikoff," Ted says, referring to the founder of CBS and the former programming chief of NBC. From Steve you get an intelligent statesmanlike style; from Ted you get high energy and imaginative ideas flying at you, and by you, like missiles. Ted Leonsis is "The Marketer."

I'm not at all surprised by his great success. In the late '70s, he coined the phrase "new media." I later sold a series of book-disk packages for his *List Magazine* to Warner Books, one of the megadeals of the software gold rush of 1984. It was, to my knowledge, the first time anybody packaged a CD-ROM in a book.

I ran into him in February 1996 at Richard Saul Wurman's TED Conference in Monterey. It had been at least ten years since I had seen him. Ted sat down in the front row next to David Bunnell and me and muttered over and over, "We're the survivors. We're the survivors." Funny, I never thought about myself that way.

For the next half hour, while some New York advertising guy wearing all black showed the audience TV commercials, Ted and I carried on a muted conversation, catching up with each other, hatching new schemes. "Time for you to do your own book," I said to him, realizing that Ted had always been one of the most entertaining figures I've ever met. For example, at TED, he told the following story: For a vacation and an adventure, he invited a group of friends to join him on a trip to Italy. He had chartered a jet to fly the party to the coast, where an exquisite yacht would be waiting to take them on a weeklong cruise in the Mediterranean. "It's costing me a quarter of a million dollars. And you know what? If I offered my friends the option of skipping the trip and taking their portion of the cost in cash, I would have wound up in Italy by myself."

As the speaker concluded his remarks, Ted whispered to me, "OK, I've got a book I want to write. How much can you get me for *Everything Bill Gates Ever Said Is Wrong?*" "For you, Ted," I replied automatically, "anything less than seven figures is an insult. But, perhaps it's not a good idea to burn business relationships. You never know who you're going to need some day." Undeterred, he began to rattle off chapter titles for next year's big best-seller.

The audience applauded, and the speaker received the ritualistic bear hug from Richard (Ricky) Wurman. Ted was the next speaker. As he rose, he leaned down and, with a toughness that is not apparent in his friendly demeanor, growled "I'm the only one in the industry who isn't afraid of him. Watch. Listen." I watched, and listened. At the conclusion of his forty-five-minute oration, Ted got his hug and left the stage having convinced the large audience of industry heavyweights (for at least a minute) that Microsoft's future in the interactive media world might be equivalent to that of a 20-watt FM radio station in central Greenland.

We made plans to talk further during the conference, but he disappeared. I called his room and found that he had checked out of the hotel early. Clearly, something was up.

Several days later I phoned him at his office in Virginia. "What about the book?" I said. "Gotta clear it with legal," he replied lamely, and hung up.

Then came the wild week in which AOL announced a series of deals with AT&T and Netscape and finally a major strategic relationship with Microsoft. I wondered how all this related to his biting talk at TED only weeks before.

"We won," he said when he resurfaced. "It's all over. We're the Number One online service."

"Right on, Ted. You're the greatest," I replied. "What about your book?"

"What book?"

THE MARKETER: <TED LEONSIS> In terms of marketing, would you rather be loved or needed? That's a question I ask all the time. Utilities are needed but they're not loved. So are cable companies and phone companies. If you're a brand that's loved, you don't even have to know who your customers are. Coke doesn't know who its customers are, but it has the most important shelf space – a position in a consumer's mind. We want to be a brand that's loved, and that's where word of mouth becomes very positive. We can send out a billion disks, but if members don't love us and tell their friends and relatives about us, we won't win.

AOL is in the entertainment and communications industry just as Ted Turner is in the news/entertainment/information business, and not the cable business. The Internet is not a market. It's a set of technological and business models that smart entrepreneurs will adapt to their businesses.

I was leading the charge at AOL against Microsoft when it was introducing MSN. I was thrilled when Microsoft originally named its service The Microsoft Network. We're called America Online. It's not our network. It's our members' network. The Microsoft Network is Bill Gates's network. That's like calling MTV the Sumner Redstone Viacom Channel. When was the last time you saw a kid walking down the street wearing a Sumner Redstone T-shirt? Branding becomes important. Since I've been here, Prodigy and CompuServe were going to put us out of business. Microsoft was going to put us out of business. Now the RBOCs [regional Bell operating companies] are going to put us out of business. We aren't threatened because we think that the consumer will always migrate to a simple, affordable, high-value proposition. If they root for you, if they want your brand to succeed, you can win.

The concept of "content" is so poorly defined. One, there's the myth that content is king. How can content be king when there are 253,000 free Web sites? If it were king, people would place a high value on it and demand their shekels from the taxpayers. What's happened is that content is not what drives a business. It's the story. It's the emotion. It's the way that the information is packaged and programmed. If you look at how newspapers started, how magazines played a role, and how television broadcast networks emerged, they were essentially picking and choosing the content that they wanted. What does a programmer do? He cancels shows. He finds talent and he packages it up. Nobody's doing that on the Web right now; whether or not people want to consume information and consume content in new ways remains to be seen.

My son, who's seven, is already living in a nonlinear digital environment. He spends more time on the computer and with videogames than he does with television, so he'll be trained to want to live in the more granular, interactive, on-demand world.

The concept that publishers are content providers who can repurpose existing content like a Hollywood studio is ludicrous, especially when you look at what Hollywood does. Studios open their movies in theaters, and then package them up and sell them to HBO and Blockbuster and the networks. Magazine publishers and newspaper publishers looked at the Internet as being an ancillary revenue stream. They would repackage their content and make it available in CD-ROM, then put it on the Web or America Online. That's proven not to work, because this medium demands more. Content is not the end-product. Content is the activator of the conversation and the community.

Esther Dyson jokingly says that I am the world's biggest bartender and essentially I pour the same beer as everybody else, but when people come into the bar I use content to activate the conversation, and my job is to provide context and navigation. That's where the value will accrue. The two big hits in cable, MTV and HBO, essentially take other people's content and transmit it over someone else's pipe, but they package the materials using their own brands and market those brands as a destination. No one is doing that yet on the Web. We're seeing the first glimmers of that with some of the search engines and some of the packagers. Certainly AOL will continue to try and do that.

The Web is a lonely, cold, ice gray place. Going from site to site is like going from empty restaurant to empty restaurant. First we have to build a sense of community, so that when you're in a site you know who else is in that site with you. Not only will you go into that site and come back for the camaraderie, but you will stay longer in that site than in other sites. One of the big issues that advertisers and transactors face is that people go in and out of sites. They're browsing. This is bad for a business model. What we have is an anti-market. Browsers are free, Web sites are free, and access is, for the most part, provided by corporations. No money is changing hands, yet everybody holds on to the myth that advertising will follow. Advertising will follow when there are brands and a site can show that people spend time there, that there's repeat activity, and that it has become a community. *60 Minutes* has a viewership; people spend the hour with *60 Minutes.* People spend thirty minutes with *Friends* or *Seinfeld.* That's not happening on the Web today.

What we are going to have in the near future is an infrastructure that enables chat and enables the avatars and the people-to-people aspect of the Web. Whereas today the aspect is people-to-content, the big win will come when you have people-to-content-to-people. Once you have that you'll get some accountability, and then you can start to overlay advertising. The big hit will come in the transaction area.

The Web is a daytime phenomenon. People get their high-speed access to the Web through TCP/IP networks at their companies, which are paying for access. The Netscape homepage, for example, peaks at about four o'clock. On the other hand, AOL is a prime-time medium. Most of our usage occurs from seven to eleven in the evening, and is at 14.4-kps or fewer, so we have to optimize for this narrowband world. That consumers are coming to the Internet is a myth, at least in the evening. Fewer than a million people, at max 1.25 million people, are paying for direct-dial Internet access from their homes. Netcom is the big Internet service provider, with three hundred thousand to four hundred thousand members. We have added that number of subscribers to AOL in a month. That's because we are programming an environment.

Our strategy at AOL is to become a lifestyle brand. We want to have the permission to be a media company not unlike Disney – to be on TV, to do books and magazines, to sell T-shirts and other branded products in malls, and to show that we represent something regardless of the transition medium. When DBS [digital broadcast satellite] came out, no one said to Ted Turner, "CNN is at risk. There's a new distribution method." He said, "That's great! I'll get millions more people that can't get cable who are subscribing to DBS." The companies that understand marketing and brands and how to weave together areas of interest and communities of interest will win in the long term.

We call the online world "new media" but at some point this won't be new media. It will be *the* media. When you look at the transitions in media history, it wasn't the newspaper barons who created and pioneered radio, and it wasn't the radio moguls who made TV, and it wasn't the TV execs who made cable.

Each generation had its own set of entrepreneurs. People in the mainstream are looking at the Net or at online services as being a niche business, but if we were a cable company, we would be third largest behind Time Warner and TCI. The most amazing statistic to me is that between the hours of ten and eleven at night, we're getting three hundred fifty to four hundred thousand people to log in. *The Larry King Show* on CNN reaches about five to six hundred thousand. MTV gets six to seven hundred thousand. In eighteen months we'll surpass Larry King's and MTV's ratings.

If someone had said ten years ago that in the aggregate more people would be watching a cable channel than the three broadcast networks, you would have said that was impossible. But that's what happened. Today 55 percent of all homes watch one of a hundred cable channels, and 45 percent watch ABC, NBC, and CBS. It is not out of line to say that in three years, in the aggregate, more people will be on computer, interacting over the Net, than will be watching a cable channel. The tide has shifted.

Two things haven't caught up with this. One is that, for the most part, none of us are providing acceptable levels of service or creativity. Bandwidth has had a lot to do with that, but only in the last two years have companies like AOL become the hip place to work. Look at industries that had their golden age. In the '60s, advertising and Madison Avenue were in their golden era. In the '70s the great young minds were going to Hollywood. In the '80s you went to one of two places, cable or high technology. The new interactive services business of the '90s combines advertising, entertainment, and programming like cable technology in a new way. Kids who used to want to work at Microsoft now want to program an online service or Web site or work on their own as entrepreneurs. It's just a matter of time until the talent, ideas, and the capital start flowing in. In ten years we'll look back at this ASCII world we've been living in, and AOL and MSN, and perhaps some of the new entrants, will look more and more like CBS or ABC.

For the foreseeable future we're locked in the current business model. AT&T has announced its world Net product with a lot of hoopla. It's in two hundred cities. We're in five hundred cities. The main complaint we get from our members, the reason they cancel, is that they can't get a local access-number. The phone companies and cable companies have yet to deliver on the promise to make bandwidth ubiquitous. What we've seen in our business is that every time you provide higher speed transmission rates, people stay longer because they have a more pleasant experience. My bet is that the general bandwidth is going to become ubiquitously slower rather than faster. I'm almost offended when I see people building Web sites with lots of audio, video, and graphics, because they are testing their sites in their TCP/IP environment with high-speed connections such as T1 lines or, at minimum, ISDN, whereas the average home user connects at 14.4 or 28.8. Try connecting even at 28.8 and see how unpleasant the experience can sometimes be.

I spend most of my time dumbing things down. That's one note of caution for this entire industry. Television and Hollywood have the perspective that the whole world is thirty-one years old, ethnic, single, and lives in Manhattan. The programming sensibility of television is very New York. We've developed the same kind of prejudices on the Web. We have a Cambridge/Berkeley/Silicon Valley outlook. That's not what makes things mainstream. Vanilla ice cream is mainstream. McDonald's is mainstream. You can't be clubby and cliquey and inward. I read *Wired,* but I'm in the industry. I love *Wired,* but I don't believe that it is an inclusive publication. In fact, it's an exclusive publication. That's what a lot of people do on the Web. Rather than make it for Everyman and Everywoman, they overcomplicate it. What we've learned at AOL is the simpler, the easier, the better.

I'm "The Marketer" because I don't care about what anyone in the industry says. I care only about what our members and consumers say. As a marketer you have to provide service and value to consumers. Then you have to lead them from one place to another so they continuously buy your services. In our business, when we become inbred, we drink our own bathwater. We're a business in an industry that has the luxury of having intelligence in the network, where you can talk to and communicate to consumers all the time. I have learned that if you package things, and if you build a brand, you can overcome any kind of technology and make the transitions from generation to generation of technology. People could consider us a marketing and programming company. I don't think anyone, if you mentioned AOL, would say that we don't have enough members, or we don't have enough buzz, or we're not mailing out enough disks, or we don't have our ads all over the place. I'm extremely conscious that this is a brand business.

For example, I went shopping with my wife in a mall. We bought Coke from the grocery store. We went next door to a Blockbuster, which was doing a promotion with Coca-Cola. We bought suntan lotion at a CVS pharmacy, where there was a big cooler of Coke. Then we went next door and I bought a slice of pizza and got a Coke. As we walked back to the car, it stuck with me that Coke was everywhere. That's what we're doing with AOL. It's on Windows 95. It's included with every modem. It's shrink-wrapped with every computer and in magazines about the Web. AOL will become an impulse buy, a product providing the service that you need access to, where trial is important. I believe we are the first company, the only company, committed to making the brand and the trial ubiquitous to all consumers.

Our main competition is the weather. Our usage goes through the roof when we have big snowstorms. When spring arrives, we see some dips in usage. A second area of competition is leisure-time activities. There's a battle waged every night in the home. You finish dinner, then what do you do? Do you talk with your husband, wife, boyfriend, girlfriend, kids? Do you watch television, read a magazine, or go online? Some people do all at once.

What strikes me most is our usage pattern. Thursday night is the highest TV viewership, and it's our worst night. We're competing with Jerry Seinfeld, so I'm much more concerned about *Seinfeld* than I am about Bill Gates. No one's going to turn on the network to listen to Bill Gates, but 20 million people have a date every Thursday night from nine to nine-thirty with Jerry Seinfeld. We're not that good yet. We will be. If we look at that kind of compelling programming as our competition, we can become a new media. If we look at CompuServe and other online services as the competition, we'll be setting the bar far too low.

The Lover: <Dave Winer> AOL is in a major struggle to keep up with its growth. If you want to understand where AOL is at and why they get a bad rap, you have to understand that.

THE WEBMASTER: <KIP PARENT> A lot of people talking about the Internet don't know what they're talking about or say the same type of stuff. Leonsis is an interesting guy to see. He has vision, and he's able to communicate it. If I'm going to listen to a speaker, he's the kind of speaker I want to hear.

THE SEARCHER: <BREWSTER KAHLE> Ted is a marketing extravaganza. He is good at spinning a tale that is amazing, fun, and based on real numbers. Credited with inventing the term *new media,* Ted seems to thrive on pushing technology into the mainstream.

THE CATALYST: <LINDA STONE> I've always thought of Ted more as "The Seller." He could sell anything to almost anyone. How can a person be the mayor of Vero Beach, Florida, the CEO of Redgate, and the president of America Online? Ted is the consummate relater. He made me a little nervous when I first met him because he's so smooth, and there's something about someone that smooth that makes you wonder what's really going on.

THE PRAGMATIST: <STEWART ALSOP> 90 percent bullshit, 10 percent brilliant.

THE IMPRESARIO: <RICHARD SAUL WURMAN> He seems at first like the electronic car dealer to the world and says things I don't really want to hear but are correct.

<JOHN MARKOFF>

THE SCRIBE

THE ORACLE: <PAUL SAFFO> *Markoff is a special kind of infonaut. He has an academic's curiosity and doggedness, but his wonderful practical streak, much to our good fortune, means he's writing in* The New York Times *rather than in some dry academic journal. The important thing about Markoff is that he doesn't just get the scoop. He gets the scoop behind the scoop. He tells us about something we didn't know was happening, then goes down another layer to what it means in the larger context.*

JOHN MARKOFF covers the computer industry and technology for *The New York Times.* He is the coauthor of *The High Cost of High Tech* (with Lennie Siegel, 1985); *Cyberpunk: Outlaws and Hackers on the Computer Frontier* (with Katie Hafner, 1991); and *Takedown: The Pursuit and Capture of America's Most Wanted Computer Outlaw* (with Tsutomu Shimomura, 1995).

John Markoff (alias "Scoop") is in a class by himself. No one writes about technology the way he does. David Bunnell, no slouch as a computer industry journalist, says, "I know people who say the only reason they read *The New York Times* is to read Markoff. A technology writer who sells newspapers – that is remarkable."

Markoff is "The Scribe." He creates his own stories. He gets the scoop. Never will you find him crawling on the floor searching for crumbs of intellectual property. He is knowledgeable, almost professorial. He's a pro, a working journalist who covers all the bases and gets the job done. Just as important, he is an enthusiast. It matters to him that he can buy a notebook computer with a 150 MHz CPU speed. He wants that new disk drive with 256K cache.

Markoff and I have an interesting relationship. With regard to computers and software, I do whatever he tells me to do. No questions asked. In return for my complete and utter supplication, Scoop is my tech-support guy. I call him at least once a day at *The New York Times.* No story is too big, no deadline too urgent: he drops whatever he is doing and tells me how to reinstall my system software, lectures me on the intricacies of TCP/IP protocols, advises me on setting up an email bozo filter.

There are only two exceptions to his extraordinary solicitude. If I lapse into DOS talk, he'll quietly sigh in resignation and say, "What do you want from me? Call Dvorak." Then there is that unmentionable word, which, if uttered, guarantees an instant disconnect of (a) my telephone to Markoff's telephone, and (b) Markoff from his senses.

And what might that word be? To be explicit would risk my friendship with Scoop and, more important, void my lifetime tech-support contract. One day while I was on my farm sitting on the porch and watching the corn grow, I was talking to Markoff on the phone as a thunderstorm began. "Scoop," I said, "it's pouring. Hold on while I close the windows."

Click.

Then there is Markoff's secret, which he bared to me while we walked in the Arizona desert in 1984 during Esther Dyson's PC Forum. Although we were attending a high-powered computer industry conference, from the conversation you would have thought that we were at a 1968 SDS meeting in Berkeley. Scoop told me something remarkable that has remained unknown to his friends, his sources, his masters at The New York Times Company, and the computer moguls whose IPOs, mergers, buyouts, and bankruptcies he covers.

"I am a Marxist," he confided. That's the scoop on Scoop, and it may explain why some executives at the companies he covers are frequently unhappy about his articles. (Today, by the way, he proclaims himself a political agnostic. But then, didn't Marx claim that he wasn't a Marxist?)

Next came the bombshell that his reporting for *The New York Times* is not to be taken at face value. Deeply embedded in the text is Markoff's daily secret message – in code! I didn't believe it when he told me. I spent the next five years voraciously reading his column, attempting thousands of acrostic combinations. I was getting nowhere. It was only two years ago when Danny Hillis let me beta-test one of Thinking Machines' powerful CM-5 parallel processing computers that I became the first to break what is now known as "The Markovian Acrostic."

Check out the following lead paragraphs from his *New York Times* article (Section D; Page 4; June 13, 1996):

> **Microsoft Prepares to Improve Its Threat to Netscape's Rule**
>
> The Microsoft Corporation will take another Step in its effort to overtaKe the Netscape Communications Corporation in the market for Internet software when it presents a number of new technologies to 300 corporate executives at a meeting Thursday in San Jose, California.
>
> But Netscape moved to preempt Microsoft today, saying that 92 of the nation's largest 100 companies were already using Netscape's products. Netscape, based in Mountain View, Calif., also detailed its own strategy, describing the next-generation versions of its NaVigator program for browsing the IntErnet and its Suite Spot server Software for the World Wide Web.

The Scribe: <John Markoff> We are in the Model T phase of this new and interesting ecology, and there are all kinds of innovations and new protocols that will permit different kinds of human interaction. When we go from limited bandwidth into real broadband stuff, the Net will get very interesting. But we are too close to make a judgment that the Internet is as important as fire or more important than the printing press. You have to give it time to see where it fits in the social milieu. There is evidence that the Internet may be an interim step, paving the way for the next big thing. We are still only halfway through Nicholas Negroponte's grand shift, from wireless to wired and from wired to wireless. We need to see how wireless technology is deployed before making grandiose judgments. The Internet is just a platform, the way the PC was a platform and the Mac was a platform. The Net is the next platform, but I don't think it's the last platform.

I was optimistic about the grand promise that the Internet would create a multiplicity of communities, until about a year ago. The Internet as it is today lacks the necessary bandwidth to give you a real community. Communities are as much about smell and texture and touch as they are about intellectual content. The Net is not going to be a substitute for the family and the close-in community. We're talking Yellow Pages here.

The World Wide Web has enabled a whole series of things because it was accessible to mortals – allowing you to point and click instead of typing a set of arcane command sequences – and because it resonated with whatever particular thing was happening. People were looking for the next big thing beyond personal computers, and the Web took off. It met some key minimum standard and then became a standard that is going to rival the personal computer. But it's not the last one. The Web created a platform for innovation, so innovation and growth moved away from the PC to this new thing that's bubbling along.

But there are a couple of flies in the ointment. People say that there are 30 million people on the Internet. Let's deconstruct that number. The actual number of people who can get to your Web site at any given moment is not 30 million, because maybe 20 million of them use some sort of electronic mail system that might not be compatible and might have a gateway. So that cuts the figure to 10 million, which has to be broken down even further. The real figure is probably a million people. This is not a number to sneeze at, but it's certainly not 30 million. Until the next leap – the Web is put into a consumer appliance, like your telephone, or your television, or something you can carry around with you, where it really is accessible to everybody – it is still a playground for yuppies and intellectuals and engineers and people who work with computers, and is not societywide in any sense.

There is a tension between distribution and centralization. David Gelernter's centralized vision was remarkable because he really was out in front of it. When he wrote *Mirror Worlds* in the late '80s, no one had any sense of the power of computer networks. David had this idea of mirror worlds, just the way

Ted Nelson had the idea of hypertext, but he couldn't implement it. The world rushed right by David. His notion that there will be terminals in supermarkets was the vision of a group of anarchists in Berkeley back in the early '80s, called Communion Memory, made up of Lee Feldenstein and his gang. But public terminals in public spaces make no sense. Silicon is free, so why would you want to share it? Why wouldn't you want your own? Why would you want to have to plug it in somewhere rather than have the data coming out of the ether? Practically as well as sociologically, it will make more sense to carry something. You carry a notebook with you right now, so why wouldn't you carry something you could perhaps talk to, something that could understand you?

Too much computer power is coming too quickly to think that the keyboard is going to be the interface in five or ten years. A grand inversion is going on in the computer industry. In the past, the people who built and designed and purchased supercomputers were the people – or institutions – who could afford them: the military, the Pentagon, large corporations. In the future, the fastest computers will also be the cheapest and will arrive under the Christmas tree first. The military and large corporations will follow. That is the nature of the technology.

Everybody thinks that Bill Gates is radically innovative, but if you look at the personal computer industry today and compare it with the mainframe industry of two decades ago, there were eight architectures at that point, IBM and the seven dwarfs. In the PC industry, we have two architectures. It is less innovative now than the mainframe business was. There is less competition. There are a million dwarfs making boxes and a couple of guys making software. This is going to lead to a huge computing crisis, and nobody sees it.

The nature of the computer has changed entirely. I buy into Kevin Kelly's point that the computer is basically a tool for communication. We saw inklings of that in wordprocessing as a communications vehicle. Communicate directly with someone, and the machines disappear entirely; that's the ideal. Why should you be tied to this machine at all? It should be tied to you: you should wear it, which is what the people at the Media Lab are pursuing.

Voice recognition has been a Holy Grail for thirty years. The interesting thing is that, along with Moore's Law, there's Joy's Law [named for Bill Joy of Sun Microsystems]. Both are geometric. Joy's Law is the same kind of geometric procession in MIPS, millions of instructions per second. Very quickly we are going to reach interesting levels of computing speed in something you can carry around in your hand, where it can do super-computer kind of stuff, such as a huge dictionary that can recognize speech. Then all of a sudden you are free of the imprisoning keyboard, the imprisoning mouse. It's going to happen.

What comes out of Disney-ABC, Westinghouse-CBS, Time-Warner-TCI-Turner? This is a period like the late 1960s, when the perception was that the only way you could survive was if you were the largest. What is motivating these guys is essentially the perception that mine is bigger than yours. Will this ultimately lead to the same disastrous explosions that capped the merger period of the '60s? Moving large blocks of capital around is uninteresting; there's no value created. Netscape Corporation is an example of the process that has been marked by the rise of the personal computer, the workstation industry, the networking industry. Over and over again technology, largely spun out of government research programs, is being adopted for commercial use. The result is the creation of technologies that are changing the world. This is where the interesting stuff is happening. The renaissance is in the Valley, not in New York, and it doesn't look like it's slowing down, which is the one sign of hope. But I don't understand the interaction between the corporate giants. They are playing Monopoly, going around trying to put hotels on all the squares.

It's too early to bet on any particular technology. A corporate giant that wants to protect itself will have to take a cover-your-bases strategy, dabble in everything, and be prepared to commit heavily in something that seems it will win. If it's the Net, the corporate giants have to be there, but they are just going to be followers. They want to be tariff takers, the bridge-toll collectors of this new technology. I suppose they can capture it, although there is some hope that because the technology is interactive it won't be the kind of McLuhanesque global village we saw in the '60s and '70s, where there was one source broadcasting to millions of people. Perhaps, just the way personal computers made desktop publishing possible, this technology will democratize the ability to create content, and content will come from the grassroots. You will be able to create small design houses and production houses, outside the control of the gigantic, vast operations. The technology may move quickly enough so that it will be a decentralizing force. Obviously there's a tension there.

The idea of convergence is a myth. You have collisions, but you don't have convergence. Marx had a vision of the pianist as the performer who produced something that you couldn't turn into a commodity. Then there was this other thing, the recording, which was the commodification of the pianist's art. But they were two very different things. Maybe in the twenty-first century, when you can commodify everything, when everything becomes content, you will have this leveling process, and we will become entirely commercial beings.

Perhaps convergence means the coming together of all these spheres of creation, writers writing, performers playing, scientists creating, with this new world that Negroponte talks about, which is expressed best by saying it's all just bits. If it's all just bits, it's like money. There's an exchange mechanism, and everything is taken to the same digital level, and you have a very flat world. It's multimedia, but it's this gelatinous stuff. Maybe that is the convergence – running the unique spheres of human activity through the Cuisinart of digitization. Maybe this is capitalism's last revenge, so that the universal commodity is not money, as it was in eighteenth- or nineteenth-century capitalism, but bits. Where does that lead? Technology does not substitute for creativity. It enhances creativity in places, but not if it's flattening the world and is the ultimate leveler.

A classic moment in the evolution of the Internet took place at the 1995 Neiman conference when Esther Dyson was talking about what the Web means for commerce with *New York Times* publisher Arthur Sulzberger, Jr., and Sulzberger said, "We're the shopkeepers, and we're here, and we're your worse nightmare." There is a lot of truth to that. A small anarchic community of wireheads and hackers made the mistake of giving fire to the masses. Nobody is going to give it back. It is paradise lost. This wonderful community is not a community anymore. It's a society. It is a city on the Net, and in the back alleys of this electronic city, people are getting rolled. It is no different than being in New York. Let me be a couch potato if this is what Internet activity is about.

As an example, go to the chat lines. Anybody who has been around the Net for more than five years bemoans the declining standard of discourse because it is not an elite phenomenon anymore. It has become a mass phenomenon. I thought that the Net would be able to support both elites and mass culture and they would coexist. Now I am not so sure. This is what sociologist Herbert Marcuse predicted, a one-dimensional society, where everything becomes level, and there are no elites.

THE GADFLY: <JOHN C. DVORAK> Markoff is the journeyman reporter who should be a book writer. Get out of *The New York Times!!!*

THE SEARCHER: <BREWSTER KAHLE> John Markoff is one of the more insightful writers alive today. He does much more than journalism; he routs out the new trends that are about to come up. His front-page coverage of publishing on the Internet in 1991 was way ahead, even of the trade press.

THE PUBLISHER: <JANE METCALFE> John Markoff is the voice of the Digital Revolution. If John says it's important, it is.

THE SCOUT: <STEWART BRAND> John is the voice of sanity in an often insane field. There's no more exemplary journalist around the computer business.

THE CATALYST: <LINDA STONE> Markoff is one of the people I look to for help in educating me about what's going on, to be a step ahead of me, to be putting things together for me. Markoff was one of the first people who started pointing to the Internet. He was excited about Mosaic almost before anybody knew what it was.

THE SOFTWARE DEVELOPER: <BILL GATES> John's a great journalist. He's been around for a long time.

The Competitor: <Scott McNealy> John is probably one of the most trusted and respected technology reporters in the business. You trust him to respect your opinion, to respect your off-the-record comments, and you expect him to understand what you're talking about, and not misrepresent – or even worse – represent inaccurately the industry trends. If there was one guy out there who I'd grant an exclusive interview to, if I could only give one, it would probably be John.

<John McCrea>

The Force

The Webmaster: <Kip Parent> *John McCrea has been a tremendous force at Silicon Graphics. He was able to rally the engineering and marketing people in the company around the Web, and he managed to build the WebFORCE product line into a rapidly growing business within the company. It is a tremendous success. John is definitely someone who sees the big picture and has a vision. He rallies people around him and makes things happen.*

John McCrea is the manager of Cosmo, Silicon Graphics's next-generation Web software product line.

Networks and computers have been around for a long time, and network computers have been connecting people around the planet for a long time. For Silicon Graphics's John McCrea, the connectedness that is occurring and accelerating right now is interesting. John is one of the people leading the drive toward a new medium. He sees the Web as the key enabler to bring about 3-D hypermedia: virtual reality modeling language, or VRML. He's not the typical Silicon Valley guy. I know John because through his efforts, Silicon Graphics has provided technology support to Content.Com, Inc., the Internet publishing company I have formed with David Bunnell. Part of his job is to seek out the right start-ups (HotWired, for example) and provide Silicon Graphics technology as a way of getting the word out about his products. Unlike many of his colleagues, he lives in San Francisco, and his interests are oriented more toward the arts than toward engineering. It's refreshing to talk to him.

John entered the computer business late, joining Silicon Graphics in 1993 right out of Stanford's MBA program. In 1980 he went to MIT with the notion of becoming a physicist, and fairly quickly he realized that there were lots of other people who would be better physicists and that it was not an exciting time to be in physics. His second passion was the arts, and strangely enough it was possible to pursue creative writing and other art forms at MIT, a school known for engineering and science. "The '80s were the lost decade for me," he says. "I was doing everything from moving to Ireland to work on a novel to doing fund-raising for a school in Oregon. In '91 I had a 'born-again' capitalist experience, went to Stanford business school, and fell in love with Silicon Valley. I worked a summer at Tandem, then ended up at Silicon Graphics. So I am not a computer industry insider, by any means."

In early '95 John thrust Silicon Graphics into the Internet market with the WebFORCE server product line. Today he is manager of Cosmo, their next-generation Web software product line. "Who knows where that will lead," he says. "I was the product manager for the Indy workstation, and the Web thing came on really strong. It was obvious that we had an opportunity, and I went forward and defined what we would do and pulled together the team that would build the first Web authoring tools and the first Web system. It has grown into a multi-hundred-million-dollar business for us, in both servers and authoring workstations. I lead much of the business, and the marketing effort behind it, and I work with the engineering teams that are building the next generation of products."

John McCrea is "The Force."

THE FORCE: <JOHN MCCREA> At a technical level, VRML is a file format. At a higher level, it is a way of doing 3-D graphics over networks. 3-D graphics are coming to a Web where people have become comfortable with a page-centric view. But VRML will take the page-centric view and pop it into another dimension, with the potential to make the experience more like the physical world. This fundamental shift brings a sense of place to something that has absolutely evaporated the notion of space. While evaporation of space is a powerful concept, much of the information suddenly loses context. Introducing the notion of space to the Net via VRML has the potential to make it more compelling and appealing to a larger audience.

Increasingly you will see 3-D objects that you can move around and look at from different angles right inside your Web window. Your Web page will have text and pictures and 3-D in a little window. This is the intermediate step to a more major shift that happens when, instead of encountering 3-D as if it were just another type of media, like a picture or a movie clip, what you see in the window is a 3-D world. This world is like the outside world in that you can choose where to go and steer yourself through it, flying or walking or whatever. You get to where you want to go in the same clicking fashion as with hypertext, but now it's hypermedia. I click on a door and stuff comes to me. I click on a window and stuff comes to me. That stuff could be more 3-D or a video clip or a picture or text. It is a major shift in your experience of that information set. It is not better than text. It's different.

Rikk Carey, one of the original leaders of the VRML effort at Silicon Graphics, contrasts the Web with a library. The differences are significant. On the Web you can't go to a section of the library and see all the books related to a topic, or see how big they are, or get a sense of the style of the book from its cover, or what it looks like inside. You can't even go inside the library; you have to stand outside. By typing an address or hitting a link, you shout up to a window and ask for a particular page. Mysteries happen behind the scenes, and moments later the page you requested is held up to the window. You never see the book and you never see the chapter. You see only the page.

The Web today, a world organized by bookmarks, is a very different model from what we human beings, who live in a 3-D world and have a spatially oriented memory, are used to. When you recognize, for example, a picture of a house in a field, you immediately know something about that house and field. Suspending your disbelief, you think of the real world. When you enter a 3-D environment under your own control and can move through it as a virtual world, you have to get a certain frame rate up, considered to be a minimum of twelve frames per second for reasonably smooth motion. At that point, your mind is no longer interpreting a still image and figuring out its worldliness. When you're moving through something, you're experiencing it, and a powerful cognitive shift occurs.

At Silicon Graphics, we searched for how we might be able to make VRML happen. We were working for years toward what would eventually be called VRML. That effort was originally called "Inventor." Inventor was the first object-oriented toolkit for developing 3-D applications. It was open and cross-platform. When Mark Pesce and Tony Parisi were talking up the vision for VRML, the search for the technology brought forward Gavin Bell, a member of the Inventor team at Silicon Graphics. He drafted a proposal based on Inventor that became known as VRML 1.0. The spec came out in early 1995 and, probably most important, was adopted by a small group of people who felt passionate about it. At Silicon Graphics a small team broke off and started working on the VRML products. That effort gave birth to the VRML 1.0 browser.

Silicon Graphics basically took the lead role in starting a new industry around VRML. The specification, the first parser, and another piece of enabling technology were thrown out over the firewall into the public domain, and about seventeen different companies started making VRML browsers because it was relatively easy to do. Now at least a half-dozen companies have VRML products based on that technology. Microsoft was able to get one by licensing it from a small company.

Where do we go from here? We now have worlds that you look at and fly through, and are inhabited by creatures. One of the first was fish swimming, with sound that is spatial and 3-D. Moving around, you feel you are in the space. Creatures come up to you, and if you click on them, they do something different. What happens when I, as a viewer of this content, can begin to build this myself, when I can take different, almost robotlike parts and put them together? I can start to have things that represent me in this world. Or I can interact with a representation of someone else in the world. It really is a shift, a blurring the line between application and content.

The whole notion of live content is like the notion of artificial life. It's not something that people are thinking about right now, but wait until you start to exist in these worlds. You'll be walking down the street of a city that doesn't exist, and walking into stores that don't exist, but interacting with people who do exist, represented to you in a unique way on a computer screen and with agents that are programmed animated characters. We are at the beginning of trying to figure out what it will mean. What happens to the robot avatars when no one is looking?

Microsoft is a company to be taken seriously. Its fortune has been built on proprietary formats and closed APIs [application programming interfaces], but the Internet is forcing it to behave in a different way. A number of battles will be fought, and Microsoft has stated an intention to go open, a complete reversal of strategy. The evolution of VRML, from 1.0 to 2.0, was a defining moment in the new era of competition around open standards. Microsoft proposed something called Active VRML, which is in no way technically related to VRML. It was a complete reset of how one might do 3-D. Of course, innovation is great, so the more the merrier, but the way Microsoft presented Active VRML raised questions and concerns within the online community. They haven't figured it out, but they want to throw something out there and slow the process down and confuse the market. But the community of interest around VRML rallied and joined battle for VRML 2.0, which was initiated by a Silicon Graphics proposal called Moving Worlds. The battle between Moving Worlds and Active VRML is now playing itself out. Moving Worlds is fast becoming the standard, with support from Netscape and Apple. VRML 2.0 products such as Silicon Graphics's Cosmo Player are now coming to market. VRML is an open file format, and because 3-D is complex, file format actually has a lot of implications for what you need to make an authoring system and a viewer. At the end of the day, VRML is a file format. Silicon Graphics invented the file format, essentially extracting elements from Inventor.

The rivalry between Java and VRML got a lot of attention. The reality is that they are not competitive, but are perfectly complementary. VRML is a file format for doing 3-D, and Java is a programming language. Early in the rise of hype and interest around Java and VRML, both sides, Silicon Graphics and Sun, started thinking about how they could be complementary. Both companies are cooperating or mutually endorsing each other's technologies. In fact, Silicon Graphics is working with Sun to bring 3-D and multimedia to Java, based on the work with VRML. We're bringing to market Cosmo 3-D, which is a VRML 2.0–compliant API for the Internet. Cosmo will allow developers to create platform-independent 3-D applications in Java or in more traditional programming languages like C++.

People are making interesting analogies about the Web. One is that the Web is becoming the world's largest disk drive. I like that, except it doesn't paint a very exciting picture of the content. The analogy of the world's largest library doesn't excite most people because they find libraries fairly boring. Another analogy is that the Web is more like a CD-ROM than a disk drive. But with CD-ROMs, you can't change the information. The Web is more like a CD-ROM with immediately updatable information through databases. At Silicon Graphics, we're trying to take the Web from a static, page-centric, download-then-view model and make it dynamic and experiential, where the bandwidth will eventually make it totally live, with streaming. A lot happens when you go from page-centric to worldlike with the combination of 3-D graphics and audio, and the interactivity that Java brings. These technological changes are happening so quickly that one of the great challenges is to match a marketing strategy with product development.

Because the Web is evolving so rapidly, our strategy has to morph at a minimum of every three months, and in some ways on a weekly basis. A year ago Silicon Graphics focused like a laser beam on the Web because we saw the Web as uniquely visual and engaging – different from the Internet that had come before it. Now we are bringing our core technologies in 3-D graphics and streaming media to the emerging open platform of the Internet. We focused on the problems people were having in implementing homepages or sites on the Internet. When you view the World Wide Web as a medium, you realize that there are only a couple of ways to make it economically viable: a pay-per-view model or advertising. In the case of a corporate site, the content needs to be compelling enough that people want to come to what is essentially a corporate message center.

Creating engaging content that generates interest is where you get economic value. When you make content that is media-rich, you need the tools to build that content, and you need servers to serve that content. The more media-rich it is, the more traffic it generates, the harder a job the Web server has. Silicon Graphics's value proposition for that whole space is the ability to make the best possible content, with servers designed to get that content to a large number of people efficiently and reliably. Because databases are now involved, it is not enough just to get up a homepage. Now you need to have a Web site where you're doing real business. When you're doing real business on the Web, you want to capture information, you want to customize the content, and you want to do transactions.

Whether you can do a hundred thousand, one million, or ten million hits a day on the server is an important consideration, but database performance and reliability are also concerns. Another concern is the applicability of Web technology to the enterprise, or to business processes that have nothing to do with sending out a corporate message or generating advertising dollars. The Web can become a universal front end because the Web client is really the world's first universal interface to information and applications.

The growth of this part of our business is tied to an interesting synergy between Silicon Graphics and our customers. First, the Web browser spread like wildfire onto every desktop at our company. Then we created the first set of tools for easily building Web content, and they spread like wildfire. Now we have a situation at Silicon Graphics where outside the firewall there is a handful of Web servers; and behind the firewall there are more than two thousand. So the whole company is being run with the Web. Existing customers and potential customers want to know how we do it. Innumerable executives from around the world have traveled to Mountain View, California, to see how a true information-age company is run. The powerful notion behind this is that operating system religion is irrelevant. You can have whatever operating system you want. You can build Web infrastructure with much of your existing infrastructure. You don't have to throw out your mainframes or your Unix database servers or your Macintosh desktops. It's a wildly exciting time. People looking at this Web stuff for the first time find it a little intimidating because so many different technologies have been brought together. In reality, putting the Web to work for their business can be implemented very easily. A number of our customers have borrowed our systems – for example, a workstation with all the Web-authoring tools and site-management tools – for a weekend and in forty-eight hours they have implemented the beginnings of an intranet.

Creating the best possible content outside the firewall is the issue. The IS department – those unfortunate souls who have to build the information infrastructure for a company and are usually blamed when there are problems and rarely thanked when things run well – doesn't care about the best possible content. They care about needing to train, retrain, and hire IS people. When we show them that we have two thousand servers up internally, and two-hundred thousand URLs, all of which are managed by five people, they are amazed. These five people can do it because the Web has an unusual balance of centralized control and decentralized empowerment. Everyone can create their own content, and the IS organization, if it wants to, can control the framework in which that content gets deployed.

I first heard the word *content* used in the way that I think about it now in 1993, when the notion of multimedia was rippling through the Valley. *Content* is one of many interesting words that are now commonplace, at least for those of us in this industry. When we were launching WebFORCE, Silicon Graphics's product line for the Web, I thought about how to describe a professional Web authoring and serving system to somebody totally removed from Silicon Valley. Think of all the words that need definition. *Web. Authoring.* What is authoring? Even though *content* and *authoring* are old words, the way they're used now seems to suggest something different. As technology changes, we need to develop new ways to express ourselves. Otherwise, we only see ourselves through a rearview mirror. I've been struggling to find the tools, the vocabulary, the instrument that could express exactly what I'm thinking and feeling about the changes in communication we're currently experiencing. Somehow, I don't think I'll find it in the written word.

THE SEER: <DAVID BUNNELL> John is not really "one of us." He is a well-rounded, cultured, artistic, educated person who just happens to be at Silicon Graphics. He would be successful anywhere.

THE CONSERVATIVE: <DAVID GELERNTER>

McCrea is right at the center of one of the hottest technologies – Web servers – of modern times. The machines he markets are the foundation of the Internet, the towers that support the bridge.

<Scott McNealy>

The Competitor

The Genius: <W. Daniel Hillis> *For the last decade, I have heard nearly every year that Sun was facing a great problem. Somehow it has always managed to stay ahead. Now it's clear that Sun and Scott are flying high and everyone is wondering how they do it. They did it by hiring smart people and letting them take risks, and they moved fast enough to stay ahead of their mistakes.*

Scott McNealy is the cofounder and CEO of Sun Microsystems, Inc.

"I like to compete," Scott McNealy says, "by the rules. Fair and square. Toe to toe. I don't like my competition, I'm not elected to like my competition. I'm paid to deliver a return to my shareholders by following the rules of business, by following the rules of commerce, by following the rules of the local land, by staying ethical, moral, and legal, but burying my competition. That's what I get paid to do, and that's what I love to do. A good clean legal body check is as exciting as scoring a goal."

I was predisposed to like Scott McNealy, who has been CEO of Sun Microsystems since 1984. When I entered his office and saw him surrounded by hockey sticks and other memorabilia of the sport, I realized that he was a major-league hockey fanatic. Since my goal in life as a teenager was to play right-wing for the Boston Bruins, Scott is someone I can relate to. But am I intimidated by him, sitting in front of his impressive array of hockey trophies? No way. I like a challenge; I'm ready for anything he's got.

These days, Scott has a lot more than hockey on his mind. He's the driving force behind the leading network-computing company, Sun's bread-and-butter business. More surprising is his role as leader of a team of world-class computer scientists who distinguish themselves by making a significant contribution to the state of computing as a whole, as well as to Sun. You wouldn't expect a Silicon Valley body checker to carry on in the R&D tradition of Bell Labs, Xerox PARC, GE's Sarnoff Center, and IBM's Watson Center.

Scott claims, however, that he is not a visionary but rather a good businessman who stays focused. "I leave the vision thing to the gurus and scientists," he says. "What I do is articulate what our people think is the right answer." There are plenty of visionaries and gurus to choose from at Sun. Scott can look to Bill Joy or James Gosling or Eric Schmidt or John Gage or Lew Tucker – just to name a few. His role is to interpret and articulate what the visionaries are saying, evangelize these visions, and put together the resources to take advantage of the discontinuities of the "paradigm" shift caused by a new technology, which happens in the computer industry every few years. "I'm on the bully pulpit," he says. "Fundamentally, the CEO's job is to figure out what the vision is, not necessarily create it. Develop a plan that uses company resources to best take advantage of that plan. Get it approved by the board, then go on and execute it, deliver the numbers to the shareholders, and get yourself reelected another year. That's my job. I decide who's on my staff, I charter them, and I approve the plan, and away we go. Then I spend the rest of my time evangelizing – where we're headed and why it's the right answer."

The current prominence of Java – a programming language for the Web – is a good example of the benefits that Sun derives from supporting internal research efforts. Java, originally developed by Sun engineers in 1991, is a highly interactive language that allows users to download small applications – called *applets* – and run them on any type of computer, using the "Java Virtual Machine." Java is the first "network-smart" and "platform-independent" programming language around. Though the Internet has been important to Sun since the company was founded, until recently the Net was not seen as the main plank of Sun's continued success. The explosive growth of the Web offered opportunities that the company has been able to vigorously exploit. Java is becoming the standard for Web programming, opening up completely new market opportunities for Sun. By changing the way in which applications and *content* are written and delivered to desktop computers or "clients" – across a network – Java offers the possibility of altering the entire competitive landscape to Sun's advantage. In this regard, Scott is going after what he refers to as "the desktop hair ball" of computing, and he clearly has Microsoft in his sights.

Scott McNealy is "The Competitor."

THE COMPETITOR: <SCOTT MCNEALY> At Sun we believe in the network-computing model. We're not wired up and married to the host-based centralized computing model, and we're not all tangled up in the desktop hairball – that is the desktop computing model of the Intel-Microsoft world. Everything from the first computer we shipped a long time ago goes out with a network interface, and every desktop, server, application, software product, and service product that we've ever offered has been network-centric. That's probably our biggest advantage. Our second biggest advantage is that we own all the implementations of the key components based on openly published interface specifications. We have our own microprocessors. We own the user interface and the networking interfaces, in the sense that we implement TCP/IP, Corba [common object request broker], and all the other network protocols. We have the technologies that allow you to run your network environment. Then we have servers and desktops to help you go out and deliver the value of the network computing environments. We have all the pieces that really matter to the customer.

There are two kinds of companies: product companies and trading companies. Sun is a product company. Our integration services and capabilities are all focused around network computing and our products. We are not like a trading company, which services any product, or writes software for any product, or trains you on any product. We do software development, we do integration, we do training and consulting on our products, around our products, for our products, and we help you integrate with other environments. We sell in highly focused markets, which are tightly related to each other. We do not do the services for other companies' products. Only IBM and DEC seem to want to do both. Everybody else is in either the integration business or the products business.

Since 1985 we've said "the network is the computer." That's been a nice little tag line. We got off on tangents and invented some other tag lines, but we came back to the original one, because it is the right one. The network is the business, the network is the future, and the network is what matters. So we say the network is the computer.

I'd love to evangelize and make credible the myth that the computer is disappearing. The more people who leave the computer industry, the better, because we're here to stay, and we're going to be one of the Big Three computer players, if you will. In the same way that the automobile industry consolidated around three players – General Motors, Ford, and Chrysler – the computer industry is going to consolidate. I'm not talking about the integration-trading-reseller channel. There will be lots of resellers in the same way there are a lot of car dealers. There will be only a few integrated product companies, such as Sun, that do microprocessors, operating systems, user interfaces, networking pieces, and do the final assembly and integration of desktop and server and client-side computing environments.

We want to be one of those three. Two of the survivors are what I call "General" and "Motors," Intel and Microsoft. They have all the pieces to make the Wintel computing environment. They just don't seem to work together very well. IBM will be Chrysler, going back to the government for loan guarantees on a regular basis. We will be the Ford Motor Company of the computer business, with our integration from the microprocessor all the way through service and support.

Silicon Graphics is going to make a nice division, at the very high end, of one of the Big Three computer businesses at some point. You might think of SGI as the sport-utility vehicle of the computer industry. The product line could be very profitable, but needs to be part of a larger organization. There aren't going to be niche companies in the computer business in the same way that there aren't any car companies that specialize in two-door sedans or four-door convertibles. You've got to be a broadly global player with volume. Scale really matters in our business.

Unix is the enterprise-server environment for databases, for large hardware data warehouses, and for file servers, Web servers, and security servers. All of the features of Unix make it the best scalable enterprise-server environment. Unix has also won on the power desktop for CAD engineers, software developers, and Wall Street traders, because of its multiprocessing capabilities.

What has won on the corporate desktop has been the Microsoft environment. Within that particular environment, we've given everyone a mainframe on the desk or in the lap. Everything's there except the halon fire-retardant and the water-cooling system. You've got a file system. You've got a disk farm (i.e., massive amounts of storage). You've got a 32-megabyte, 32-bit multitasking, multithreaded, symmetric multiprocessing, scalable desktop operating environment, with a backup medium known as a floppy and a software distribution mechanism known as a CD-ROM player. You've got all the middleware and the bells and whistles and configurations. PCs are like thumbprints. No two PCs in the world are configured alike, and they are a nightmare to administer. If you want to keep kids off drugs, give them Windows 95 and tell them to get it up and running on your current home PC. That will keep them at home for a long time.

The challenge and the opportunity is to come up with a new paradigm for client-side computing. That's where the Java model makes sense. You can deliver a Java-based computer that has no disk drive, no floppy, no CD, no operating system, and minimal memory; then you can use the network to store files, applications, data, video, audio, Web access, security, and billing. All these activities can be handled in a server room by a trained professional. This is the way technology can be driven into a ubiquitous usage model. The obvious example is the telephone. When I give you a telephone, I don't give you a handset and a switch on your desktop and say, "Program the switch, configure the switch, load software into the switch, write software on the switch, back the switch up, and carry the switch around with you." If we were doing that, we'd never be able to make a phone call.

The new model of the Java client for the network terminal, or the network computer, is a Java Virtual Machine run in a browser environment. You just turn the machine on, click, and down comes your word processor. You create your application, send it back, and have it filed. You download video. You go out and surf the Internet. You do whatever you want to do, but when you're done, everything is stored and managed in the server room. You never run out of disk space, and you never have to worry about your battery running low. You always have a datatone.

Think again about the phone. If you pick up a telephone and don't get a datatone by the time you get the handset to your ear, you're angry. Contrast that with turning on your Wintel computer. A little part of you goes, "Yes, it booted. It's working today." When it crashes every day, which it does, and you can recover something from your file, you're thrilled to death. When was the last time you got cut off during a phone call, other than cellular, and how does that make you feel?

That's the difference. We believe that the datatone model of computing, where the hard work is done *for* you, is the model that allows you to execute content on your desktop. You still get the power of a microprocessor, dedicated to you. With Java you don't have to buy Intel. You can buy a chip that does long division properly and has the Visual Instruction Set. You can buy four of them, strap them together, and really have some horsepower on your desktop.

You don't even have to carry a laptop. You check into your hotel room, and there's a network workstation sitting next to the fax machine or part of the fax machine. You dial up, call your server – either in your company or at your service provider – and log in to your server room. You load your applications. You don't have to worry who made that Internet terminal, because as long as it's run on the Java Virtual Machine, your applications will run, and you can browse. You can do everything you can do on your own computer. The problem today is, if you use Unix, you can't use Mac; if you use Mac, you can't use Windows; if you use Windows, you can't use the other two. But in our environment, one computer does it all.

The Java phenomenon creates a couple of challenges for Microsoft. First of all, the Java client says that for most computer users, the desktop operating system is a negative value-add. There's no reason we mere mortals should have to mess around with ten million lines of code just to type our names. There's something wrong with that picture. A big part of Microsoft's net worth is tied up in keeping people dedicated and committed to the desktop computing mode. The other challenge is that in Java, you can write a desktop productivity tool in what I call "subset" mode and then publish it on the network for free.

By contrast, the "superset" model is represented by Microsoft Word. One CD, one stocking unit, one tested unit, is available for everyone to do publishing. Every known feature on the planet you can possibly imagine is embedded into it, and it comes with a stack of manuals. You have to get in the car, go to the store, buy it, bring it home, unwrap it, stick it in, and download it into your machine. Then you've got to figure out how to work it. You've got to have a superset of every possible known feature.

Think about the Java applet role. When you're on your network client, your Java client, you click on Word Processor and download a four-function word processor. It comes down in a heartbeat, because there aren't many lines of code. It has four functions: Backspace, Delete, Cut and Paste, and Print. If I need right-hand justification, I can download that. If I need a spellchecker, I can download that. If I need a new font, I can download that. That's subset: an object-oriented, scalable, robust, enhanceable kind of environment.

In this new model, I can probably get that applet for free. Some really powerful author, a single individual, will write a wonderful word processor, put it out on the network for free, and get millions of users. Then McDonald's will pay this guy a million bucks a year to put golden arches around the border of the applet and get ten-million-odd exposures every time anybody wants to use a word processor. There might even be a "click here if you want a burger" button on the word processing applet. I'll deal with that for a free word processor rather than spend hundreds of bucks a year with Microsoft. I get the kind of application that I can use and that doesn't need documentation.

This puts huge pressure on Microsoft's billion-dollar apps business. With Java Office or Java Word or Java Excel potentially out there for free, or near free, we're challenging Microsoft to buy into Java. Those guys in Seattle have a lot to do: launch satellites, buy the Bettmann Archives, get Marilyn Monroe locked up and proprietarized. They must be seriously trying to figure out how to support a $56 billion market cap. I'd be a little agitated, too, if I had to figure how to do that. I think we've got upside here.

Every device that has a microprocessor and a network port will be an IP address on the Internet – they will have connectivity to all the devices and networks on the Internet. They will run the Java Virtual Machine, will be able to execute content, will be able to browse the Internet, and will be able to download content from over the network, anywhere, everywhere. This means that every hub, router switch, printer-copier, set-top box, game machine, nomadic computer, desktop computer, server, automobile – you name it – will have a network port. You can download a game to your kids in the back seat of the car; when they get bored with it, you can download another one. When your car doesn't start, you can download diagnostics, or checklists, on what to check to make your car start. This kind of executable content will be downloaded to you at these different IP addresses on the Internet. Today, on average, we have less than one IP address per citizen on the planet. With our model, people will each have a half-dozen or a dozen IP addresses. Every cellular phone in Europe today is an IP address. This is just an extension of the Internet.

The Web is the biggest online library on the planet, by a lot. It turns out that Web interfaces and technologies are how Sun is going to publish information out on the network, so that anybody and everybody from any machine can view it. This is a powerful new paradigm.

Inside Sun we now publish most of the information that we need to share among ourselves on our own internal Web, the Sun Intranet. We use the network to run the company. We have about 16,500 employees. We do a couple million emails a day, so that is the killer app. That's the way people communicate. I certainly like email better than I like voicemail. It's hard to speed-read voicemail. It's hard to print voicemail. It's hard to cut-and-paste voicemail. It's hard to intuitively forward and copy people on voicemail. People tend to have very little filter between brain and mouth. Because they can't type well, they tend to have great filters between brain and fingertips. So with email you get something more concise, readable, and manageable.

Every project at Sun has its own Web page. In fact, we're moving to the point where we want every employee in the company to have a homepage. I do a McNealy report radio show every two weeks at Sun, which we record digitally and put on a server.

The favorite section is my pet peeve section, where I rail on about any particular pet peeve I have. Then we send everybody email. They click on it and up comes a browser page, and they click on that and listen to the audio streams. We're using the Web, Web technologies, the Internet, and email technology to run this company. I believe that the reason Sun has gone from zero to $7 billion in fourteen years is our use of the network.

THE MARKETER: <TED LEONSIS> I had the good fortune at Redgate of working very closely with Sun. When I came to America Online, I saw Scott one day in the waiting room. He had come to talk about some big strategic issues, but he brought with him the local sales manager. It was great to see this CEO of a multi-billion dollar company go from thinking big thoughts and strategic alignments to trying to sell us some workstations. You have to admire Scott. He's a big thinker, but he executes.

THE CONSERVATIVE: <DAVID GELERNTER> On the one hand, I wonder how Sun will survive. Its market is people with a professional interest in computers, and that market is becoming peripheral to the computer business. Unix, developed around 1977, is dead. It was a great idea at the time. On the other hand, the sophistication with which Sun has exploited Java is stunning. This is one hell of a smart company.

THE PRAGMATIST: <STEWART ALSOP> I think of Scott as a prankster. He loves to needle people. He gets pleasure in making people angry, but not in a mean way.

THE GADFLY: <JOHN C. DVORAK> The most quotable man in the industry. Outstanding at making interesting observations and doesn't care about the consequences as much. Spends too much time bashing Bill Gates.

THE IDEALIST: <DENISE CARUSO> Scott McNealy comes across as the eternal fratboy, but he's wicked smart. Back in 1985, when I was covering Silicon Valley for *Electronics,* Sun launched a sales campaign called "The Network Is The Computer" – which nowadays is a pretty good description of the global Internet. Whether or not he came up with the slogan, he was dead right about where the future was headed. I'll bet how right he was surprises even him.

THE SCRIBE: <JOHN MARKOFF> Scott's a remarkable business strategist. The Java strategy is a brilliant gamble that may eventually provide Sun with an end run around the entire Microsoft monolith. At critical junctures in the computer industry he seems to have pulled these strategies out of his hat: open systems, SPARC, and "all the wood behind one arrow" have all served to keep him one step ahead of the Hewlett-Packards, Digitals, and IBMs in the workstation business.

<Jane Metcalfe>

The Publisher

The Catalyst: <Linda Stone> *In so many ways Jane is the heart of Wired. She's the president, and she's an effective businessperson. Her energy has been core in building that organization.*

Jane Metcalfe is the president and cofounder of Wired Ventures. She is also a board member emeritus of the Electronic Frontier Foundation.

"You have three *Wired* people in the book," David "The Seer" Bunnell said in an accusatory tone as he sat on my living room couch, as we were having drinks before dinner. "What's that all about, John?"

The key ringleader of the "radical front" of the digerati was on my case, and the subtext was clearly political, an indirect swipe at *Wired,* a publication that, in the front's eyes, has a propensity for promoting the commoditization of the emerging digital culture.

"Louis Rossetto and Kevin Kelly are obvious choices," I explained. "Louis is highly visible as cofounder and editor of *Wired* and HotWired; Kevin is executive editor of *Wired* and author of a seminal book on the digital revolution, *Out of Control.*" Jane, I thought to myself; why did I put Jane in the book?

I first met Jane, Louis Rossetto's partner in *Wired* and in life, on the beach at Cannes, in January 1995, at a sumptuous luncheon hosted by Dr. Huburt Burda, the German billionaire and media magnate. Among the guests were a dozen or so young German executives wearing dark business suits and holding cellular phones. Seated to my left was Lord Weidenfeld, to my right Oskar Prinz von Preussen (general manager of Burda New Media and director of Europe Online), the great-grandson of Kaiser Wilhelm II.

Across the table, locked in rapt conversation with Dr. Burda, was a glamorous beauty who, despite the enchanting surroundings, was all business as she presented a smörgåsbord of projects as investments. Her success speaks for itself. Eight months later, Burda New Media made a seven-figure investment in the financing of HotWired.

"Jane is a brave woman," Denise Caruso says. "She has sallied forth in an area that is populated by people who take one look at her and think, 'Oh, a bimbo.' She's about as far from a bimbo as you can get. Polar opposite. In *Esquire*'s 'Women We Love' issue, Jane was 'the woman we'd most like to exchange email with.' It must be hard to be that pretty and that smart. Jane is probably more responsible for the success of *Wired* magazine than almost anyone else, even though she operates so much behind the scenes." She may be less visible than Louis Rossetto, but she is a powerful presence whose day-to-day activities are concerned with building Wired Ventures, the umbrella corporation that owns and operates *Wired,* HotWired, HardWired, and other companies on the drawing board.

Jane has thought a lot about how the digital revolution can empower people to fashion their own futures. "The information you absorb in society," she says, "is no longer necessarily going to be chopped up and fed to you first by your teachers, then by the national media. It could come at you from a variety of different areas. You could pursue it according to your interests, as deeply as you wanted to go. You could link it to other things and build your own picture, form your own opinions, and stimulate your own thinking. The idea that you can piece things together from so many different sources so easily, that you can publish, broadcast, or otherwise distribute your ideas and have every bit as much of an impact on other people's opinions as national media or film studios, is incredibly exhilarating."

Jane went to a small private girl's school in Kentucky. Although the curriculum focused on ideas, it was still within the confines of fifty-minute periods divided across a variety of subjects and was geared toward preparing students for college exams. Jane sees our educational system as being completely out of sync with our industrial, business, and economic needs. "At this point," she says, "preparing students for college no longer seems like a valid goal for education. The information society clearly does not require people who can answer test questions well. It requires people who can think. The promise of multimedia, the promise of interactivity, is being able to follow your thoughts, to learn how to think laterally and connect with other things."

"OK," I said, returning to my conversation with David Bunnell. "Jane's in the book because I want to get to know her."

"Good answer," said "The Seer."

It hasn't happened.

Jane Metcalfe is "The Publisher."

The Publisher: <Jane Metcalfe> When Louis and I launched *Wired* in January '93, the only people who were talking about the Digital Revolution in the national media were Bill Clinton and Al Gore. We wandered onto the stage at a time when the searchlights were trying to find something to illuminate the issues and understand what the new vice president was talking about. *Wired* came out with flashy colors and a new way of writing about what was happening around us. As such, it also represented a generational change: the end of World War II leadership in government and corporations and the dawning of a new generation of entrepreneurs, technologists, and politicians. We confused them at the beginning. We infuriated them. They were particularly annoyed that something important was coming out of San Francisco instead of New York. At the beginning there definitely was some fear and loathing, and some people are still complaining about the design. But they're all reading the magazine.

It's trite to say that *Wired* is talking about the convergence of media, computers, and communications. What we are really talking about is a fundamental shift in society that is being led by technology but is infiltrating every aspect of society. Technology, invented in labs, gets absorbed by business, and as business takes it on, it starts to spread throughout society. Often, at that point, artists are attracted to it and pioneer it, champion it, stretch it, push the boundaries of it, and use it to bring a different message to the public. It's a three-pronged approach that has a multi-layered response from the society it's impacting. *Wired* is really about this change. It's led by technology, absorbed by business, and spread by artists. But it's not about technology.

The Web is likely to become a lot more like television than like books, at least as long as screens are such a fatiguing interface device. As new technologies come online – streaming audio, streaming video – big media companies will move in and we'll all be vying for the attention of Web audiences. The Web started out as a text-based intellectual space. Now it's going to have to compete with MTV. Print is still a remarkably colorful medium for delivering ideas and analyses. While images are powerful in conveying certain ideas, words allow you to go much deeper and much further. Stewart Brand said that intellectual elites, the people capable of grappling with the ideas of the Digital Revolution, are going to take charge and have the power, but I'm not sure the Web is going to be the medium through which they do so.

Teleconferencing is much more likely to be the kind of medium through which ideas are propagated. Look at the business networks that exist today. Whether it's Ford or General Motors or Matshushita, businesses have their own internal networks, through which their experts and senior executives communicate. Those types of systems are going to become more and more powerful. It will be interesting to see if you can have a system that's less business focused and perhaps more intellectually focused. Once you work out the jaggies and slowness, teleconferencing becomes an expressive medium in which a lot of exchange can take place. And with teleconferencing systems springing up at Kinko's shops around the country, they're bringing this power to the people, and turning teleconferencing into a consumer communication tool.

Television is stuck in a mass-market mentality that is antithetical to the explosion of opportunities for special-interest programming and niche markets. What will be interesting is when the Internet meets television. The result is going to be driven more by the Internet than by television because people will be coming at it from an I-want-to-see-what-I-want-to-see-when-I-want-to-see-it and I-want-to-be-able-to-communicate-with-others point of view. Television has been so driven by advertisers' needs that the two media (TV and online) are going to be locking horns to figure out how those needs are going to be incorporated when people choose exactly what they want to see when they want to see it.

The trend among advertising agencies and advertisers to want to own content is both interesting and scary. Advertisers see that the media world is changing very rapidly, pushed by technology, steered by content owners, and paid for by advertisers. They're concerned because they're being asked to support this medium, but they haven't in many cases gotten what they wanted out of it – or even figured out what they want out of it. Their response is to try to own the content themselves, directly. In the next couple of years, we're going to see some real experimentation in sponsorship models. Some of it could turn out to be wonderful patronage of the arts, a de Medici model, in which advertisers say to the content providers, "We'll give you guidance about what would be good for us, and we'll give you the money and the editorial space to develop your ideas." Of course, it could also turn out to be a disastrous mistake, as marketers delude themselves into thinking they are entertainers, as opposed to staying focused on what they're trying to accomplish, which is selling their product. I am very concerned about editorial integrity if sponsors want to manipulate the programming. Our society has a long way to go before we are truly media literate – and this blurring of editorial and business interests is something we need to watch very closely.

The relationship between publishers and advertisers is undergoing a lot of change. Print, radio, and television are all mature media, which are pretty well understood. Media companies are clear on what they offer, and advertisers are clear on what they want back. Advertisers know how to measure response to an ad and how to judge whether or not they're getting their value. Now translate that experience into an entirely new medium in which the old rules don't fit but you don't have any new rules yet. When you launch a Web site, the pitch to an advertiser is, "Hold my hand, and we'll jump in together." It's been a cooperative experience in which the publisher, the content developer, says, "Here's what I can do." The advertiser tries it and says, "OK, here's why it doesn't work. Here's where I want to go next." I'm not sure how long that's going to last, but if you look at the cable industry, it took MTV and CNN quite a long time to build their advertising relationships and turn a profit. Advertising is no longer the company's public image and message, crafted by an ad agency. It's not a billboard or a TV commercial the company can hide behind. That barrier between customer and company has become much more porous. The minute you put up a Web site, you've got to keep it fresh and changing. You have to show you're a company with ideas and that you're responsive to your customers. Otherwise you've just cemented your site into a mausoleum, and people will never come back. That's the big challenge for both agencies and clients.

At the moment, ads on the Web are primarily in the form of banners. Clicking on the banner takes you directly to the advertiser's site or to additional pages that fill out what the advertiser is trying to say. The big challenge is to get people to click on the banners. The other model we're seeing more and more is animation – a moving icon or text that broadcasts a message and also clicks through to the advertiser's site. The Web at the moment is a little like television with a direct-marketing arm, so in a way, it's back to a broadcast model for advertisers, but with back-end fulfillment opportunities. The fulfillment is a lot bigger than just order taking, though. People can get product specs and have their questions answered. You can correlate their tastes with other people's tastes, and propose merchandise they might like. Customers can provide feedback to manufacturers, participate in product design or focus groups, and eventually get products and services tailored to their specific profile.

Louis Rossetto describes the content on the Web or the Internet to date as being like twenty-five years of public-access programming. Now we're starting to see a couple of different developments. One is the evolution and emergence of new multimedia auteurs who shoot their own video, score their own sound, and craft their own experience. Then there are the media professionals with a background in broadcast, audio, film, or print, who bring with them some of the intellectual baggage from working in another medium and have to try to figure out how to adapt that medium to the new one.

Until now the tools have been very accessible, though restricted, of course, to the people who have computer and Net access. Anybody can learn HTML. But the emergence of object-oriented programming languages like Java will make much more complex applications available, and you're going to see a split again. The explosion of people who are learning HTML and creating personal homepages is great, but those pages aren't going to look nearly as exciting or sensational as those made by engineers who can do the Java programming and can use the applets and the animation and so forth. There will be these jags of technology, when a new thing that only engineers can use is designed and then filters down through an interface-design process until it becomes accessible to a larger public. Meanwhile, the pioneers are out developing the next edition of the latest technology, which will be difficult to use and therefore inaccessible to the bulk of Web users.

More and more people are encouraged to check out the Net. Once some sort of critical mass has been reached in people's minds, then people, whether they're programmers or advertisers or users, will be more comfortable segmenting into their natural interest groups and into more identifiable niches. People are used to thinking of Internet users as eighteen- to twenty-four-year-olds, pimply faced adolescents, and egghead researchers. I don't think that was true even at the beginning. There has always been an incredible diversity of interests on the Net, which is clearly becoming more a reflection of society as a whole than of any particular group.

A recent study says there are 24 million people on the Net, or on online services, and 17 million on the Web. We're starting to see numbers at which content creators feel comfortable saying, "I can't be all things to all people. I can't expect everybody who has a modem to want to come to my site." So I'm going to create material from a particular point of view with a target audience in mind. That's an encouraging sign.

However, the cyberworld we inhabit is still pretty homogenous. I've been thinking about Brian Eno's statement that the problem with computers is there's not enough Africa in them. And Peter Gabriel has been talking about the north-south divide and how technology and music can help bridge that gap. What happens when you take the technology out of the labs of the people who've designed it – primarily Western engineering types – and plunk it down in the middle of a place where it's completely alien? The Net is a global communications medium that is being used only by a very small percentage of the real world. What happens when the Net starts to reflect the diversity of the entire globe? It's going to be fascinating. People will talk a lot about the signal-to-noise ratio and then start to be segmented out, but the Net will change and grow faster at that point.

People are increasingly looking for experience. There are so many barriers that distance us from experience. I don't read a book anymore; I read a book review. I don't experience a speech live; I watch it on television. People are desperate for firsthand experience. To an extent, we can use the Net to create that experience, to penetrate the solitude of one person, one computer, isolated up on the twenty-eighth floor of an office building. That's really interesting. According to the people who run the cybercafés, many of the customers who come in and pay to use the computers have Internet connections at home, but they come out because they want to share the experience. This is a trend that starts to counter the isolating technologies of the twentieth century. We'll be looking for unifying experiences in the twenty-first century.

My big hope for the people who are designing our digital future is that the things they talk about and care about become implemented in the products they produce. So much of the technology of the twentieth century was deployed without conscious thought about its impact. Who knew that cars would lead to freeways, which would lead to the creation of suburbs and the subsequent death of our inner cities? Or that cars would lead to increased air pollution, gridlock, and freeway shootings? If there's anything going on at the end of the twentieth century, it's a desperate attempt to project into the future as far as we can how technology is going to be used and what the impact is going to be on society, and how we can deploy it rationally and consciously to reunify our society instead of split it further apart. We're all aware of the socially isolating impact of MUDs, MOOs, and interactive games, and the physical impact of carpal tunnel syndrome, reduced fertility, eye strain, and neck and shoulder stress. These are recognizable problems that people should be grappling with. As soon as we can get rid of the monitor and the keyboard, the experience becomes more integrated, and then we can go and share it, and we're not tethered to a wall with an electrical outlet. Then we can really share the experience.

Wired has been criticized for featuring business executives on the covers. Some people in our community feel that there is no place for business in an intellectual realm, an artistic realm, or even a pioneering realm, that pure research and pure art and pure science should be untainted by business. A number of people who are very communitarian and egalitarian are hopeful that the Net can be a great equalizing medium, which is certainly happening. But their antagonism toward business seems like a relic of old political dogma that does not recognize the emergence of markets as a primary influencing force in our society. Business leaders, even those who may not be considered visionaries, are sitting on piles of assets. They're going to deploy those assets in ways that will fundamentally alter the world. As much as anything, you've got to recognize the dominance of markets as an organizing principle and deal with the consequences, from an artistic point of view and from an intellectual point of view.

The Pattern-Recognizer: <Esther Dyson>
Jane's job is to market to a community and to be part of it. She is a traditional publisher in this new market. She knows how to excite people's imaginations and deliver content that audiences buy and find audiences advertisers want to sell to, which means she has to be right in the middle of it and taking its pulse all the time.

> **The Seer: <David Bunnell>** Jane is destined to be among the greatest women in the history of business. I don't see any glass ceilings in her career. Besides that, she is warm, smart, and fun.

The Judge: <David R. Johnson> Jane is an extremely lively and committed member of EFF. I particularly remember her involvement in some of the agonizing decisions about how to deal with developments in Washington. Although her basic background has been in business – and I'm sure she was horrified at the things going on inside the Beltway – she became deeply immersed in trying to think through what the right thing to do would be, and made a major commitment to do that.

> **The Genius: <W. Daniel Hillis>** Jane didn't just chronicle the *Wired* culture. She helped created it.

<Kip Parent>

The Webmaster

The Force: <John McCrea> *Kip Parent is one of the original drivers of Silicon Graphics's adoption of the Web. He developed and managed Silicon Surf, which is about taking the message of the company externally via the Internet.*

Kip Parent was electronic sales manager of Silicon Graphics until August 1996, when he left to found Pantheon Interactive. (Our discussion took place prior to his departure.)

On a business trip to Europe in early March 1993, Kip Parent was looking at technologies based on CDs and SGML publishing. He happened to visit Tim Berners-Lee at CERN in Switzerland, who said to him, "Look at this. Here's what I think the future is. It's called the World Wide Web." Berners-Lee had invented the Web as a text-based system that enabled particle physicists to share information. That very month, Marc Andreessen had released his first alpha copy of the Mosaic browser, which he developed on a Silicon Graphics Indigo computer. Berners-Lee showed it to Kip, who said, "Wow, this is what I need. I'm going to use the World Wide Web!"

Kip had recently moved to Silicon Graphics from Hewlett-Packard, where he worked as an R&D manager, because he wanted to become more involved in leading-edge technology. Silicon Graphics at that time was trying to figure out how to establish what it called an "electronic channel" with customers.

"From the first time I saw the Web in March '93," he says, "I believed that it was going to be the information superhighway and that proprietary services were going to die. Outside of the

VP I worked for, nobody else believed it at Silicon Graphics. Some of the senior people were OK about it but others said "interactive TV is where it's at and this Internet stuff isn't going to fly."

According to Kip, SGI was considering a proprietary service that didn't make sense. "I spent my first eight months there trying to convince the management that it was not a good idea," he says. "I spent eight months telling executive after executive that we should use the Internet. The response was, 'You can't use the Internet!' Or, 'What's the Internet?' The typical response in early 1993 was that the Internet was the CB radio craze of the '90s."

Today, Silicon Graphics is on the leading edge of the Internet, and until he left SGI to form Pantheon Interactive, Kip was responsible for all aspects of SGI's activities on the Web. This included managing creative, technical, production, and electronic sales staff; developing new Internet-based services; and evangelizing Internet products on behalf of Silicon Graphics at trade shows and industry conferences. He originated and launched Silicon Surf, SGI's award-winning Web site. It is one of the most accessed sites on the Web, has been featured in dozens of books and magazine articles, and is the recipient of many widely respected Internet and Web awards, including "best site" by *Interactive Age* in 1995.

Kip Parent is "The Webmaster." David Bunnell and I have worked with him as part of a technology collaboration between Content.Com Inc. and SGI. It was an interesting experience for me to check out his Web site, having produced in 1965 what I called "Intermedia Kinetic Environments" with artists such as Andy Warhol, Robert Rauschenberg, Claes Oldenburg, and Nam June Paik. On the Web, which I consider to be the canvas of the '90s, creativity is being driven not by people from the art world but by engineers such as Kip Parent.

THE WEBMASTER: <KIP PARENT> A lot of corporate guys are saying that the Web is going to implode and that 40 percent of the companies on the Web today will be gone in six months. I think they are wrong. Interactive TV is what has imploded. We may very well see a merging of the ideas of interactive TV and the Web as we get broadband TCP/IP broadcasts via TV cables. We'll see a natural merging of the technology, but it'll be far better and far more powerful than people were thinking interactive TV would be in 1993. You're really going to have the opportunity to interact with it.

So where will Netscape be in this? The real question is, How effective will Bill Gates be in scuttling it? Bill Gates is probably the biggest obstacle Netscape has. But Jim Clark is smart. One of his big talents is pulling together sets of people who can make things happen. Jim Clark came up with the idea of visual computing back in 1982. He tried to sell it to the big companies – HP, IBM, DEC – and they all pushed him off. So he started his own company and got Ed McCracken out of HP to run it. If Jim Clark has a great idea, he gets it going; he doesn't need to be the president of the company. I give him a better-than-even chance of being bigger than Microsoft in a decade. Netscape has played its cards right at this point. Gates is going to try to give away software as part of his operating systems and cut Netscape out of the market. Guerrilla tactics. That's a hard thing to do. He couldn't manage to scuttle Intuit, which had a good foothold and better software than Microsoft. I don't think Netscape is Bill's to take.

We started Silicon Surf in April 1994. At that time, there were only about five sites, and there weren't any models to follow. I read somewhere that on the first round-the-world airplane trip, the people flying the plane were mechanics. It couldn't be done any other way. From that point of view, the very first people creating the Web sites had to be very technical. There were a lot of things we had to figure out from a technical standpoint for the first six or seven months we were in business. Fortunately, we were able to draw from SGI's vast archive of high-quality graphics. We begged, hustled, and cajoled most of the content that we put online. We thought that because we were Silicon Graphics, we had to have good graphics from the start. That really paid off for us. We quickly became the de facto place to go if you wanted to see good integration of media on a Web site.

The idea behind our Web site is to bring people in to see things they can't see other places. Then we want them to ask us how it's done. We can then say to them, "It's done on Silicon Graphics, using a certain kind of software. By the way, here is how you can get it." All the way down the line we draw them in. In other areas on the Web site, we tell how our customers are using our equipment. If we are going to attract the people who really buy these $30,000 or $40,000 super desktop computers, we have to show them what their competition is doing, why their competition is going to win by going with Silicon Graphics, and why they'd better go with us, too, if they want to be competitive.

We are not just throwing print online. I look at this medium as much more akin to television than any other medium. The typical cable system has thirty to forty channels, and if viewers find one thing boring, they can switch to another channel. On the Web, there are a hundred thousand channels, and a year from now there are going to be a million. If we put unimaginative material out there, someone's going to change the channel.

The pundits who say it's going to take a long time to make money on the Internet just don't get it. We have a lead-generation form that people can fill out on Silicon Surf. They tell us who they are, what products they're interested in, what their budget is, what their purchase time frame is, what their role in the purchase process is – all the questions a sales rep would ask. This is valuable information. The Web is the single highest source of high-quality leads that we get at Silicon Graphics. Transactions are starting to come in. We are actually selling desktop systems via the Internet. For some people, the Web is the preferred vehicle. If they know what they want and feel they can get a fair price without having to go with a salesperson, they will buy online.

The catalog business is going to make the transition online much faster than any of the prognosticators are saying. I just read that the direct-mail business was worth $57.4 billion dollars in 1995 in this country. One out of every two Americans bought something via the mail last year. People are saying that the Internet might generate $1 billion by 2000. They're wrong. By 2000, it's going to be a $10 billion business. Ten years after that, catalog publishers are going to find they just can't compete. The economics are so obviously in favor of the Internet.

For example: In 1994, when Silicon Graphics was a $1 billion company, we printed 11,000 three-inch-thick paper catalogs advertising our products. In 1995, we made $2.2 billion dollars and more than doubled our profits but printed only 10,000 catalogs. Why? A year ago we put our applications catalog on Silicon Surf. Customers can go to the catalog and ask to see something about wind flow analysis. Bam, right up on the screen, within a second or two, are the thirty applications that address wind flow analysis. It's very powerful and compelling, and it's reflected in our profits.

It is the old question of push versus pull: by sending out a catalog every two weeks, you invade the consumer's space. That's powerful, but at Silicon Surf, we depend on our potential customers to think about us and come in of their own accord. I've tried combinations of active marketing. I started a publication called *Iris Online*, an email-based publication received by tens of thousands of subscribers every month. Like a catalog, it shows up in their mailboxes, but the big difference is that the mailing hyperlinks back into my Web site. Customers can look at what I've got, click, and get to the site. I want to get people to subscribe to my list so I can entice them. Since I'm not spending any money on distribution and printing, I can put more money into enticements.

I'm not sure we coined the term *intranet* at Silicon Graphics, but we started using it, and it's become the buzzword today. It came about because the only way we could maintain the culture at Silicon Graphics was to improve the communications vehicles within the company. Intranets have given us that capability. Every department in the company has a Web server. Intranets give us a competitive advantage because the Web inside Silicon Graphics makes it easier for people to publish their information or communicate within the company.

Intranets will dramatically cut paper use. At Silicon Graphics, we've cut out 90 percent of the internal administrative paperwork. When I joined the company three years ago, every employee went through a four-hour orientation, about an hour and a half of which was spent filling out forms. Every one of those forms is now online. The process is faster for everybody, the information is immediately useful, and we have zero scrap cost. Today's environment changes so fast that brochures are often obsolete by the time you get them back from the printer. Scrap costs are huge when you print your sales material. Our product line is new every eighteen months. If our sales reps have to hand out old brochures, our competitors can say, "You know, their brochure says that their top of the line is 175 MHz, and the sales rep says something else. Who're you going to believe?" Casting doubt on your competitor is half of sales. When your data is online, you can update it instantaneously and make it available immediately. Intranets make sense for all kinds of companies. It's just better economics.

THE SEER: <DAVID BUNNELL> Not too many people know Kip, but millions know his work. He doesn't need to be out front, because he is the one who is really making things happen. He is quiet, but driven, and even though he is very young, he understands how to motivate people. This guy is going places.

THE CONSERVATIVE: <DAVID GELERNTER> Kip Parent has done first-class work on making the Internet honest and serious: he counts users fairly and plays fair across the board. Hype is an enormous problem in the Internet world. If things continue as they're going now, the whole deal is guaranteed to collapse – the Internet is oversold and it under-delivers. Parent's approach to Internet seriousness and integrity is crucial.

<Howard Rheingold>

The Citizen

The Cyberanalyst: <Sherry Turkle>

Howard Rheingold sees things that others simply hadn't noticed before. And he knows how to explain why they are important and why you need to pay attention to them.

Howard Rheingold is the author of *The Virtual Community* (1993) and *Virtual Reality* (1991), and was the editor of *Whole Earth Review* and the *Millennium Whole Earth Catalog* (1995). His weekly column, "Tomorrow," is syndicated by King Features.

In the fifteen years I have known him, Howard Rheingold has evolved from a modest, quiet, thoughtful working writer/editor into the flamboyant Howard "always ten years ahead of his time" Rheingold. From his dazzling hand-designed shoes to his vividly colored suits to his TV ads for Kinko's, he has invented his own character – spokesman, communications expert, celebrity, lecturer, writer, thinker, and wise man, one of the first people to recognize the potential of a new medium for human communication.

In 1991, Howard and I had been discussing an editorial I wrote in my newsletter *EDGE #1* about electronically linked networks and The Well (The Whole Earth 'Lectronic Link) in particular. Howard was one of the founders of The Well's online culture, and moderator ("host") of The Well's earliest and most successful conference. He was foremost among a small group of hosts who created the social and intellectual architecture of Well culture and governance.

My own attitude at that time was less enthusiastic than Howard's. I could buy into the line that The Well was important, but problems remained: a Unix-based user interface beneath contempt; an artificial conversational etiquette; a lack of filters – which means that people you may not want to hear from at any particular moment are electronically in your face. No unlisted phone numbers. No answering machines to hide behind. No office to screen calls and mail. On the other hand, anyone could see that it was vibrant and alive.

The French thinker Jean Baudrillard wrote about "virtual man" in *Xerox and Infinity:* "Immobile in front of his computer, [he] makes love by the screen and gives classes by teleconference. He becomes a spastic, probably with a cerebral handicap too. This is the cost of becoming effective. Just as we can suggest that glasses or contact lenses might one day become the integrated prosthesis of a species whose gaze will have gone, so can we fear that artificial intelligence and its technical aids will become the prosthesis of a species whose thought will have disappeared."

Howard's response to my editorial was that people on The Well had discovered that a new kind of technology-assisted social contract was making it possible to do what technology alone was not yet able to do. He went on to make the following observations as we sat together in a country general store in Washington, Connecticut (fully five years before the public embrace of the World Wide Web):

> The Well serves as a communications filter as well as an information filter.

> The communications revolution will bring enormous information and communications resources to individuals, and, along with those resources, the capabilities to build new communities.

> The Well and the Internet and linked networks will grow to involve tens of millions of users worldwide; backbone sites and some local loops will upgrade to fiber-optic channels, and gigabit transmission rates will enable multimedia conferencing, video email, and other high-density information exchanges.

> Two major trends seem to be working in rather opposite directions: first, more and more people worldwide are gaining

access to vast pools of possible partners in communities of interest; second, the increasing threats to privacy and the increasingly technological ability to screen communications make it possible for people to construct "communities of exclusion" that specify, via smart cards or similar devices, who should be prevented from gaining access to them via communications; even those who have the most privileged access to advanced communications might find that their own devices will work against their best interests in subtle ways.

> In order to create a filter, you would need to know what is relevant.

From all this, you might expect that Howard is a leading technologist. Not so. Howard is distinguished among the digerati because he is perhaps the only one who is not a "cubicle person." He's more passionate about his abundant garden than he is about his computer and modem; this world is his workstation.

Howard is, and always has considered himself to be, a writer. Howard's *Tools for Thought,* his version of "what happened," written in 1984, remains one of the best books on modern technology:

"When a caterpillar transforms into a butterfly, it undergoes a biologically unique process. Ancient observers noticed the similarity between the changes undergone by a butterfly pupa and those of the human mind when it undergoes the kind of transformation associated with a radical new way of understanding the world – in fact the Greek word for both butterfly and soul is psyche.

"After the caterpillar has wound itself with silk, extraordinary changes begin to happen within its body. Certain cells, known to biologists as imaginal cells, begin to behave very differently from their normal caterpillar cells. Soon, these unusual cells begin to affect cells in their immediate vicinity. The imaginal cells begin to grow into colonies throughout the body of the transforming pupa. Then, as the caterpillar cells begin to disintegrate, the new colonies link to form the structure of the butterfly's body.

"At some point, an integrated supercolony of transformed cells that had once crawled along the ground emerges from the cocoon and flies off into the spring sky on multicolored wings.

If there is a positive image of the future of human-computer relations, perhaps it is to be seen reflected in the shapes of the imaginal cells of the information culture – from eight-year-olds with fantasy amplifiers to knowledge engineers.

"If it is true that the human brain probably started out as a rock-throwing variation on the standard hominid model, it has also proved capable of creating the *Sermon on the Mount,* the *Mona Lisa,* and *The Art of the Fugue.* If it is true that the personal computer started out as an aid to ballistic calculations, it is also true that a population equipped with low-cost, high-power computers and access to self-organizing distributed networks has in its hands a potentially powerful defense against any centrally organized technological tyranny."

Howard "always ten years ahead of his time" Rheingold: "I'm a stiff-necked Jew," he says. He's stubborn, he angers people, sometimes shooting himself in the foot at the same time. All of this makes him honest, exemplary.

Howard Rheingold is "The Citizen."

THE CITIZEN: <HOWARD RHEINGOLD> The Web is two things. Most people are concentrating on the first part, which is a control panel on the Internet. Instead of having to get under the hood and understand arcane computer codes, you can look at a graphical interface, point at what you want, click on words, and automatically be transported to the Louvre or automatically download something from the Library of Congress. This interface breakthrough makes the Internet accessible to the people of the world who aren't computer literate.

The second aspect of the Web – publishing capability – is its real power. You can sign up with a commercial server for maybe $20 a month. Using a desktop computer and an inexpensive digital camera, you can put text and pictures together, format them easily, and upload them with your modem, so people all over the world can access the material. The price of the means of production and the price of the means of distribution have dropped so drastically that we have a potential watershed, the way we had when the printing press made literacy available outside the elite of the church.

Of course, nobody would be surfing the Web if the Web didn't have a lot of interesting stuff on it. The fact is, the first two years of the Web, almost everybody who spent time putting material up did it for free, because it was a cool thing to do. Amateurism has a bad name, but most media of any consequence have been created for free by people who thought it was a cool thing to do. If tens of thousands of people don't continue to create their personal Web sites, and if all we get are the Disney, ABC, Sony, and Rupert Murdoch versions of the world, it will be an immensely impoverished medium, the way television is a powerful and yet impoverished medium.

Publishers have a lot of money invested in intellectual property and the infrastructure for putting that intellectual property into a form that can be distributed. That's had to do with owning forests and paper and printing presses. Now, with electronic means of distribution, publishers and big entertainment conglomerates spend a lot of money on content. But the tail that wags the dog is not content – it's discourse. For every book published, there's a community of people who read that book. They may read every book by that author or about that topic, and they think about that book or topic. If they had access to one another, they would talk about their thoughts. The real future is not selling chunks of content to passive consumers, but creating a context within which those consumers can be active and speak to each other. For authors, readers, and publishers, this transformation from a world of mass into a world of bits has to do not with content and something frozen, but with a continuous stream of discourse.

Another reality is that with a couple of keystrokes you can copy anything in electronic form. You can no longer count on owning the sole rights to reproduce words or images as your only means of income. The instant you put up something interesting, people can link to it from their sites and draw traffic to their sites. The only thing you can own is not a piece of property but a reputation for having consistently good material that draws people to your site first. That reputation is something you have to feed every day, and it's also something that accretes a following. It's more like a subscription to a magazine than it is like buying a book.

Can people maintain relationships with a sufficiently large audience and persuade that audience to pay them? That's the economic question being asked about the Web. Maybe the fact that you can copy anything and link to anything will ultimately destroy the intellectual property business, unless we can find an alternate way to pay the people who create property. Because copyright notions are out the window, you can't own yesterday's intellectual properties the way you used to. All you can own is tomorrow's intellectual property.

Some skill sets overlap between the era of intellectual property in the form of a movie or a book and the era of intellectual property as a stream of discourse as found on the Internet. You can be extreme and say that being able to keep people entertained in a conversation is not the same intellectual skill that Shakespeare or Tom Wolfe had, that it's more like being a borscht-belt comedian. It's an extension of what television brought us, which is discourse as a form of entertainment. That's a radical critique, and it's not totally inaccurate. However, among people who are perfectly good thinkers and writers, there is a subset who are not afraid to engage their readers and critics directly and entertainingly, in a more extemporaneous form, like a computer conference or a computer chat. It's a different craft. To craft a book or an article means going over those words again and again, very carefully considering each one. It's like creating a sculpture and making sure that every part is perfect. You can't do that with conversation. You have to think on your feet, and once you've said the words, once you've typed them in, they're gone. They're out there. You don't have the separation between you and the audience that traditional authors have. Every listener and reader can call you on your mistakes and challenge you on your assumptions.

A lot of journalists and writers irrationally fear breaching the wall between the author and the audience. There are good journalistic reasons for not allowing, say, the technology editor of *The New York Times* or *Time* magazine to be influenced by the lobbyists from the industries that they're covering. But I don't see why any journalist with integrity can't argue with anybody about anything and reveal a personal opinion in a forum, and still try to attain some degree of objectivity when writing with a journalist's hat on. Another part of the skill set is an ability to recognize that sometimes I have my journalist's hat on, which carries with it certain ethics and responsibilities, and at other times I am a person having a conversation with other people about the material that I've written. There is a place for that, and it's not just borscht-belt comedy – it's discourse. There will be stars and artists in that form of discourse, just as there are in books and magazines.

Because I sit in front of a computer, and for many years sat in front of a typewriter, alone all day, I have a need to connect with other people. When someone told me that if I connected my computer to my telephone, through a modem, I could participate in online conversation – about ten years ago, when Stewart Brand, Kevin Kelly, and some other folks had started The Well – I fell right into it, not just as a way to connect with interesting people, but also as a new way to exercise my communication capabilities.

Being online turned out to be writing as performance art. I spent hours a day having interesting online written conversations with other people. Eventually I realized that something important was happening, not just for me and a few intellectuals. It was a new mode of human communication, and like other previous media, it was going to change civilization. I wrote a book, *The Virtual Community*, to tell this to people who weren't particularly technically oriented.

An interesting thing happened as I traveled and talked to people in the industry, in communications companies, and in government. The relationship of communications to power became much more evident to me, which is surprising, because I've never been a political thinker or a political writer. The fact is that the power in the world today does not lie in weapons of destruction. It lies in the ability to influence people's beliefs and perceptions. If you want to overthrow a government, you don't attack the army, you attack the television broadcasting station. Being able to plug my computer into the telephone network and publish a manifesto, or even to upload a videotape of the police beating somebody outside my window and invite people to discuss it in my bulletin board system is a radical power shift.

Here we are, in the mid-1990s, hearing all this B.S. about the information superhighway. People are not talking about the profound power shift that could influence democracy, about the communities, about the people who need support. They're not talking about the kids in the one-room schoolhouses in Saskatchewan who now have access to the Library of Congress, or the Alzheimer caregivers, or the disabled who find support and community. We're hearing the same old stuff about five hundred channels, and that Disney buys ABC, and giant entertainment corporations that make it possible to download videos instead of walking two hundred yards to a video store. I wouldn't call it the Big Lie, but I would say that 99 percent of what most people hear in the mass media about the new medium is about the wrong part of it. It's the froth on the surface of something profound.

A critique of living in the virtual world is emerging. It's important to be aware of what we are trading in the natural world for this dazzling electronic world, and that we become aware of the limitations and pitfalls of the virtual world. The virtual world is a very good illusion-maker, and missing from it are some things that are essential to human life. But I resent the shallowness of the critics who say that if you sit in front of a computer and participate in online conversations worldwide you are not leading an authentic life. I question the premise that one person can judge the authenticity of another person's life. Millions of people passively watch television all day long. Don't tell me that having an email relationship with someone on the other side of the world is less authentic than sitting alone and watching the tube. For many people, this new medium is a way of breaking out of the virtual world they already live in.

I manage to use the computer as a means to live the kind of life that I want to live. When the weather is nice, I can carry my computer outdoors with me. I wrote *Virtual Reality* and *The Virtual Community* in my garden. After twenty years of working in little rooms, being out on the lawn in my bare feet, under the plum tree, is infinitely preferable. In that sense, having the ability to use a computer and computer communications frees me to spend a lot of time in the nonvirtual world. Metaphorically, spending the work week in the virtual world, staring at a computer screen, accumulates a lot of electrons. At least once a week, I spend my day dealing not with computers, but with plants.

The Scout: <Stewart Brand> One of the ways that The Well realized it was a community was when it caught on that it had pillars of the community, most notably Howard. Few have noticed that he wrote one of the best, earliest histories of applied computer science, *Tools For Thought.*

The Lover: <Dave Winer> Rheingold is probably one of the very few totally honest people in this business.

The Oracle: <Paul Saffo> Howard Rheingold is the first citizen of cyberspace. He is someone who followed his interests into this arena and continues today to keep pushing the edges. He is like one of those trappers in the Old West who helped open up the territory. As it started filling up with other people, he got restless and nervous and headed over the next range of foothills to discover the next frontier.

The Gadfly: <John C. Dvorak> Howard is a guy who knows how to write popular books and should just keep doing that for a living.

The Catalyst: <Linda Stone> Howard brings a combination of art, the '60s, and social responsibility to the work that he's done online and for the online community. He's a person with a tremendous amount of courage.

The Scribe: <John Markoff> Howard's a wonderful guy, but I worry that he may have taken a little too much LSD. I was very impressed that he walked away from HotWired so quickly. I thought that said something positive about Howard.

The Seer: <David Bunnell> Howard plays a very positive role in making the digital realm less threatening to outsiders. Howard is one of our finest ambassadors.

The Coyote: <John Perry Barlow> Howard had a huge effect on me. I wasn't particularly interested in computer technology. I wanted to think about new contexts for communities. Howard, one of the mavens of the Deadhead culture on The Well, was instrumental in getting me to see a new venue for community. He is an elder of my village in cyberspace.

<Louis Rossetto>

The Buccaneer

The Oracle: <Paul Saffo> *Louis popularized cyberspace. He took it out of the hands of an elite few and made it conceptually accessible to anyone who might want to participate.*

Louis Rossetto is editor and publisher of *Wired* and HotWired, and cofounder and CEO of Wired Ventures, Inc.

Louis Rossetto is playing games with me. It all started in the spring of 1995 when Louis began to take serious heat from the very *Wired* community he had created.

Louis had spent the late '80s living in Amsterdam running *Electric Word,* a magazine founded in 1986 and concerned with information processing, before returning to the United States in 1991 armed with a business plan for a new magazine. But he and his partner, Jane Metcalfe, met with a very quiet reception. It took a full year and countless rejections before they scored their first investor – Nicholas Negroponte, who personally invested the $75,000 they needed to get started. In the four years since, the runaway success of *Wired* has spawned associated ventures: HotWired, a commercial Web site; HardWired, the publisher of this book; *The Netizen* Web site and TV show; and numerous international projects run under the umbrella of Wired Ventures, Inc.

Louis created the *Wired* culture. I disagree with those who say that he tapped into a preexisting culture. It wasn't there. Louis invented it. This success puts him in the same league with such publishing visionaries as Jan Wenner of *Rolling Stone* in the '60s and David Bunnell of *PC Magazine* and *PC World* in the early '80s. It also makes him a target for those who can't bear other people's success. Thus, when Louis put corporate business leaders on the cover of *Wired* for three successive months in 1995, a number of people who have attitude toward money and business went ballistic, and Louis received heavy, sometimes abusive criticism (indeed, even from some of the people in this book). Some of those readers who considered *Wired* their magazine recoiled at what they considered to be the crass commercialization of their culture. Louis faced the wrath of readers over what was perceived as the sellout of their magazine and culture.

What was Louis to do? That's where I come in.

In the spring of 1995, I was interviewed by *Wired* about my book, *The Third Culture.* It was slated as a one-page Q&A. According to Deep Disk, my secret spy at *Wired,* just before deadline, Louis called an editorial meeting in which he decreed that from that point on, *Wired* had to take a stand and lead the culture. The new policy called for taking the intellectual high road and promoting new and interesting ideas. According to Deep Disk, he then uttered the default word that people all over the world have used for the last three decades when the going gets tough: "Brockman!"

A month later, the August 1995 *Wired* came out with not just the interview about me, but four pages of graphics in a style Louis calls a "mind grenade." The latter took one of my statements and elevated it into a call to arms. What's more, Louis personally wrote the hyperbolic headline for the interview: "Agent of The Third Culture: John Brockman is the Michael Ovitz of The New Intellectual Elite."

Very cute, Louis. Forget Sumner Redstone, Frank Biondi, Ray Smith, Steve Brill. Now he was going for the gold, for Michael Ovitz, the most important player in the entertainment industry, who at the time was the head of Creative Artists Agency. "What is Louis up to?" I asked myself. "Why am I an 'Ovitz'?"

Nearly a year later, I was still confused, and I asked my friend Danny Hillis to help me with my confusion. By that time, both Danny and Ovitz had moved to Disney. "That's fine for you, John, but what about Michael?" he asked, regarding his new boss. "If John Brockman is the Michael Ovitz of the new intellectual elite, do you think Michael is going to settle for just being the Michael Ovitz of everyone else?"

Because of Louis's copywriting talents, I am now someone worth listening to, and for that reason, his new publishing division, HardWired, outbid several New York publishers to acquire the rights to the book you are now reading.

Louis Rossetto is "The Buccaneer." Me? As Samuel Beckett wrote in *The Unnameable,* "I'm in words, made of words, other's words.... I'm all these words, all these strangers."

The Buccaneer: <Louis Rossetto> The Web is a lot of things. It's distribution, it's commerce, it's media. Our HotWired project was literally the first ad-supported original content site on the Web. Before HotWired, everyone was worried about whether the Net would accept advertising. John Plunkett and Barbara Kuhr, Wired's creative directors, invented HotWired's advertising banner, which is now the industry standard. We launched a month before Netscape launched its first Web browser.

We are Web pioneers because we believe that this is the prototype for interactive media, which we are convinced will be the dominant media of the future. It's not CD-ROM, it's not interactive television (remember interactive television?). It is interactivity over the Internet, and the Web is the leading distribution channel. In five years, for a quarter of the population, this will be their main information and entertainment source. In twenty years, it will be everyone's.

With the Web we have the ability to use all media types: sound, text, moving images, and still images. We can mix them interactively, and involve the creators of the material, the propagators of the material, and the participants on the site itself, which would include users. To a large extent the Web is the users, not as just passive receptors of information, but as actual participants in the shaping of the content and the dialogue around the content.

It's still the early days on the Web. Bandwidth is severely limited to most users, so the kinds of data we can deliver, while broad, are still limited. We can't deliver a half hour of video or put out an album of sound, because it would take forever to download. That will change.

What will come is still to be discovered. And I use the word *discover* pointedly. We're not inventing a new medium, we're discovering it, just as Lewis and Clark didn't invent the Louisiana Territory, they explored it. And what they discovered, what we're discovering, is that this is one large space, with enormous potential.

Insofar as online services can become competitive Internet providers, they have a future. If they can't make that transition, then they're history. Their unique position was that they provided an easy-to-use interface to cyberspace. Before that, all you had was command-line access, like DOS. When online services came along, they grew because they were obviously something that made connecting easier. But now with the Netscape and Microsoft browsers, the Web is the new interface to cyberspace, and the unique selling proposition of online services has disappeared.

The online services would like to believe they are content providers. Wrong. They have hosted content providers (and alienated a lot of them by not appreciating their contribution to increasing the service's user base), but they themselves are not content providers. It's like theater owners thinking they are operating studios. Media is not so easy.

Everybody talks about *content.* Everyone says, "We're content providers. Let's repurpose content. Consumers want access to content." Not true. Most of what is described as content is really raw data, and people most assuredly don't want raw data. What they lust after is *context.* They want the raw data run through the filter of human consciousness, someone else's human consciousness, who can do for it what they can't do themselves: add imagination or analysis, then deliver it in a way that is entertaining or valuable. What we are really talking about is the value added by creative minds. Creators take the raw data of the world, add their special essence to it, and deliver it to ultimate end-users. Interactivity facilitates that delivery. At the moment, the most popular media form, television, is a one-way radiator. You sit in front of a television, and it radiates you unless you flip around the dial. You can't get what you want out of the television. You can get only what the television wants to give you at any particular time.

Interactivity facilitates your access to information, to context, letting you get information when you want to get it. More important, interactivity enables you as a content creator to establish references and links to other content, which deepens the relationship of your analysis, your context, by putting it in the matrix of other people's works. This gives you an associative (and therefore a deeper) understanding of the analysis that's being conveyed.

The third advantage of interactivity, maybe the most compelling, is the connection to the other users who are consuming the context to begin with. You are no longer an isolated consumer, a passive radiation absorber. You are connected to the other people who are experiencing a particular work, or have experienced the work, today, tomorrow, yesterday. You become part of a community that is dialoguing, not just with the creator or the delivery vehicle, but with all the other people interested in the particular work. The creation of this community, the coalescence of this community through interactivity, is the real strength of this medium. It creates interest around works and around themes, trends, and ideas, and it enables works to stay alive, to evolve, to keep engaging the participants.

I have completely contradictory impulses about the question of how to reward the creators. On the one hand, the grant of monopoly on the part of the government for intellectual property seems a fundamentally wrong societal decision. We all swim in this sea of human consciousness, and some of us come up with ideas sooner than others, but nevertheless these ideas are the product of everyone's social participation. Ascribing profit to the first finder strikes me as inequitable. On the other hand, I recognize the other social argument that in order to encourage the propagation of new ideas, we need to reward those who discover them first. It's a social benefit to all of us. Otherwise, those inventions would be kept secret, and there would be a delay in their being introduced to society in general. Intellectually, I carry both competing ideas in my head, without resolving them.

As a businessperson, I am equally conflicted. HotWired as a company certainly wants to be compensated for the work that it does and the material that it puts out; on the other hand, lots of people work for HotWired, write for HotWired, and collaborate with HotWired; tracking all rights to the nth degree, to the last possible user, becomes an enormous burden. We are trying to work out a balance between our need to secure and defend our rights in intellectual property, and our desire to recognize the rights of our creators in a way that compensates them fairly without overly burdening our ability to operate in the modern world.

Regardless of what we think, a reality about the Web is that things can be copied very easily. This has good and bad aspects. It's bad because you can't seem to capture the increment of marginal revenue that you should get if you are the actual owner of the intellectual property that is copied. On the other hand, the ease of copying helps propagate your name and your ideas, and perhaps makes a more congenial market for you in the future. This suggests that compensation for intellectual property in the future may come down to being paid for delivering experience. Esther Dyson has suggested that you then may be able to add to your compensation by continuing to augment that experience in a one-to-one way, by modifying or updating the experience. Peter Gabriel's take on intellectual property when asked about Indonesia, where his discs are illegally copied, was, "Well, then I go and do a concert there, and I capture revenue that way."

One side of interactive media today is reminiscent of the CB radio craze. People are enthralled by this bright, shiny new toy out there to play with. You can build a Web page, no matter who you are, whether a corporation or an individual, without understanding what it means to build a Web page or what it means to do media in general. At the same time, there's a nascent media sensibility on the Web. That is what we're trying to participate in. The Web is a publishing platform, an environment to produce media products that other people will consume and participate in. This is the objective of HotWired.

As tools arrive and experience accretes, Net commerce is finally starting to emerge. Not surprisingly, I think most companies will eventually migrate a substantial portion of their business to the Net. Sun used to say the network *was* the computer. Now it says the network *is* the computer – and that's true for a lot of companies today. Airline companies fly tons of aluminum around, burning up millions of gallons of jet fuel every day, but their information network is what keeps the whole thing rolling along. How many warehouses disappeared and how many businesses were created because Federal Express delivered something to you overnight? These are just the harbingers. Many of the things that we take for granted as being absolutely crucial in the physical world are going to start to migrate to the immaterial world of the Net.

A simple example: The biggest expense I have as publisher of *Wired* is the physical printing and delivery of the magazine. If I could somehow get that out of the way, I'd have more resources to devote to my primary business, which is delivering context. That's true of everyone else who has to deal with the material world, especially if they have offices or warehouses or retail establishments, or walk-in facilities. It would be much easier to have fleets of UPS trucks roaming around, connected together by wireless and GPS satellites, than to build physical stores. There is a huge, compelling economic reason why a large part of our commerce is going to move to the immaterial world of cyberspace.

Tools are arriving, companies are being formed, alliances are being built, big corporations are starting to change. General Motors and Procter & Gamble, the largest advertisers, are now committing to Web advertising. Intuit lined up nineteen banks to participate in its electronic checkbook bill-paying system, while Chase Manhattan absorbed Chemical Bank and Wells Fargo swallowed First Interstate, and both closed lots of branches. They could close all of their branches in ten years. Visa has introduced ecash. Federal Express is on the Web. One of the most successful Web enterprises is a bookstore, Amazon.com. If you want to trade hazardous waste, you can turn to a Web page to find a market. The SEC has allowed a brewery to sell its securities over the Web, without an exchange, without an investment bank. I just got a prospectus for an offshore online bank. Wherever you turn, it's happening. In five years, this discussion is going to seem quaint.

Big companies don't have to invent the future. They can buy it. They have a certain arrogance. Many felt they didn't have to be involved with the risk of developing a Web presence in the early days, because in the end they could go out and buy their solutions in the event that they needed to be involved. It's like trying to sell the great book of an unknown author to a publishing house. A publisher is much more willing to let somebody else publish it, and then buy the subsidiary rights later, once the book has been proved, even if the publisher is going to be paying ten or twenty times more for those rights. This is definitely true of the media business, probably any business. Those publishing companies and those media companies that have kept out of interactive media so far, or who've been doing it in a very lackadaisical way, are going to start to get a lot more serious about it now that they see the writing on the wall.

Even big investment bankers are saying interactive media is where the big growth in media is going to be in the next five years. You have telephone companies like MCI watching their business become a commodity business and starting to divert their cash flow to content companies. My sense is that we are going to see a lot of activity in interactive media that is going to start to look more and more like real business, not just R&D. They are starting to see a real media market developing and a real commercial potential, and want to be players in the new game.

The Digital Revolution is going to have increasingly profound consequences. Fifty years ago, the Jesuit philosopher Teilhard de Chardin wrote about how technology was an integral part of evolution – you know, not only is the chicken DNA's way of making more DNA, but so is the *nest.* Digital technology and networks are part of the evolution not just of the human species, but of the planet itself. My colleague Kevin Kelly talks of the Digital Revolution as being "the earth clothing itself in a brain."

The planet is going to be networked, and a billion brains are going to be connected together, and that will have a profound impact on humans, and on the planet – unlike any that we have seen before.

I've been accused of proselytizing, but I'm not proselytizing any more than someone who looks at the horizon, sees a typhoon heading toward him, and says, "Hey, a storm's coming."

Computers are brain appliances and networks are exonervous systems that are connecting the entire human race in real time and creating a living human consciousness on a planetary scale. All I'm saying is, Take note of this, pay attention to the erupting future. Think about how it's going to affect you in your life.

THE SEER: <DAVID BUNNELL> Louis had this wonderful vision that digital culture wasn't just a subculture anymore, it was *the* culture. So he produced *Wired,* which explained this culture. Then he did a radical thing. He sold advertising to mainstream companies like Absolut Vodka and Saturn. Smug computer publishers said it couldn't be done and the readers wouldn't stand for it. But Louis was right, and they were wrong.

THE CONSERVATIVE: <DAVID GELERNTER>
Wired tries to convince people that it is a shallow and intellectually superficial magazine. Often it isn't. Often it has good stuff in it. I think it's a tremendous idea and it could mean a lot more if it took itself more seriously.

THE PRODIGY: <JARON LANIER> You don't read *Wired,* you watch it. It brought computer culture out into the light, but not far enough. There are odd orthodoxies in the magazine that are never questioned. Every issue of *Wired* has an article that suggests that the abstract world inside the computer is the same as the world outside the computer, except that computers aren't good enough yet. If you think that way, you diminish life a little bit, because computers are programmed, whereas the world outside computers is infinitely mysterious and made of this stuff called nature. When you lose the difference between computers and the world, the world becomes bland to you, you become bland to the world, and you become nerdy.

THE SCRIBE: <JOHN MARKOFF> I have a problem with *Wired*'s attitude that it is the arbiter of political correctness in Net culture, when all it is is a bunch of guys with attitude. There's no particular insight that everybody else doesn't have. They're ahead of the curve sometimes; I'll give them credit for that.

THE GENIUS: <W. DANIEL HILLIS> Louis is one of the deep thinkers who watches carefully and pays close attention to what's going on. He doesn't open his mouth very often, but when he does, you'd better listen. He's extremely thoughtful. I'm not sure he's shy. He's just a listener, an observer. You learn more by listening than by talking.

THE PRAGMATIST: <STEWART ALSOP> I have the feeling that Louis doesn't like me, but that's probably because he's ignoring me, he doesn't know who the hell

I am. I don't think he has any social skills. I send him emails and he never responds. At one point he showed me the business plan for *Wired* and I said, "This isn't going anywhere."

THE STATESMAN: <STEVE CASE> He seems conflicted. On the one hand, he's pleased that *Wired* is so successful and has become the *Rolling Stone* for the wired generation. On the other hand, you get the sense that he's a little bored with all the hype and would rather be left alone.

THE IMPRESARIO: <RICHARD SAUL WURMAN> Now that I'm over 60, I think I've earned the right to say "I knew them when." Most people think of *Wired;* I think of Louis and Jane's earlier journal, *Electric Word,* which opened the door to electronic publishing, allowing *Wired* to happen. *Wired*'s success didn't happen as an overnight miracle, but because of an astonishing amount of work, passion, and risk.

THE CITIZEN: <HOWARD RHEINGOLD> If I had wanted to work for an asshole, I would have worked for myself. He taught me that the only way an editor truly has creative control is by being the publisher.

<Paul Saffo>

The Oracle

The Scout: <Stewart Brand> *Nobody in the business gives better quote than Saffo. Every journalist who calls him gets someone who is familiar with the news flash of the day and its deeper significance. Paul speaks with succinct eloquence.*

Paul Saffo is director of the Institute for the Future, a twenty-nine-year-old research and forecasting foundation located in Menlo Park, California.

"For most of this century we have viewed communications as a conduit, a pipe between physical locations on the planet. What's happened now is that the conduit has become so big and interesting that communication has become more than a conduit, it has become a destination in its own right – what in the vernacular is called cyberspace."

"This is interesting stuff, Paul," I said. We were having dinner with John Markoff, Cliff Stoll, Stewart Brand, and Howard Rheingold at City of Paris restaurant in San Francisco. Paul Saffo is a rapid-fire quote machine, a walking-talking sound bite, an instant headline for the next journalist who calls looking for an expert opinion for tomorrow morning's story. He's good.

Paul is also Silicon Valley's resident intellectual. He's the big-picture guy who articulates the trends. He is preoccupied by the long-range implications of the Information Revolution for business and society. Paul is a senior member of the Institute for the Future, a nonprofit think tank that consults a wide range of business and government entities, including telecommunications and consumer companies.

In between bites of steak au poivre, Paul predicted that the dance between laser-enabled conduit and processor-enabled computing power will continue over the next couple of years. Just as the processor shaped the last decade, the device shaping this decade is the communications laser, and it is the advent of ever-cheaper, more powerful lasers that is setting the stage for an access revolution. Each new processor advance – each new version of the Intel chip, the Motorola RISC chip – will create new communications demand, and each new communications advance will create a greater demand for more powerful processors. How does this change in the relationship between communications and processing affect our lives? "*Content* is the second most stupid term used today in the information revolution," Paul said. "The first most stupid, of course, is *information*. I agree with Jaron Lanier, who says that information is nothing more than alienated experience. *Content* evokes this notion of denatured, indifferent, unchanging information that is somehow a commodity. That may be what content is, but this business is not about selling commodities."

According to Paul, *content* is about selling unique things. It is about understanding. It is about things that touch and change people's lives. "The scarce resource in this business is not content, but context," he continues. "We have this hangover from the bad old days when there was a shortage of conduit and content. Now that content is hyperabundant, it is essentially valueless. The thing that people will charge monopoly rents for is not content but context, the sense-making ability to take this ocean of information and turn it into something useful that actually touches and changes our lives – and entertains us."

Paul gives talks that verge on performance art. He is in great demand as a consultant for companies in a myriad of businesses that want to zero in on the future. He may deny the efficacy of "convergence" among media, technology, and publishing companies, but he is convergence personified. As Stewart Alsop says, "Paul is a connections guy: he knows how to connect things up, he knows how to connect people up, and he knows how to connect ideas. He's a human switch."

"Paul, it's time to write a book," I said after absorbing his soliloquy, which was impressive both in its intelligence and in the confident manner of its delivery. "I *am* writing a book,

John, and I have an agent and a publisher," he replied somewhat testily. "Don't you remember when I came to your office five years ago? You turned me down flat."

I had completely forgotten. "Of course, I turned you down," I said, winging it. "You weren't Paul Saffo five years ago, and it was four years before the Internet hit big. The future's more interesting now than it was in the past. So are you."

Paul Saffo is "The Oracle."

THE ORACLE: <PAUL SAFFO> Without a doubt, the main event of this decade is laser-enabled access. First there was access to information by individuals, but now, and much more important, a new kind of access is emerging: instead of people accessing information, we are moving into a world defined by people accessing people in information-rich environments. The fact that the Web exists is proof of that trend. But social spaces like MUDs (multiple user dimensions) will be the next big thing.

It is important in this revolution to be constantly on guard against developing hazy utopian notions that our lives are somehow going to be better. The Internet, at the moment, feels democratic and open, and everybody is accessible, but it is certain that as the Internet matures, walls and blocks and passwords and exclusion zones are going to arise, and people are going to create elite environments that others are not allowed into. At the other extreme, people are going to be talking closely with others whom they should not be talking with. It is not always a good idea to put an extreme fundamentalist into the same space with someone holding the opposite views. You will not have constructive communications. This stuff is not utopian. It is social dynamite. It is tremendously unpredictable. Most of the benefits will be positive, but there will be negative impact.

Repurposing is a disastrously oversimplified concept. At its best, repurposing amounts to nothing more than intellectual strip-mining of an old medium, in a desperate attempt to beat one's way into a new medium, to figure out the formula that will cause people to get excited about it. We tried to repurpose old radio shows into television, but this wasn't enough to excite consumers. Television took off when we created new content designed with the subtleties of the emerging medium in mind. The same will be true this time around. There is something larger than repurposing afoot, and that is how you take old stories, old ideas, old themes, and breathe new life into them. The stories that may have the biggest life in the new medium may be the stories that weren't the biggest hits in the old medium because they were told slightly ahead of their time or told in media that didn't quite make sense for the story. So you have to hoard all that old stuff – there are diamonds hidden in these huge intellectual tailings of information.

One would not even recognize the diamond in the tailings if one looked today. It's a good idea to hold on to intellectual property, but I wouldn't rush to get it typed up to dump onto the Internet, or even put into digital form, until I had a sense of which parts are going to be worthwhile. Otherwise, you might end up with the intellectual equivalent of having put everything on microfilm in the 1960s because you thought libraries were going to buy it. Just as one would be embarrassed to have a warehouse full of microfilm canisters today, the same may prove to be true of digital technologies. Putting intellectual property into digital form is not what's critical.

The one thing about intellectual property that will not change is the complete chaos of intellectual property laws. Our intellectual property system, copyrights and trademarks and patents, traces its origins back several centuries and is held together with the equivalent of baling wire and duct tape. The temptation for lawyers and politicians when faced with rapid change is to create a new system that throws out all those old things. Lawyers do an even worse job when they try to create a legal regime that anticipates something not quite here yet than when they try to codify after the fact. So, God save us if lawyers and legislatures manage to do that, because the system has a regenerative, self-healing quality. We will figure out the proper legal regimes as the environment continues to evolve.

The revolution afoot today is the ultimate fantasy for writers who have harbored grudges against those folks who stand between the writer and the reader. Without a doubt, new communications technology will be used to disintermediate some of those players, at least in the short run. It will be at least as big as the advent of desktop publishing in the mid-'80s. The Web today is like desktop publishing. It is a way for writers and other creative types to cost-effectively reach ever smaller audiences with specialized information. A small number of people out of the large number of people trying to do this will actually find a way to make a steady living at it.

But you will not disintermediate all the middle people in this business: digital technologies make it ever cheaper to be a middle person in this process. It may be that we all end up being middle players and the notion of disintermediation proves to be largely a phantom.

Just how big this revolution is depends on your time frame. If you are looking at a one-year period, the advent of the Web over the last twelve months is not a terribly big deal. If you look at twenty to thirty years, the events of the last three years probably are comparable to the advent of the printing press, encompassing the advent of the PC, the invention of the Internet, the growth of global nets. If you look over a hundred-year period, it is as big as the events swirling around the Renaissance from about 1428 to 1515.

To understand what this means for culture, you have to ask the question: Is this a big revolution or not? Humans are fascinated with change. But amid all the change going on, the things that don't change, the constants, are vastly greater than the things that are changing. Even in periods of rapid change, it is the constants and the continuity that set the stage for innovation. Culturally, this is the latest step in a long cultural, intellectual tradition of taking raw untamed technologies and turning them into compelling media that touch and change our lives. That's a slow evolutionary process. More precisely, it is like a process of punctuated equilibria, as the evolutionary biologists would say, where you have periods of fairly rapid change followed by periods of consolidation. We happen to be in a period of very rapid change. The consequence, as Professor Tony Oettinger said more than twenty years ago, is that the microprocessor is the solvent leaching the glue out of our social institutions. The consequence is a fundamental rebalancing of social contracts, business structures, organizational structures. Everything is up for grabs, but is not all going to change at once, and if we all live our lives one day at a time, it is all very manageable.

The impact of digital technology on commerce, buying and selling, hanging out, socializing, money – all those things – is still barely under way. We are taking one more step in the process of a steady abstraction of what we mean by *money.* Once upon a time, we bartered, trading actual physical objects; then somewhere in the Fertile Crescent someone had the idea of using symbols to represent those physical objects so you didn't have to carry a sheep in your pocket every time you wanted to do business. There has been a steady process of abstraction from coinage to paper currency. The most interesting step happened in the hill towns of northern Italy, where the right combination of technologies and social needs, trade with the east and across the Mediterranean, conspired to set the stage for modern commerce as we have known it for the last four hundred years.

The signs of it are all around us today. All the modern words of commerce – *credit, discount, value* – have Latin roots. All came from northern Italy. Italy was so much the center of it then that Herr Fugger, the head of the most powerful financial house in all of Europe, sent his son to Italy to be educated. If you read passages from books of the time, you'll notice astonishing echoes of today's issues. We worry about how we move money safely over the Internet. The same thing happened back then in Italy. There are wonderful records of correspondence between people who were setting up triangular trade of sheep and sheepskin and tanning materials with Egypt and Tunis and into Italy. It's exactly the same process. We are going to go through the same confusion in terms of value. Back then, a lot of people got rich and a lot of people lost their shirts. If I were a businessman trying to get on with my job today in an industry touched by electronic commerce, I would feel a bit like John Jacob Astor, who was reported to have remarked while sitting at the bar of the *SS Titanic,* "You know, I asked for ice, but this is ridiculous." There is enormous opportunity here, but it is also going to be enormously disruptive for people trying to get on with business.

We are seeing old businesses being changed in subtle ways by the Internet. The first businesses that are really going to take off in this world are the catalog companies, for the simple reason that the World Wide Web is a perfect way to do catalogs once you solve the problem of the cost and awkwardness of the machines people use to do the accessing.

There is an important subtext here. The notion of buying and selling things in a digital age evokes visions of people in some celestial casino trading information, but what this really comes down to is a more efficient way to buy and sell stuff and move stuff around the planet. In the end, if it doesn't lead to getting a better stereo system or a fancier car or a better household appliance, it will not last for long.

I am uneasy about all the executives who are betting on digital convergence, for the simple reason that digital convergence is not happening. We are seeing convergence certainly at a narrow technical level. There are processors in everything, and the communications laser is making bandwidth ubiquitous. But convergence at a broader technical level seems to be leading to something quite the opposite, which is digital divergence. If you look across the patterns of industries today, there is a unifying theme. The core businesses of television, Hollywood, consumer electronics, the personal-computer industry, and the consumer electronics industry are imploding. In the personal-computer industry, PCs are mere commodities being sold at commodity prices. The people who are winning are the ones who can commoditize their products. The ones who are losing are the ones who sell unique products, like Apple. The core business of consumer electronics – TV, VCRs – is flat, with no prospect of growth. It is clear that the core businesses are in trouble, but interesting things are happening at the margins. As the industries are dying out, they are also overlapping, and what seem to be the margins are actually the centers of entirely new industries that will shape change in our world twenty years from now.

In evolution, species often get very large just before they become extinct. As I look at executives wheeling and dealing and making their companies bigger, on the one hand it looks like they are leveraging scale to take advantage of ever larger global opportunities. On the other hand, it looks like they are once-fierce competitors huddling together for comfort as the world crashes in around them. For big businesses today, to make it into the environment that will exist twenty years from now, gathering their resources together to find a way to leverage them as best as possible is the only way to go, but in the end leverage will be how to turn those large companies into small companies that are in the position to take advantage of the emerging opportunities at the start of the next decade.

Jaron Lanier's observations about sedimentation and the dangers of picking the wrong standards are extraordinarily profound. We look at this stuff as bright and shiny and new, but it is clear that someday it will be old and it will hang around far longer than anyone wishes. We will be stuck with DOS and Windows for longer than anyone would want. Ted Nelson, paraphrasing Lord Acton's phrase of a hundred years ago, observed about Microsoft that all power corrupts and obsolete power corrupts obsoletely. In our rush to standardize, my fear is that we are going to end up settling on standards that will come back to haunt us in the future. We are performing a great unwitting experiment on ourselves by introducing all this digital technology into our lives. Where it ends up is anyone's guess. But wherever we end up, we are in for a fascinating and utterly surprising ride.

THE GADFLY: <JOHN C. DVORAK> Saffo is a futurist and, like all the rest of them, is wrong most of the time.

THE GENIUS: <W. DANIEL HILLIS> Saffo is the Alvin Toffler of his generation.

THE CATALYST: <LINDA STONE> Paul is a futurist and a presentist, too, because he understands what's going on in the present, and can describe it, and can help clarify it for everybody. Sometimes understanding the present is more helpful than going into the future.

THE SCRIBE: <JOHN MARKOFF> Saffo is the industry's dancing bear. He has the ability to conceptualize ideas and articulate them better than anybody I've seen. Paul gave me the best pull quote of my career. It was in a Sunday "Week in Review" piece on "Net Sex," and his quote was, "There's a lot of heavy clicking going on out there."

THE SEER: <DAVID BUNNELL> Paul Saffo is really on top of the futurist thing. He is the only one in this profession who actually knows what he is talking about and has the capacity to not let his ego dictate his conclusions. He is hard to pigeonhole.

THE IDEALIST: <DENISE CARUSO> Paul Saffo is quicker with a quote than anyone I've ever known in my life. He is a fountain of the most arcane, yet somehow appropriate, information. And he is as allergic to hype and puffery as I am, though he's much more polite when he calls people on it.

THE STATESMAN: <STEVE CASE> Paul Saffo is very bright and a terrific speaker, and has a unique ability to capture the essence of what's happening in an engaging sound bite.

THE IMPRESARIO: <RICHARD SAUL WURMAN> He gently slides past all of us astonishing connections, whether from the medieval soothsayers or the inarticulate predictors of today. Everybody's choice as a speaker and as an observer. Paul's middle name should be Homework.

<Bob Stein>

The Radical

The Oracle: <Paul Saffo> *Bob Stein is the professional maniac who is not afraid to go off and do something that seems absolutely absurd to everyone else who does not have his vision. People like Bob make things happen. He is the publisher born before his time, born before the printing presses were good enough to do the things he wanted to do.*

Bob Stein is founder of the Voyager Company.

"There's a great need for some competent intellectual who understands Marxism and what Lenin and Mao added to it, who can apply that method of thinking to the digital transformation that's taking place." Bob Stein, CD-ROM and Internet publisher, is presenting a discourse on radical politics to me. "Somebody needs to write a political economy of digital culture," he continues. "We could use it. We need the [French sociologist Fernand] Braudel who wants to extrapolate forward with these technologies and try to really understand them."

I first heard about Bob in 1988, when his company, Voyager, released what is considered to be the first consumer CD-ROM, *Beethoven's Ninth Symphony,* while also launching the Expanded Book Project.

After arranging licenses for the rights to dozens of titles, Bob moved his company from Santa Monica to New York. In New York, Voyager continued to play an important role in encouraging major houses to enter the electronic publishing arena.

For the inhabitants of corporate America, Bob is hard to read. He runs a business, and he strives for economic success, but as David Bunnell, himself an unrepentant '60s radical, notes,

"Everything about Bob and his company flows from the fact that he marches to a different drummer. In a digital world filled with money-grubbing, heartless capitalists, Bob is doing work that enriches our culture and will endure long after the garish mansions of high-tech billionaires have crumbled and returned to dust."

Thus, you will find on the Voyager list a distinguished array of Modern Library literary works. You will also find a CD-ROM by award-winning journalist Mumia Abu-Jamal, who sits behind bars on Death Row, convicted of murdering a police officer. *First Person: Mumia Abu-Jamal – Live From Death Row* is evidence that Bob doesn't check his values at the door when he walks into his company every morning. He will devote as much space on Voyager's Internet Web site to anti-censorship forums as he does to his own commercial line.

Bob thinks deeply about the social ramifications of the communications revolution. He understands that the big battles looming in the digital realm are not the browser wars or open-versus-proprietary operating systems and platforms. "The subtext of what's happening is that we are changing the way that humans communicate with each other," he says. "This transition is going to take much longer than people talk about, and it may be a hundred years, two hundred years, before it settles out. This profound shift is more significant than the invention of the printing press, and the deep implications of it won't be known for some time. A thousand years from now, humanity will look back at the late part of the twentieth century as the time when something big started."

The big battle will be over how the Internet is shaped. Will it be a common carrier like the telephone system in which each individual has access, or will it follow a broadcast model like TV in which only a few have the ability to make content available? According to Bob, the media companies want to control the Internet in a way that is comfortable for them, that ensures their ability to make profits. These companies favor the broadcast model. "If an unknown in Nebraska has the same power to reach everybody as somebody at 75 Rockefeller Center," he says, "that's unsettling for somebody who's trying to make money. It's clear how the companies will organize themselves. What's not clear is how the people will organize themselves to maintain the freedom that we have right now on the Internet."

Bob Stein is "The Radical."

THE RADICAL: <BOB STEIN> The excitement about the Internet is that it is a common carrier. There are hundreds of thousands of Web pages created by people who are unknowns, and suddenly they're on the Internet on an equal basis with Time Warner and Sony.

What excited me from the beginning was letting authors express themselves in new ways, letting people see works in new ways, and letting them communicate with each other. I've been willing to use whatever technology has come down the pike, whether laserdiscs, videodiscs, CD-ROMs, or the Internet. The reality is that every medium has a unique capability. CD-ROMs are good at giving you a fairly large amount of audio-video and textual data in one place. If you want to give somebody reasonable-resolution video, high-resolution audio, and text, there is no other medium right now that does it like CD-ROM. A lot of the programs that I'm interested in producing require two hours of video, an hour of animation, and four hours of audio. Someday we'll have capability on the Net and we'll distribute products requiring high bandwidth that way.

For now, one of the keys is localness. I can have a book in my hand on the subway, and I read the first twenty pages. When I get off the subway, I curl down the corner of the page and take the book with me. I sit down at my coffee break, take out the book, and open it up again. It's all there and it's instantaneous. I can have a CD-ROM with me all the time. It has bookmarks and things like that. It's nowhere near as good as a book, but it's almost there. The Net requires me to be connected to a telephone, and it's not personalized in the way that it needs to be. For things that require twenty or thirty hours to go through, like a CD-ROM, it's nice to have them local, to own them and be able to have them at your beck and call. The Net is best for things that are much smaller to absorb. It is better for sound bites than for two-hour audio programs. That will change over time, but negotiating that divide will be interesting.

I assume that the future for all publishing is on the Net. In terms of Voyager, clearly we're not so established in any form of publishing that we could ignore the Net. We must establish ourselves as a leader, as we did in CD-ROMs. There's no way we could stay only in the CD-ROM world and survive. Our Web site gets, on the average, ten thousand hits a day. I'm happy with that number at this point. One of the nice things about having a company that's up and going is that we can put people to work on our Internet site, and most of what I'm doing now is Internet stuff. We're still evolving and growing, and we're not sure what direction we're going to go in yet.

Will today's hot content providers or filters, the HotWireds or Yahoo!s, be the same ones in existence five years from now? I tend to think the filters are more valuable than the content providers, unless the content providers are doing something unique, and of long-term value. The topical stuff we see from companies like HotWired makes it hard to believe that providing content is a prescription for success in the long run on the Net. The content providers who will end up being successful on the Net will be able to create material that you go back to over and over again.

Whenever a new technology comes to the fore, people glom on to it and do what they can. In capitalism, the tendency over a very short period of time is for the market winners in the first year or two to be co-opted and made into businesses so there's no longer any room for the individual. First you get a Netscape – originally built as Mosaic on a university campus for work-study money – going public for $72 million. Next we have Yahoo!, a wonderful little site on the Internet, which basically kept track of all the other sites, and overnight it became a business. The window of opportunity for individuals is shorter than we'd like it to be.

Another much deeper concern in the long run is the contradiction between the technologists, who keep making and improving their technologies without thinking about their social implications, and the rest of us, who have to live with these technologies for the next hundred generations. The analogy is the car, although what we're doing is more significant than inventing the car. Sometimes when I give a talk I ask the following question: If you had the opportunity to invent the automobile, with foreknowledge of what it was going to do to society, not only in technical and environmental terms, but in social and economic, would you invent it? I'm always amazed at the answer I get. The first part doesn't surprise me. Basically they say they would, because if they didn't, somebody else would. What I find more surprising is the hostility that comes from the audience when I ask, because they don't want to hear the question. They don't want the responsibility of having to think about the long-term implications of something as fundamental as the creation of the automobile or, what's probably much more significant, the development of new communications technologies.

The time must come fairly soon when poets and philosophers and artists, and the rest of us ordinary people, try to think about what we are inventing with these machines and how we're using them, in terms of the kind of society we want to have. If we continue on the same path, making machines without understanding the broader social framework in which they exist, we'll end up with something truly frightening.

At a conference I attended someone said it's becoming increasingly less common for architects to design structures that actually get built; instead they are designing virtual buildings. The reason is that there's not a lot of money out there for real buildings, so it's natural that architects would try to build where they could, which is in the virtual world. I was struck by how easily this went down with the audience I was in, because I was very disturbed that we're willing to accept that as a reality. It's not as if millions and millions, if not billions, of people don't need better housing, more beautiful public buildings, and better factories to work in.

The question is, What do we want in the real world? If we want to use electronic mail to lead to discussions that take place in physical places, with people looking at each other and talking to each other, I think it's great, but not if there are not enough people talking to each other face-to-face. I love my machine. I love the fact that I can use it to talk to people all over the world, but we can't use this technology as a replacement for physical communication or physical presence. I'm somewhat suspicious of the movement toward developing a sense of community on the Net. I would much rather encourage the development of communities in the real world.

What people think are technical questions are really social questions. What society does with machines is up for grabs. This is especially true in education. There are those in the educational community who would just as soon use computers as baby-sitters and trainers of kids; there are others who would like to see these machines basically as intellectual prostheses to empower children. Between these two extremes, we've got what's going to happen, which is a social question rather than a technical one. Until there is a good discussion about what we should do with these machines, I don't see how using them in the schools is going to bring great benefits. If the schools are good before they get the machines, the machines don't change them very much. The kids who like computers will use them; lots of other kids won't. It's the schools that aren't good where the machines sometimes have a much bigger effect.

The short-term picture of what is happening is quite complicated because there is a cauldron of conflicting interests. You have people who are excited about the pure technological issues, who keep raising the ante every year, or every week. You have people who are excited about the possibility of making money using these advances, and who are thinking very short term. You have the broad masses of us who are just excited about the access we're getting to traditional material and content, and also about the new content being created and the way people are able electronically to talk to each other online. What I find most interesting is watching these different groups battle with each other. The Internet is going to be a place of tremendous struggle over the next several years.

The Pattern-Recognizer: <Esther Dyson> There seems to be some fundamental dissonance between running a for-profit company and what Bob Stein believes in, and I think that must make him uncomfortable.

The Publisher: <Jane Metcalfe> Bob Stein is widely acknowledged as a pioneer in multimedia development, and if it weren't for him, people would not have understood the creative opportunity quite as early as they did. But a lot of his ideas are still locked in a previous generation of political thought, though; they seem to be less and less appropriate to the world we live in now.

THE CATALYST: <LINDA STONE> Bob Stein can inspire you and he can piss you off, and he can do it at the same time. At some level, Bob is shy. He's very soft on the inside, and it causes him to be very hard on the outside, to protect himself.

THE CYBERANALYST: <SHERRY TURKLE> If I was having a meeting, and I wanted somebody, in the most politic and kind way possible, to stir things up, Bob Stein would be on the invitation list.

<Cliff Stoll>

The Skeptic

The Software Developer: <Bill Gates>

There's certainly a need, as people get caught up in the excitement of all this stuff, to have someone who can take the opposing viewpoint, and point out, in some cases correctly, that it's all still fairly hard to use and fairly expensive. Let's not lose sight of what was good about the previous way of doing things. There's definitely a role there and I think he's done very well positioning himself as the devil's advocate. Sometimes I think he underestimates how, over the next few years, the industry will do a very good job getting rid of some of the limitations he criticizes. His book, Cuckoo's Egg, *was my favorite of his two books.*

Cliff Stoll is an astrophysicist and the author of *Silicon Snake Oil* (1995) and *The Cuckoo's Egg* (1994).

"When I'm online, I'm alone in a room, tapping on a keyboard, staring at a cathode-ray tube. I'm ignoring anyone else in the room. The nature of being online is that I can't be with someone else. Rather than bringing me closer to others, the time that I spend online isolates me from the most important people in my life – my family, my friends, my neighborhood, my community."

Cliff Stoll didn't think this way back in 1994. One of a large and varied group of weekend guests, Cliff was sitting in front of my computer in the study, typing like a man possessed, on a beautiful, sunny June afternoon.

"Come outside, Cliff," I said, "and join the party."

"Can't, John," he said. "Been away from home three days and already I have at least two hundred fifty email messages to answer. It's going to take me all afternoon."

"Are they from people you know?" I inquired.

"No," he replied, "but they took the time to write and I feel a personal obligation to answer each and every one."

Drastic action was required. "Cliff," I barked, shifting into my U.S. Army command mode, "you *will* get offline, you *will* turn the computer off, and you *will* move your ass outside. *Now!*"

In 1967, Marshall McLuhan faced a similar predicament as he dealt with the negative impact of sudden fame. When I asked him how he found the time to keep up his voluminous reading and also answer mail, he exclaimed with a laugh, "Answer my mail! Just reading it would take ten hours a day." Compound this situation with digital communications and the accessibility we all have to each other, and you begin to see how Cliff, since the publication of his best-selling *The Cuckoo's Egg,* had gone from Internet God to Digital Martyr.

"Cliff is often given short shrift because he is acting as a very spontaneous critic of the Net hype," says Mike Godwin, counsel for the EFF and Cliff's close friend. "What a lot of people don't realize is that, first, Cliff is coming to this position from a base of knowledge about all the positive things the Net can be. The second is that he is not nearly so negative as he is commonly presented as being. What he wants us to do is ask critical questions – not to assume, for example, that putting computers in the schools or an Internet connection in the schools is necessarily positive. That's quite salutary. In Cliff you see one of the first people who had to grapple with a wide range of ethical and security issues on the Net, and these are expressed in both his first book, *The Cuckoo's Egg,* and his current one, *Silicon Snake Oil.* Unlike virtually every other critic of online communications, Cliff knows what he's talking about. He's used the medium. He deserves a lot of credit."

Cliff walked outside, away from the sea of digital information in which he was drowning. I don't know if it was the beauty of the day, the attention he received from the bright teenagers who had read his first book, or just the walk alone with a dog and his thoughts through the pine forests and cornfields, but Cliff never went back into the study. He didn't answer his email. He didn't even finish reading it. When he left for the airport two days later, he handed me drafts of the first two chapters of a new book inspired by the experience of the past two days, which quickly evolved into *Silicon Snake Oil.*

Two years have passed, during which time Cliff has become a father – twice. He's the one who stays home and takes care of the babies. The digital agenda has faded into the background. "I love computers and I use them all the time," he says. "I've got a half-dozen computers in my house. But this cult of computing gives me the heebie-jeebies, the sense that if you don't have an electronic-mail address, if you don't have your own customized homepage on the World Wide Web, if you don't have your own domain name online, then you're being left behind, that progress is going on without you. Human kindness, warmth, interaction, friendship, and family are far more important than anything that can come across my cathode-ray tube. While I admire the insights of many of the people in the world of computing, I get this cold feeling that I speak a different language."

Cliff Stoll is "The Skeptic."

THE SKEPTIC: <CLIFF STOLL> For a scientist, the Internet is hard to get along without. It lets me send messages from one place to another, lets me pick up on the latest happenings in astronomy, and lets me share not just my thoughts, but data and hypotheses with other astronomers, whether about Jupiter or climatic change. On the other hand, I have been able to do all of those things quite well without the Internet. People did astronomy, science, and physics – damn good astronomy, science, and physics – without computers and without the Internet. There is a lot of talk about how essential the Internet, electronic mail, and Internet relay chat are for doing science and research, but it's hard for me to point to an example where great astronomy, great research, came out because of the Internet. For physics and science and research, do I need immediate communications? Or might it be more important to have a sense of what is worthwhile, what is important, and what isn't?

In astronomy, this means I want to think hard about the messages that I receive. I want quality stuff coming across my computer and into my work life. In that sense, the Internet might not be so great for me. It brings me terrific stuff, but it also brings me loads of drivel and dross and mediocrity. My computer doesn't know how to separate the two, so I end up having to work hard to figure out what's good stuff and what's lousy stuff. Rather than saving me time by providing fast communications, the Internet is wasting my time by forcing me to edit out lots of valueless dreck from a constant stream of messages. At the same time, the immediacy of the Internet takes away my time to reflect on my work. It makes me react to what's happening inside of my computer and across the network, rather than think about what's happening in the universe at large and on the planets that I'm studying.

The Internet is said to be growing from its present infancy into a wonderland where there will be commerce and lot of information. I don't believe it. The Internet provides lots and lots of data, but data is just words and bits and bytes and numbers. Unlike information, data has no content, it has no context, it has little utility, it lacks accuracy, it lacks pedigree, and it lacks timeliness. Most of all, it lacks usefulness. The bulk of what comes across my modem connection simply has little use for me.

This information highway, which delivers damned little information, is said to be the roadway to power in progress. After all, information is power. I don't believe it! Information isn't powerful. Information isn't power. Powerful people are seldom informed. Who's powerful? Look at some of the powerful politicians. Presidents. Prime Ministers. Generals of armies. They don't sit behind a computer reading stuff off the Internet! Hey, who's got the most information? Librarians do! It's hard to imagine a group of people with less power than librarians. Information is power? The whole idea is false.

Nor is there a connection between information and knowledge. Knowledge, dare I say wisdom, which we ought to be seeking, is, for the most part, not information, but a sense of understanding, a sense of judgment, a sense of when to ignore information. Moreover, what turns the cranks in my head is not information, but ideas, hypotheses, creative solutions that I might not have come across before. I can't get those from a computer. I can get those only by thinking.

The Internet is perhaps the most oversold, overpromoted communications system ever created. It is little more than an uppity telephone system. In fact, it's somewhat less than that. At least on a telephone system I can call anyone I want to, worldwide. I can't do that online! I can't call my mom on the Internet. She doesn't use a computer. I can telephone her. The telephone system reaches 98 percent of the people in North America. How many are on the Internet – 10 million, 3 million? Suppose it's 30 million. That's only 10 percent of the population.

The World Wide Web makes it easier to graze around the Internet. The Web makes it even faster to switch channels on the Internet. On the Web I can jump anywhere I want, quickly, so I'm told. But most of the time when I jump from one place to another, what I get is waiting, waiting, waiting. I watch a little ball turn around, a little clock, and I watch my life dribble off my modem at 9600 baud while something is being downloaded or some network connection is going slow. We are told that someday this will be fixed. Sure, the *SS Titanic* might come into New York Harbor as well. The French may repay the war debt. DeSoto may come out with a new car in another year or two.

An essential aspect to studying, to thinking, is context. It's not enough to look at just a sentence in a book or even a paragraph in a book. I want to read the whole book, to get the ebb and flow of the storyteller, to understand where the story is leading. I don't want just little bits from things. The nature of the Web and hypertext destroys context. We literally surf, from one place to another, without going to any depth. If television is the vast wasteland, then the Web is a phenomenally surface-shallow hole of mediocrity. The homepages that I find are monuments to narcissism. I suspect this infatuation with the fad will decline and people will find some use for it. Like the Internet, the Web is a terrific solution, a great solution to a nonexistent problem. Someday we will find problems that the Web solves.

It follows from a sense of economic principles that publishing online is cheap. At the same time, the cost of paper is skyrocketing. A curious phenomenon is that every year publishing online gets cheaper, and publishing on paper gets more expensive. A real obvious result of this is being ignored by almost everyone – namely, that people who have valuable things to say that others are willing to pay money to hear will publish in print. Those who have things to say that have least value, the least commercial value, will publish for free, online! It's Gresham's Law:

bad money drives out the good. In a system like the Internet, where most of the coinage is made out of lead, where most of the files have little value, one would be a fool to spend gold coins. You hoard the gold coins and spend your lead nickels on the Internet, since it's the land of the cheap, the home of the free.

Look at the vast amount of governmental data. Stuff that we would walk past if it were on a bookshelf is online. It will be just as boring online as it was when it was on paper. The stuff that is truly valuable, the stuff that you need to know and that you're willing to pay money to find out, will get published in print – because copyrights can be enforced, because there's a sense of permanence about it, because a book is blessed with the veneer of authenticity.

I suspect that, rather than ending publishing, the Web and the Internet will take the lousier manuscripts out of the bookstores and put them online. Good authors will continue to publish real books. Science fiction authors will continue to yearn to get published in hardback. Nonfiction authors will continue to smile when they see their book on a bookshelf. Why would somebody publish terrific ideas online? Somebody else will swipe them and publish them. It happens in science all the time.

Publishing online probably will flop, but who am I to say? Publishers and authors have not made any money off electronic rights other than those to computer games. Nobody's made any money off the Internet rights to anything. But then nobody's ever published a book online, largely because try as you might, you can't read it from a computer. A book is one fantastic device that has been honed and evolved over the centuries into a potent tool for information. It's user-friendly, it's portable, and it's cheap. We have a terrific distribution system for it. It's available to every person who's literate. What more can you ask for? Books are terrific, and I don't think they'll disappear in the near future or in the far future either.

Hypertext is not an adequate substitute for a book. Books have their own hypertext: an index, contents, a footnote, a cross-reference. When hypertext is essential, it's there. When I dug a sewer in my backyard, I needed to know the correct slope for a sewer. I decided to go online and search the Web. I started the browser running, but couldn't find the answer to this obvious question. I went to my public library, got a copy of the Uniform Plumbing Code, the UPC, looked it up, and there it was, a damned useful piece of information. What did I find online? I found thousands of obsolete programs but I couldn't find anything about plumbing.

It costs less than a thousand dollars to make a Web page and put your message up. Therefore, you find lots of commercial messages online, but damn little commerce happening, not just because there's no trustworthy way to exchange money, but because of the marketing triangle. We know, intuitively, that you can get anything either cheap, fast, or good, but you can't get all three at the same time. You can get cheap fast food, but it's not going to be good. You can get good fast food, but it's not going to be cheap. You can get cheap good food, but it won't be fast, because you'll be cooking it up on your stove. This applies to information as well. Those who expect to make gobs of money off the Web and the Internet will have a curious awakening. It won't be rude, because they won't have invested that much, but it will be a curious awakening when they realize the dirty secret of the Internet: people online are phenomenally stingy. They'll spend lots and lots of money on hardware, but they'll avoid spending seventy-five cents on a long distance phone call to another county to log on. They're looking for the cheapest possible way to get things. When online services offer information that people need to pay for, they suddenly discover that not many people want it any longer. They are unwilling to pay even token amounts.

It will be a long while before there is a lot of online commerce. One thing the Internet is missing are salespeople. When you're online, you see catalogs of great stuff. Catalog sales pale in comparison to genuine retail sales. Why? Because there's a trust between the salesperson and the customer. The customer can go back to the salesperson and complain if what was purchased doesn't work. In doing business online, how do I know that a company is going to exist tomorrow, or next week, or next year? In dealing face-to-face, there's a sense of trust, of camaraderie, a realization that the salesperson works for the customer as well as the business. It's an idea as old as commerce. Yet somehow in computing we think that we can avoid salespeople by selling online. I expect that in the next five or six years we'll realize that the great predictions of online malls and Internet commercial bonanzas evaporated into thin air.

I am more at home with plumbers and carpenters than with the gurus of the digital culture. I have the feeling that the world of tomorrow will not be that of the information age. Most of the jobs that we see around us today – bartender, waiter, senator, movie actor, salesperson – do not require computers, probably don't even require faxes, and oftentimes don't require telephones. I suspect that twenty, forty, one hundred years from now, those jobs will still exist, and we'll still need competent, capable people to work them.

THE CITIZEN: <HOWARD RHEINGOLD> Who doesn't like Cliff? He's off-the-wall and charming and nuts. I completely disagree with his brand of Luddism. We need criticism that can discriminate the good from the bad points of new technologies, not a meat-ax approach.

THE IDEALIST: <DENISE CARUSO> Cliff Stoll reminds me of Tigger, the character in *Winnie the Pooh* that has the spring in his tail. I have never seen anyone except a two-year-old with that much energy, intellectually and physically. Or, I might add, as prone to sailing off in different directions.

THE STATESMAN: <STEVE CASE> Cliff Stoll is hyperkinetic. It's unclear to me how genuine his current passion is about the negative aspects of this medium. He has some serious concerns about it, but he has, I'm sure deliberately, overstated the case so dramatically that it now lacks some credibility.

THE DEFENDER: <MIKE GODWIN> A lot of people think Cliff is a curmudgeon or a crank. What he really is, I think, is a holy fool – the guy who sees that the emperor has no clothes and refuses to shut up about it. Such people can be uncomfortable to be around – they specialize in shaking the rest of us up – but Cliff's passions for both knowledge and wisdom, his genuine commitment to leaving the world a better place than he found it, and his irreducible humanity and idealism make me very proud to number him among my closest friends. I love the guy.

THE PATTERN-RECOGNIZER: <ESTHER DYSON> Cliff Stoll is an idealist because he wants everybody to be perfect and he wants everything to be nice.

THE SCRIBE: <JOHN MARKOFF> Stoll is a character, an extremely clever itinerant astronomer, who led me astray eight years ago and started himself on this weird magical mystery tour, which doesn't seem to have ended yet.

THE PUBLISHER: <JANE METCALFE> I'm puzzled by Cliff Stoll, and *Silicon Snake Oil.* Part of me wonders if it isn't his loss of enthusiasm for the sort of labyrinthine development of the Internet that he chronicled so well in his previous book. As these things become business they somehow become less interesting.

<Linda Stone>

The Catalyst

The Seer: <David Bunnell> *Linda is uniquely knowledgeable and plugged in, in a way that makes her one of the best friends you can have.*

Linda Stone is the director of the Virtual Worlds Group in the Microsoft Advanced Technology and Research Division. She has spent more than ten years in high tech, working primarily in multimedia both at Apple Computer and at Microsoft.

"In real space, each place we go has a different sense of place. Places offer mood, personality, and context. When we choose where we want to take a walk or have dinner, carry on a conversation or shop, we do so based on how a place dovetails with how we're feeling, who we will be with or what we hope to accomplish. Likewise, how we dress and how we generally present ourselves impacts the impression we make on others. In part, our lives are a process of developing, tuning, and refining who we are... both to ourselves and to others. At the moment, our cyberspace identity is our email signature."

Linda is a visionary both within Microsoft and to the industry at large. She is also extremely effective in making things happen. Her vision of the Internet is a place that embraces humanity and serendipity and supports rich social interaction, as well as recreation, information, and productivity. She's been promoting this view for years; it is only very recently that the rest of Microsoft has come to the Internet party and thus realized that Linda's work addresses some of the big societal (and business) issues we all face in the immediate future.

"Multimedia," Linda says, "makes it possible for us to create a sense of place and a sense of personal identity in cyberspace that makes use of sounds and pictures as well as text. This takes us to multimedia virtual worlds. Virtual worlds can bring a social and cultural context to the Internet. For better or for worse, chat and social interaction on the Net account for more than 30 percent of hours logged. People crave contact and connection with other people. People-to-people communication is likely to be a killer app on the Net. Virtual worlds are a substrate for people-to-people communication."

Linda began her high-tech career at Apple in 1986, moving to Microsoft in 1993. For years, she has been working at the intersection of art, culture, and technology; to it she brings a background ranging from art to education, cognitive psychology to hardware and software development.

At Apple, she was involved in business development and market development for multimedia, working with developers, the creative community, and the New York publishing crowd. Apple was testing the waters and wanted to understand what a multimedia developer community would look like, what types of products might exist, where multimedia would be sold, and how the industry would take shape. "For a long time, the big joke was that multimedia was a zero-billion-dollar industry," she says. "Multimedia has evolved in some predictable and some unpredictable ways. The same will happen with the Internet."

As director of the Virtual Worlds Group, she has worked for software wizard and industry bon vivant Nathan Myhrvold; she cofounded and has executive responsibilities for the group that developed Microsoft V-Chat and Comic Chat; and she is continuing to develop virtual worlds – multiuser, multimedia environments that run on MSN and the Internet. Linda believes that the person-to-computer interface that was a key focus in the early days of the computer industry is, in today's world of the Net, being superseded by both person-to-person and person-to-self user interfaces. She describes the person-to-self user interface as the way we define our virtual selves, everything from our email signatures to our Web pages to our avatars – all of the things that contribute to our status and reputation on the Net.

Linda is a people person, one of the nicest in the industry. She's also very smart. She is a catalyst: she makes friends, stays in touch with key industry people, and attends major industry events to wave the flag. She's at many events I attend, proselytizing her work with Virtual Worlds and talking to everybody – customers, competitors, friends, and critics of Microsoft.

Since the beginning of 1995, Linda has also seemed to play a role as Microsoft's unofficial goodwill ambassador to the industry. In this regard, Linda, because of her own personal authority, is a strategic corporate asset. No one wants to criticize Microsoft when she is within earshot. No one wants to personally offend this Microsoft executive, who talks openly and affectionately about her years with Apple, and who confides that she used to think of, and nurture, her PowerBook as her child. Linda told me that when she moved to Microsoft she began using a Toshiba laptop. I didn't have the nerve to ask her what, if any, emotional bonding had taken place.

Am I being rational? If so, does it go even deeper? Is the "goodwill ambassador" bit another brilliant smokescreen? Isn't Microsoft Number One because *all* its actions are strategic in nature? When Linda comes up to me at a conference and says, "Hi, John, great to see you!" my wheels start spinning: *who* is after *what*? Has Nathan Myhrvold, aka "The Chef," heard about my mother's recipe for "Brisket Brockman"? (Guess I'd better call my trademark lawyer.) Does Linda's group want to license the exclusive rights to the "Brockman Avatar," that is, the sixteen poses they videotaped at the Microsoft V-Chat launch in New York? (Will they ask me to sign a nondisclosure if I am the product?)

Linda Stone is for real, she's genuine; she's "The Catalyst," the people-to-people communicator.

THE CATALYST: <LINDA STONE> Effective interplay between content and technology is necessary for us to realize the potential of multimedia. Content with poor technology results in inadequate performance and poor usability. Technology without attention to content may perform well, but it is unlikely to have a purpose. Try to imagine a musical recording, a movie, a book, or a magazine article without something creative to say. Empty. So it is with so many CD-ROMs and much of what we see on the Web. Multimedia is more interesting when content and technology work well together. Multimedia products are often loaded with beautiful images, and high-quality video and audio. Yet even the most perfectly produced multimedia product can leave us cold. It is ultimately point of view and interface that breathe life into any media. When the technology works, it disappears – it becomes transparent in a way that facilitates the content.

In 1989, an article I coauthored was published on CD-ROM, *The New Papyrus.* In it, I made the point that the interface is the product. Domino's Pizza is still my favorite example to make this case. We don't buy it for the technology – pizzas are pretty easy to make. We don't buy it for the content – there are many other pizza companies to choose from. We buy Domino's Pizza for the interface. When we call Domino's, we are always greeted quickly and courteously by an efficient person who offers us delivery of a hot pizza in 30 minutes with a free soft drink. The interface is the primary reason most people patronize Domino's. The interface is the product.

With the proliferation of content, the interface and the point of view will be the product. Think of all the Web sites, imagine all the content being generated. How will we ever sift through it all? The interface will be key. The articles, images, and sounds will have to be adequate. The technology will have to be functional. The interface and the point of view will be crucial differentiators.

In my group, artists and programmers work closely together. Most software companies struggle to create a culture where this can happen effectively. Often, there is a kind of mutual disrespect. Programmers always think that artists are a commodity. Artists think programmers are a dime a dozen. It is hard to create a culture where both sides learn and understand how to acknowledge each other, how to listen to each other, how to recognize the very different kind of intelligence each contributes and how to make equal contributions to a project. This is a big part of what my team is doing. With the Virtual Worlds Group, it's been my job to provide a vision, develop a plan to execute that vision, and bring together a team capable of working together to evolve the vision and to drive creation and production. In less than two years, my group has deployed two products and is well on the way with a third. At every turn, we strive to ensure that the creative side and the technical side are working together in a way that allows us to realize our vision.

Virtual worlds are multimedia, multiuser, social meeting places. These worlds are going to be places where people can live on the Net, a sort of home base for the part of our lives we will spend online. When social interaction is integrated into other activities on the Net – games, shopping, information browsing, learning – all these activities can become more engaging. When I first looked at a seemingly endless stream of beautifully produced 3-D shopping malls that had no people, no sense of culture, and no sense of spirit, I thought, Whoa. This place called cyberspace is going to be one lonely, sterile place I won't want to be. There's something wonderful about choosing to go to Soho or the Upper East Side, about going into a neighborhood that has a sense of culture, a sense of place. It seems to me that if we are going to spend more of our lives online, in cyberspace, cyberspace needs to have more humanity.

V-Chat and Comic Chat are both multiuser, multimedia environments in which you can either create a graphical representation of yourself, called an avatar or a character, respectively, or choose a premade avatar. All avatars have the ability to gesture. Instead of existing solely as text, or as a body that is still and lifeless, you have an embodiment, an avatar or character, that has some personality, complete with gestures and idling behavior. When you speak to someone, when you say hello, you can wave. When you ask how someone is, you can smile or flirt. You can be playful in conversation. There's a sense of presence. We have found that this is addictive and very compelling.

The Virtual Worlds Group has worked on both graphical chats and virtual worlds. Virtual worlds have persistence, or a sense of history. This takes us beyond synchronous chat to a world that can evolve, a world that has a life and an existence both when we are there and after we leave. In a virtual world, we can "put down roots," rent a cyberspace apartment, and have a different kind of online life. Virtual worlds can have neighborhoods with distinct personalities. Links can exist, allowing people to move back and forth between virtual worlds and the Web. Virtual worlds can give social context to shopping or information browsing or other activities we might want to do on the Net. Statistics indicate that people spend a tremendous amount of their time online socially interacting with each other.

There are a number of trends that are pushing us to make the Net a rich social place. I will oversimplify to make my point quickly. Before we had automobiles, people were centered in a neighborhood. Because it was hard to get around, one got to know the people nearby through school, work, and worship. Once transportation became accessible, people began to work farther from home, worship farther from home, go to school farther from home. As a result, we have become much more cut off from each other. Many of us don't know our neighbors, or we see them only on the weekends or in the summertime when we're outside gardening. But we still need to connect with each other, and people are now going to cyberspace to reach out to their friends and loved ones and to meet new people.

I'm interested in how technology can be used to enhance communication, and to enhance and enrich our lives. I'm fascinated by the degree to which the computer can help people express themselves and also connect with each other and relate to each other. As a former educator, I'm interested in how people learn, and how people communicate. The Internet is not just about creating highly produced, beautiful information. It is also about creating avatars, places and spaces people can customize and make their own. When people invest in who they are in relation to others and invest in or contribute to a community, they become more committed to how the community evolves. If we expect a sense of community to develop on the Net, people need to be able to participate fully rather than just retrieve information or exist in someone else's creation.

People talk a lot about community. At a talk I attended recently, someone said, "Look at all these buildings. We've created a digital community." To my mind, a community isn't buildings; it's people, places, and their relationship to each other.

Will the increasing presence of technology in our lives bring about the dystopic visions of many science fiction authors or will it serve to enhance our lives and our relationships to one another in some way? It's up to us. It demands our best efforts and intentions.

THE SOFTWARE DEVELOPER: <BILL GATES> Linda's doing very creative work with Virtual Worlds and the kind of social interactions you have there. She's put together a great group. I'm very optimistic about the work she's doing.

THE GENIUS: <W. DANIEL HILLIS> Linda's working on the most important near-term problem for the Net, which is how to use it to enhance human interaction. A lot of us were inspired by Neal Stephenson's *Snow Crash* and said, "Hey, that would be neat." Linda's doing it.

THE IMPRESARIO: <RICHARD SAUL WURMAN> I remember sitting in Tokyo in a restaurant with Linda, Max Whitby, and Chris Cerf. Even though we all knew each other, Linda brought us together – it wouldn't have happened without her. That's one of a number of meetings where her sensitivity to personalities, backed up with her interest, allowed some new thoughts to occur.

THE CYBERANALYST: <SHERRY TURKLE> Linda Stone has a clear and focused mind. She is an exemplary dialogue partner.

<Lew Tucker>

The Evangelist

The Searcher: <Brewster Kahle>

Lew Tucker is Javaman. I've watched as he handled thousands of companies as Java's third-party evangelist. If the intensity of "Internet time" is a test of character, Lew passed the test.

Lew Tucker, trained as a biologist, is the former director of Advanced Development at Thinking Machines Corporation and is the director of JavaSoft's Corporate and ISV Relations for Sun Microsystems, Inc.

I kept hearing about Lew Tucker for years, but never in the context of computers or the Internet. It was about love. I call it "Ottavia's Dilemma."

I refer to my friend Ottavia Bassetti of Milano, "the Princess," as I call her, who had spent a few years in Cambridge, far below her station in life, working as an associate of Danny Hillis at Thinking Machines. When Ottavia showed up one summer's day in 1992 to visit me at Eastover Farm, she was perplexed. She was ready to go back home to the Palazzo (right off Via Monetepoleone) and resume her life in Italy, which included helping her father in his campaign for mayor of Milan.

"I'm lost," she said, with an accent worthy of the best of Fellini. "What am I to do? Live in a small apartment in Cambridge, spend my life programming parallel-processing computers?" "Of course not. So what's the problem?" I replied. "Oh, there is this boy at Thinking Machines. I don't know, I just don't know," she said softly. "Princess," I said incredulously, "are you out of your mind? Get rid of him. Get on with your life. Go back to Milan. You weren't born to live in Geeksville."

Three years later in San Francisco, I am hosting a dinner that includes Cliff Stoll, Mike Godwin, Stewart Brand, and Jaron Lanier. We are waiting patiently for Sun Microsystems's director of JavaSoft's Corporate and ISV Relations and anxious to hear about the implications of "executable content." Finally, he arrives with his lady, who apologizes. "We are so sorry to be late. The baby was cranky," she says in that familiar Italian accent, worthy of the best of Fellini. Then she turns and smiles at Lew Tucker, "The Evangelist."

The Evangelist: <Lew Tucker> When I first heard about Java, I knew that it was the answer. Java was the missing link that connected a number of ideas that had been forming over the years in my head and through discussions with friends and colleagues. Central to these ideas was the concept of "executable content." Executable content involves the delivery of content along with the means by which you interact with it – that is, content tightly linked with software which allows the user to view it or manipulate it in some way. Take for example VCRs and videotapes. While I'm watching the mandatory FBI warning about unauthorized copying, I would like to see my VCR reading in software that would allow me to view the film in any way I choose. This software would be specifically designed for the film itself and distributed with it on the videotape. Once the tape is loaded, I might choose to see the full four-hour director's cut, the ninety-minute theatrical release, or a twenty-minute condensed version. In terms of the Internet, if I were accessing a personal portfolio of stock information, instead of getting an ordinary list, along with the data I'd receive a spreadsheet program that would allow me to manipulate and analyze the portfolio according to my own wishes. This direct delivery of software with content is what I believe is necessary as we move into the digital information world.

When you talk about executable content, you face the following problem: how does the provider know what system the content is going to be viewed on? Today, software is system-dependent. Java is designed to be architecture-independent and run on almost all platforms. Application writers who write to the Java platform don't have to worry about the fact that the user is on a Windows system, a Unix system, or a VCR. Instead, from the developer's point of view, Java allows one to write to a single standard software platform, the Java Virtual Machine.

With Java, in addition to getting content from somebody, you're also getting a program. How do you know it doesn't have a virus? How do you know it isn't going to steal personal information that you have on the system? Java is designed so that the program is actually checked during run-time to make sure it's not doing any damage to your system. The Java environment puts constraints around each program running the executable content in a kind of a padded cell, prohibiting it from accessing files or opening up unauthorized connections.

Because Java is network based, communication is an integral part of Java applications. For example, say you had a Java-based encyclopedia or part of an encyclopedia that is six or twelve months old. Since the software is intrinsically network based, the program can send messages back to the publisher, and get an update and include it automatically. Content is no longer a static thing; it's dynamic, because it uses the network to connect to servers and with other content sources. To be able to do all of this seamlessly, you need standards.

People who are publishing on the Net now use HTML. It is independent of whatever browser or viewer is being used. It's ubiquitous. You can get it with every system today, and it is what has made the World Wide Web so popular. It is limited, however, because it's really just a description language for a page. Additions made to HTML allow it to deal with forms and other ways of interacting, but it is limited by its origin as a page-description language.

Java allows programs to live on top of HTML pages. Because a Java Virtual Machine is installed inside a Web browser such as Netscape Navigator, programs can be run on any machine that runs Netscape. This marriage of Java and the Web is what is causing the enormous popularity of Java and its adoption by today's major computer companies.

Another important attribute of Java is that it's dynamic. In order to construct a browser today, you have to know in advance all the different formats of the data that the browser is going to support. If you don't support that particular kind of format, then you need a helper application, already installed, in order to be able to view that data. The notion behind Java is that when a Java-enabled browser encounters a data type or an image file format that it doesn't understand, the browser can get the code off the Net to view that image format, download the code, and allow you automatically to view it. This opens up a tremendous new playing field for innovation. People who are content providers may find that they can't display the data in one of the traditional HTML formats. Now they're free to invent new formats, because when they invent the new format they also invent Java code that goes along with the content. Java is one of the main enabling technologies on the Internet today and is going to open up a whole range of services that can be provided on the Internet.

Java is also being applied inside corporations. Businesses are finding that keeping their desktops up to date is extremely costly. With Java they only need to have a Java-enabled browser on the desktop. Services or applications to be deployed come across the network from the servers themselves. A user who wants to fill out a travel form or an expense report can at the time of executing the form get the program itself. This means that if an application needs to be changed, the system administrators don't have to reinstall all the software on the desktops. They change the software, which is on the server, and it is automatically downloaded the next time people want to file a form.

A number of vendors are also talking about developing a kind of Internet terminal designed to run the Java Virtual Machine. This shields the application writer from the specifics of the hardware. All they have is a Java-enabled browser, and applications will come over the Net when they are needed. This development is going to have a long-range impact on the entire software industry. Today, publishers are creating software products that typically sell in the $200 to $400 range and are getting tremendously complex. Most people never need to use all the features built into a typical application. One of the properties of Java is that it's a very simple language. It's designed for building very small applications to deliver functionality just when you need it. This aspect of Java is very powerful and poses a great challenge to the software industry as it is today. The distribution model is about to change. The traditional software channel is disappearing.

On the Internet, the cost of delivering products to the consumer is approaching zero.

This change in the distribution model, coupled with the ability to have applications that are very small, dynamic, and updatable by themselves, may lead to a restructuring of the software industry. I believe we will see movement toward a leasing model. If I want to use a particular piece of software to create a presentation, I may need that piece of software only for a couple of hours every month. Why I should have to own it? With a leasing model, whenever I need to use that piece of software, I would get onto the Net and request the very latest and greatest. I would pay for that usage. The next time I came back, I would get the upgraded version automatically.

Vendors themselves have an interest in doing this because it puts them much closer to the customer. They're able to see exactly what the customers are doing with the software, what features they like, and, at the same time, they're able to reduce their distribution costs. Software vending machines will be available on the Net. The downward spiral of software prices, coupled with the ubiquitous nature of the Internet, indicates that the number of different software players will grow. A lot of innovation in software has been stifled by the fact that we've had very big players in the software market; they've dominated distribution channels. It's difficult for a small garage shop with an interesting piece of software to get it out to the market. The Internet levels the playing field. With the reduction in distribution costs, the small players will be able to compete very effectively with the large ones.

Wherever I go, invariably I get asked the question, Why is Java so popular with developers? A lot has to do with its origins. Java was originally designed by James Gosling as a programming language for consumer devices, an area where you simply cannot afford software bugs – you're talking about having millions of devices out in the field. Gosling therefore designed Java as a simple-to-use, object-oriented language. Java has many features that make it easier for programmers to build practically error-free applications. It incorporates features from other popular languages such as C++, Smalltalk, and Lisp, and is therefore familiar and easy to learn. The explosion of interest in Java happened when it became linked to HTML and the Internet.

Sun's Java Web site is now getting around one hundred thousand downloads of the Java Developer's Kit a month. That's a lot of interest. Developers really see Java as the new platform for Internet computing. Java addresses the issue of platform-independence and reduces the development cost of new applications and services.

Java's popularity and potential have attracted widespread support throughout the computer industry, and Sun has adopted an open policy that allows everyone to share a common set of programming interfaces. Even Microsoft has "embraced" Java as a key element in its Internet strategy. What is really important, however, is that for the Java revolution to succeed, these interfaces must be open and available on all systems. This is the only way that we'll get applications that can run anywhere. Microsoft would like to make Java simply a part of their Windows environment and force the developers to write code that only runs in their environment, but this runs counter to the whole idea behind the Java revolution.

Java is quickly evolving from a language for Web computing to become a common software platform covering a wide range of devices. This change, I believe, will have a profound effect on the computer industry. Applications will be written once and run everywhere. Executable content, applets, and agents will be able to move freely about the Net without regard for the underlying hardware or operating systems. Handheld devices, pagers, telephones, and other communication devices will allow us to access the Net from anywhere. Java opens up a whole range of new opportunities. The Net as we know it will fundamentally change as innovative developers exploit the new possibilities.

THE CONSERVATIVE: <DAVID GELERNTER> At Thinking Machines Corporation, Lew Tucker helped create one of the highest-powered computer science research environments ever built. Though Thinking Machines was a losing proposition commercially, it contributed a great deal to the intellectual capital of computer science; Tucker was one of the people who made that possible.

THE GENIUS: <W. DANIEL HILLIS> It's no coincidence that you've got a guy that was trained as a biologist working on getting a language for computers to talk to each other on the Net. He's helping create the first really complicated thing on this planet since biology.

<Sherry Turkle>

The Cyberanalyst

The Pattern-Recognizer: <Esther Dyson>
Sherry Turkle probably understands better than anyone how people transfer their emotions onto the Net: sometimes they go through the Net to other people, but sometimes they just stop at the Net and start having an emotional involvement with the Net itself.

Sherry Turkle is a professor of the sociology of science at MIT. She is the author of *Life on the Screen: Identity in the Age of the Internet* (1995); *The Second Self: Computers and the Human Spirit* (1984); and *Psychoanalytic Politics: Jacques Lacan and Freud's French Revolution* (1978).

When MIT psychologist and sociologist Sherry Turkle was first experimenting with the Internet virtual communities known as MUDs (multiuser domains), she came across a character named Dr. Sherry. This Dr. Sherry had a room set up as an office in the MUD where it was said she interviewed people and handed out questionnaires about the psychology of online life. Turkle was taken aback by this because Dr. Sherry wasn't her or hers. "It was like someone else had used my name as a trademark to mean 'cybershrink,'" she recalls.

This was what Turkle has called in her work an "evocative" experience, an experience that causes you to think about things in new ways. And it offered particularly rich food for thought for Turkle, who has always been at the forefront in the enterprise of examining our interactions with the machines we create. In her landmark book *The Second Self,* Sherry looked at the impact of the personal computer on the way we learn and on our psychological makeup.

There she focused on the one-on-one of person and machine. In the wake of MUDs and other online virtual communities, she turned her attention to how computer-mediated communication has led to dramatically changing concepts of identity, relationships, and community.

Sherry is "The Cyberanalyst." I met her in the late '80s, when she came to New York from Boston to give a Reality Club talk. Since then, I have seen her mesmerize audiences at PC Forum and TED conferences. Don't misread the MIT affiliation. Sherry is a humanist; her background is both literary and psychoanalytic. I place her in *The New York Review of Books* crowd. Such is her fate that she wound up on the cover of the April 1996 issue of *Wired.*

Sherry had a mixed response to the virtual double she encountered in the MUD. She tried to tell herself that having someone create a character by using your name as a trademark was the highest compliment that could be paid in the new virtual world. But she couldn't feel at peace about it, because Dr. Sherry wasn't just a trademark. It was a person, or several persons, talking to people, interacting online.

Then a friend asked her, "What if Dr. Sherry isn't a person at all, but a bot?" A bot is a kind of robot or artificial intelligence that you can build on a MUD to interact with as though it were a person. In other words, Dr. Sherry might be a program, an artificial intelligence. "Faced with the notion of a double that might be a person or might be an artificial intelligence," Sherry says, "I realized that I was in a brave new world. I'm still approached by people on the Net and off who say things like, 'Was it as good for you as it was for me last night, Dr. Sherry?'"

THE CYBERANALYST: <SHERRY TURKLE> One of the things that interests me is the way experiences on the Internet bring philosophical ideas down to earth. For nearly two decades I have been interested in how people make personal connections with ideas, bring ideas into their daily lives. My particular focus has been on the "appropriation" of ideas about the self. The first time I explored this was when I studied the widespread infatuation with Freudian ideas in France that began during the late '60s.

There was a special drama to this new French rage for things Freudian because for the preceding half century, the relationship of France to psychoanalytic ideas had been overtly hostile. With a few exceptions, French philosophers and psychologists, French psychiatrists, and the French public spurned Freudian ideas. But by the mid-1970s, psychoanalysis, particularly as interpreted by a French psychoanalyst, Jacques Lacan, had become quite the rage. Why were things happening this way? What was behind this reversal in Freudian fortunes?

I saw it as an intellectual puzzle, and I went to France to try to solve it. As I came to see things, the May–June 1968 student-worker uprising, almost universally known in French folklore as "the events," turned out to be an important element of the story. The May events had brought large numbers of people to see the personal as the political. And then when the events were over, there was a kind of void. Lacanian psychoanalysis was highly politicized and had theories that tried to bridge the social and the individual. It provided ways to "think through" the problems that had been raised but not resolved by the May events. When I wrote *Psychoanalytic Politics,* I was able to track how the psychoanalytic ideas that caught on – Lacanian ideas about the interpenetration of identity and language, self and society – were those that offered concrete images that facilitated this process of "thinking through." These ideas served as almost-tangible "objects to think with."

During my research I developed a method – how to study ideas in everyday life, ideas as they "hit the street." In this case I was studying psychoanalysis as understood by people who had never been to an analyst or read a word of Freud.

All of this might seem very far from the world of computers, but from the very first days of my joining the MIT faculty in 1976, I was struck by the way computers were carrying new ideas about psychology and philosophy and making them part of everyday understandings. Psychoanalytic ways of seeing the world had been carried by the power of concrete images, and I had thought of them as "objects-to-think-with," but computational ways of seeing the world were actually being carried by concrete objects. I began to look at the way computers were provoking new ways of looking at mind and life and intelligence.

For example, I found that playing with computer objects (including computer toys and games) influenced how children thought about life. Traditionally, children considered the question "What is alive?" by thinking about whether a given object moved "of its own accord," without an outside push or pull. But in the presence of computer objects, children think about the problem of life rather differently. The question becomes not whether objects move of their own accord, but whether they can think of their own accord, whether they are programmed by themselves or by somebody else, whether they know, have intentions, can *cheat.* Computers changed the terms of the discussion about life. And what is true for children is true for adults, although it takes different forms. In *The Second Self,* I wrote about how, in the presence of programmed computers, adults focused on people's spontaneity and lack of "programming" as central to what made them special, and they looked to evolution as central to life. But today, in the presence of computers that in some significant ways do evolve, people are not so sure. The ground is shifting.

The question of how we talk about being alive is a good example of a fundamental philosophical problem being brought down to earth by the presence of the computer. There are others, too, including what is special about people. Twenty years ago, the idea of talking to a computer in the role of a psychotherapist about private, even intimate matters struck most people as very disturbing. They felt that such conversations with a machine were not appropriate. I find that today the most common response to the idea of a conversation with a computer psychotherapist is, "Let me try out your program. It can't hurt. Maybe it'll help me." I call this attitude a new pragmatism. People take the idea of some sort of computer intelligence as a fact of life. What needs to be worked out are the details of how to relate to the new entities. The new pragmatism poses the question, "What are the things that we are willing to render unto the computer as its appropriate domains?" Our sense of what's appropriate in our relationships with computers versus those with people is eroding.

For many years as I looked at the computer as an object that provokes new thinking, I concentrated on the stand-alone machine and what it evoked as a person related to it one-on-one, person-to-computer. But by the late '80s, it was becoming clear to me that experiences on the Internet, where people relate not *to* the computer but to each other *through* the computer, were becoming central to the story of how computers are changing the ways that we think. Experiences on the Internet are bringing a whole new set of ideas "down to earth." This became a central theme of my most recent book, *Life on the Screen.*

For example, while living in France in the 1960s, I had my first exposure to ideas that stressed that the self is constituted by and through language, that there is no simple, centralized unitary ego, that each of us is a multiplicity of parts, fragments, and desiring connections. Sometimes I jokingly refer to such slogans as my "French lessons." I had some intellectual appreciation for what this way of looking at things was about, but my understanding was pretty abstract. This disjuncture between theory and lived experience has always been one of the main reasons why multiple and decentered theories have been slow to catch on – or when they do, why we tend to settle back quickly into older, centralized ways of looking at things.

But many of these same ideas no longer seem abstract or esoteric when you immerse yourself in life on the Internet. For example, the idea that you are constituted by and through language is not an abstract idea if you're confronted with the necessity of creating a character in a MUD. You just have to do it. Your words are your deeds, your words are your body. And you feel these word-deeds and this word-body quite viscerally. Similarly, the idea of multiplicity as a way of thinking about identity is concretized when someone gets an Internet account, is asked to name five "handles" or nicknames for his activities on the system, and finds himself "being" Armani-boy in some online discussions, but Motorcycle-man, Too-serious, Aquinas, and Lipstick in others. In *Life on the Screen,* I argue that just as the events of May–June 1968 in France brought Lacanian and Freudian ideas about politics and the personal down to earth, experiences on the Internet are concretizing a set of ideas about the power of language and the decentralization of the self.

It is important that questions about the psychology of the Internet not be taken in isolation from the way in which our psychological culture is more broadly rethinking the notion of identity. There is a movement within psychology to redefine healthy identity not in terms of a core identity – of a one, of the integration of self into a one – but as someone who is comfortable with the many aspects of self, the many roles that we all play. We no longer talk so much in terms of integrating these roles as of being able to make smooth transitions and having easy and fluid access to all aspects of self. This is a new kind of language. A language of nonpathological multiplicity. On the Internet, people are cycling through many aspects of self as they cycle from window to window. They play somewhat different aspects in different online environments, they present themselves in rather different ways. Of course, this is true of many people's daily life. But the Internet is bringing it home, and in a surprising twist, it is life on the screen that is concretizing the phenomenon, bringing it "down to earth."

We increasingly live in a world where you wake up as a lover, have breakfast as a mother, and drive to work as a lawyer. In the course of a day people go through dramatic transitions, and it's apparent to them that they play multiple roles. Well-functioning people, successful people, happy people, have learned to work through all these roles, to cycle through them in productive and joyful ways. On the Internet you can see yourself functioning with seven windows open on your screen, literally assuming different personae in each of those seven windows, having all kinds of relationships, cycling among and being present to all of these roles simultaneously, having pieces of yourself left in these different windows as programs that you've written which represent you while you attend to another window. Your identity is a distributed presence across a series of windows. Increasingly, life on the screen offers a window onto how we are in our lives off the screen as well: we are people who cycle through aspects of self. But, of course, life on the screen takes that quality of "cycling through" and raises it to a higher power. I think that this is one of the most compelling things about online life: it is so different, but in some profound way we recognize it.

We're too far along in the game to characterize people who live much of their day in this way as aberrant or unhealthy. We are going to work in offices that exist both virtually and physically; we are going to have ongoing relationships that are in both realms. Using the metaphor of cycling through windows to think about the self can no longer be seen as a way of talking that is reserved for "nerds" or "techie types" or "MIT-niks."

People's concerns about online life – that people will lose themselves there, and in particular, that kids spend too much time there – mirror concerns about videogames of a decade ago. In my opinion, the two phenomena have a lot in common. At the beginning of adolescence, young people have always been confronted with an overwhelming set of new circumstances. There's a new body, new social demands, new peer pressures, new relationships to forge with parents. At this point, with all of this going on, young people have traditionally sought a safe place where they could have a sense of total mastery and a place where they could experiment in relatively consequence-free ways. Our culture presently offers precious few such spaces. Life in the world of a videogame or in the confines of online life are such spaces. So computer experiences – to the extent that they offer not just feelings of mastery but the kind of world in which people feel contained and safe – were made for that moment in the developmental cycle. There's no question that when young people find gratification and containment and a safe place to experiment in computational experiences, they may look "addicted." But if the parenting has been good, if they have confidence and self-esteem, and good feelings about their physical body, they are able to move beyond the place of safe mastery. They move beyond videogames to the world of people in which nothing is ever black and white, in which everything is a shade of gray. And now, when it is online life that offers safe places, they start to move from online to offline experiences. They learn to use what they have learned online to make better relationships offline.

Of course, the need for a safe space, the need for a "moratorium" where you can try new things out and work through troubling issues, does not end with adolescence. We revisit the issues of identity over and over in the course of adult life. In my view, cyberspace is one of the key places where these issues are being played out. It is a big part of what makes the Internet so compelling.

In the years when I was studying how personal computers carry philosophy into everyday life, the ideas that the computer carried were about the mind as machine; today, when my focus is the Internet, the ideas that computer-mediated experiences carry tend to be about notions of identity as multiplicity and of society as a web. But, of course, new ways of thinking about such matters do not come to us quickly. These changes take time, proceed with fits and starts. Indeed, I think that we live in a time where we stand betwixt and between the worlds of the modern and postmodern, the mechanical and post-mechanical. Anthropologists call such betwixt-and-between times "liminal." We must learn to live in such times, to embrace the process of rethinking that they engender. It is not productive to yearn for a romanticized past or to glamorize a "future-perfect."

When a new technology is powerful enough, it causes a period of disruption, when a lot of things are up for grabs. For example, with the explosion of online life, we see people preoccupied about how we should think about identity, authenticity, and physical presence. Some people start to talk as though we are already in some idealized digital future, while others fear that we are being "sucked into" virtual reality. The former group tends to devalue the past; the latter group tends to wax nostalgic about a golden age that never was – when people were completely "present" to each other in direct, transparent communities. Between the hype and the fears, between people saying we're already in the future and people longing for the past, I believe that we are missing something really splendid about where we actually are. We're in a moment of creative upset. People who spend time in cyberspace environments where they create avatars who have a "physical" presence experience their bodies in both of these realms. People who have significant relationships "through" their avatars experience their identities in new and complex ways. We are rethinking the notion of what is real.

One of the things that seems most clear to me is that we are not being sucked into the virtual and we are not going to live completely in the physical. We are going to learn to live between two worlds. Already we see that once people meet virtually, they want to meet in the physical realm. Communities that begin in cyberspace start to grow in other places as well. And people who are "offline" friends do more and more of their socializing online. It goes in both directions, and this is how it should be. The challenge is to build a life that embraces all of the possibilities for relating to each other. These are very early days, and we are going to see more and more permeability between the real and the virtual and much less a sense of a boundary between where the physical realm ends and the virtual begins.

One important lesson in all of this is to remind us that people construct the meaning of our technologies. These meanings are not inherent in the technologies themselves. For example, when I first lived in Paris in the late 1960s, I lived with a French family that had just gotten a telephone. The telephone was considered an alien and alienating intruder. They saw its use as essentially for medical emergencies. Its technological mediation was experienced as cold and impersonal. Yet another kind of technological mediation was considered intimate. Important communications, significant communications were conveyed by what was known as the *pneumatique.*

When you sent a *pneumatique,* you wrote a letter and brought it to the post office. There, a postal worker put it into a system of hydraulically powered underground tubes that wove through Paris. The letter came out at the post office in the quarter of Paris where the person destined to receive the letter lived. And then, another postal worker hand-delivered the letter. For me, recollections of the *pneumatique* serve as a reminder that whether a means of communication seems intimate or alienating depends not only on what is intrinsic to the object, but on the social construction of that object. And at the same time, I think that the *pneumatique* has lessons to teach us about what is so compelling about our digital communications. The *pneumatique,* so tied up with hydraulics, with underground pipes and clunky valves, has a kinship with digital communications.

The *pneumatique* took its emotional power not only from how quickly it could be sent and received but from the way it communicated a feeling of intimate, hand-to-hand access. There was a sense of a direct connection between the hand that made physical strokes on a piece of paper, the hand that brought it to the post office, the hand that brought it to its destination, and the hand that received it. With email, we are getting back into a means of communication where, although physically no bodies touch, we have the immediacy and the urgency of the *pneumatique.*

With email, we allow ourselves to speak more informally, we respond quickly; it is a medium, like the *pneumatique,* that is experienced as standing between a letter and a conversation. All kinds of new things are possible. At MIT, most of my students are away from home for the first time. They're very anxious to separate from their parents and to show their independence.

One student described how he was studying for a test very late at night, and his mother, who had just gotten an account with America Online, sent him an email, the first she had ever composed. He wrote her an email in return, telling her that she had done it right and mentioning that he was going to be up all night studying. She, having insomnia, was further experimenting with AOL at four o'clock in the morning and saw that he had responded to her mail. She typed back a note in reply. He was still up studying, so he sent another message. And so, they had a back-and-forth email correspondence-cum-conversation about the pressures of being at MIT and about his anxieties about his first college examination. It was a conversation they never would have had without email. This son would not have found it appropriate to place a telephone call to his mother to discuss his plans to "pull an all-nighter" at MIT or to talk about how frightened he was. Yet with email, all this was possible. It enabled them to be close; the mother felt connected and the son felt comforted. New technologies are rich with possibilities. Our job is to use our self-understanding to exploit them in the way that most enhances our lives.

The Coyote: <John Perry Barlow> Sherry is an academic who has a strong background in rigorous sociological investigation. The methods of traditional academic sociology are going to be critical in maintaining a continuity from the old understandings to the new understandings. She's the only other person I've run across who is thinking about what may end up being the central issue of cyberspace: What is the self?

The Citizen: <Howard Rheingold> One of the very few people who has actually done long-term research into what computers seem to be doing to our minds.

The Seer: <David Bunnell> Although I like her ideas, I don't have time to read the books she writes. I wonder about the people who do.

The Genius: <W. Daniel Hillis> Sherry is really interesting. If you describe to me what she does, I wouldn't guess that I would like it, but I find her books fascinating to read. She reflects back what we're doing and shows it to us in a different light; often from the psychoanalytical angle, and sometimes with a psychoanalytical French accent.

THE MARKETER: <TED LEONSIS> I fell in love with Sherry Turkle on the big screen at the TED conference. Her books are right down the strike zone on what we've been talking about: this new kind of identity that you create, the cyber-personality. I encourage anybody who's going to program and try and make a business in the consumer arena to read her books, because she's got her finger on the pulse of what people do, as opposed to what they say they do, online.

THE IMPRESARIO: <RICHARD SAUL WURMAN> Sherry has brought personification into electronic communication. Much as Lou Kahn asked a building or a brick what it wants to be, she is asking seemingly simple-minded but prophetic questions of electronic communications – what it wants to be.

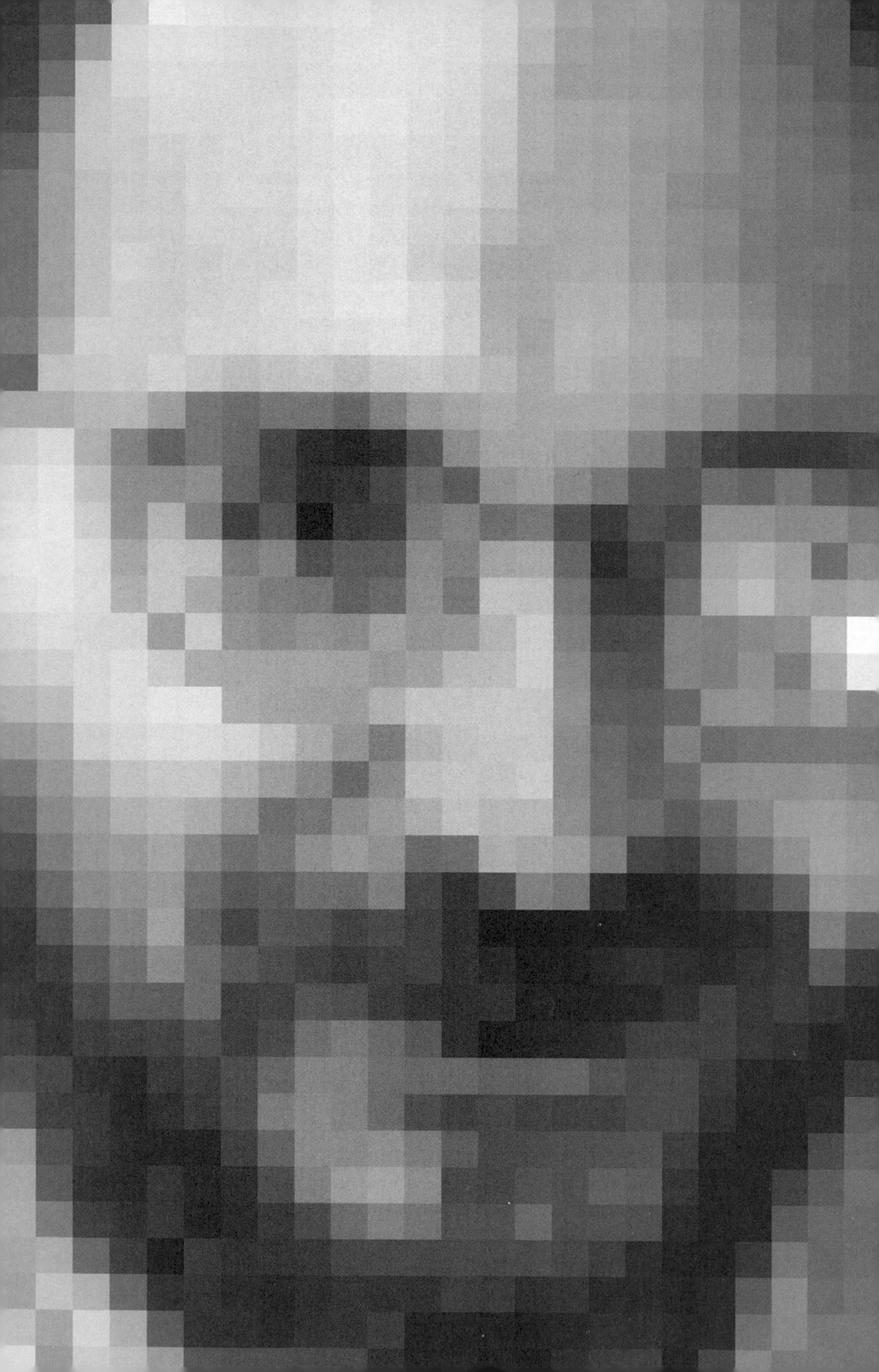

<DAVE WINER>

THE LOVER

THE STATESMAN: <STEVE CASE> *He's come out of nowhere to emerge as one of the poets of cyberspace.* DaveNet *is always quite engaging, and his ability, his willingness, to open himself up to say whatever's on his mind is quite impressive.*

DAVE WINER is a software developer and the publisher of *DaveNet*.

Part of the *DaveNet* Web site, January 17, 1996:

Big Fear in MacLand

Almost 80 percent of the people coming thru hotwired.com are using Windows, and that percentage has been going up steadily. The relative advantage that Macintosh used to enjoy is dissipating. The opportunity to grow significantly by being the best net client has faded.

We need a strategy for this thing! Is it finally clear that it isn't going to come from Cupertino? I've been saying this for over a year now. We're going to turn the platform in a whole new direction. Get it more in line with what's happening in the world around it.

We're getting into Windows. We have to. There's no Java for the Macintosh. Big fear in MacLand - Mac Netscape 2.0 may go golden without Java support. Big fear and big anger. How did this happen? Who's screwing who?

So if you're a net content developer, like I am, there's a Windows machine sitting next to your Mac now. The need for this just happened in the last two weeks, in my life at least. I'm always late for these platform things.

Every couple of days, a printout of an email like this lands on my desk. A new issue of *DaveNet* has arrived.

Dave Winer, software developer, is also webmaster, author, CEO, and janitor of *DaveNet*, a publishing phenomenon that is an example of what's possible on the Internet within the constraints of current technology and within the constraints of revenue models for doing business on the Web.

DaveNet is an ongoing rant – at Apple, at Microsoft, at the Web community at large. The subject, usually topical, depends on his mood. A typical *DaveNet* may start out with Dave commenting on a rock song he's listening to at 5 A.M. Then he may start "singing," even "crooning," the lyrics – his brave attempt at creating virtual karaoke in ASCII text.

Having warmed up, Dave begins to roll. He tells Gil Amelio, the new CEO of Apple, how to reorganize the company. He opens a debate between Microsoft and Netscape software engineers on open standards. He tells the online services not to read his email. He lectures the industry and the government on the First Amendment. He falls in love and ends friendships. He stirs the pot and gets people going at each other. All this is suffused with his signature message: love.

Did you report a $700 million loss last quarter? Did you write the strategic plan for the coming year for your company and leave out something called the Internet? Dave understands. He loves you. Dave shares your pain. He has a dream: you are a child sleeping in the safety and comfort of his loving arms; he carries you to a lush green cliff high above the sea and gently awakens you to a sparkling new day radiating positive energy. He wants to share this with you and with a thousand other close friends, including your employees and competitors. You can have his scripting language. It's free. Everything beautiful is free. We are all free. Did you come home early from an Apple developer's conference and find your wife in bed with a guy from Seattle? Dave knows. He counsels you on how to love the passion they feel for each other.

All this comes in an eminently readable voice, which makes it hard to put down. Unless you are the kind of person who considers Dave's occasional violence to the English language a cause for alarm:

> The *www.suck.com* parody stung a little. They mocked me. PS I love you! they said. Get it? A Beatles song. Cute! Very nice. I do love you, yes, but I've never said it before. I felt it was too early in the relationship. Everyone I knew said how cool it is (notice, only two *o*'s) to be mocked by *www.suck.com.* I became a bit more self-conscious about my writing. Maybe I should stop using so many *o*'s?
>
> Maybe they're right - that too many *o*'s is not a goooood thing?
>
> What about it?
>
> No way!
>
> Coooooooooool.
>
> And to all the people who say I use too many *o*'s - get a life! There's hunger in the world. They're censoring the net. AIDS is ripping up our culture. Why do you have time to care how many *o*'s I use? Hmmm. Not likely. I don't usually give advice but this time I'll make an exception - give it up.
>
> The geeks are buzzed.

I loooooove *DaveNet.* And since it comes to me as email, I don't have to waste time logging on to my Internet service provider and finding Dave's site, which inevitably takes minutes. Dave sends it to his personal list of about one thousand industry insiders. It is also available (and archived) on his Web site, where it is read by another thirty-five thousand people. If you are among Dave's privileged one thousand, you know you are in good company, but you never get a look at his complete mailing list. Every *DaveNet* carries your name in the address list, along with a dozen other addressees. The other names and email addresses are always different. This week you are on a list with Jean-Louis Gassée and John Doerr. Last week you were in the company of Bill Gates, Howard Rheingold, and Marc Andreessen. Next week, it may be Mike Markkula and Ted Leonsis.

Dave knows about communities. In fact, I sense from what he tells me that one reason he lives on the edge of the continent, in San Francisco, is to get as far away as possible from the community he came from. He takes from that world, and brings to *DaveNet,* the agitation and the tumult that occur in a real community where people interact with each other in real time and physical space.

DaveNet shows that content is community. Many people pay lip service to this concept, but Dave executes. *DaveNet* is a real community. First, everybody who receives *DaveNet* knows everybody else, either personally or by reputation within the industry. Second, a response to a *DaveNet* issue will be read by the people who count in the industry. Third, Dave encourages response, emotion, and passion. People go at each other over issues that matter to themselves, to each other, and to the wider world. Such a discourse within this community can have real consequences.

Today's conventional wisdom is that the name of the game is market share. Piss on a hydrant in cyberspace and in three years you may be one of the survivors who will emerge from the wreckage to dominate the biggest market in history. Watch how the media conglomerates hemorrhage cash, how the start-ups plan to lose millions, how the online services continue to cover the reported losses by floating more stock.

"What's nice about *DaveNet,*" Dave says, "is that I don't need any money to do what I do. I don't require an editorial staff, and I don't need a printing press. Therefore, I don't have anybody telling me what I can write. I also have a lead time that is the envy of every journalist in every other medium. If a news story comes out and I get it first, I can be out on the street in ten minutes. There's never been a medium like this, with that kind of immediacy. It changes the way news happens. It also changes the way opinion happens."

Dave's dream in his software life is to have a great collaboration between people who don't necessarily work at the same company. "Software is not a corporate thing, by nature," he says. "It's an individual thing, and the corporate interests, the guys in the suits, get in the way."

Dave Winer is "The Lover."

THE LOVER: <DAVE WINER> I wake up at about four o'clock on the mornings I'm going to write, and I put on some music. I tend to listen to albums, or one song over and over again. I warm up by writing an intro that's about the music. I usually leave that in because I think it helps the reader warm up, too. I also want at some point to write more about music, and have music be part of the stuff, so I like leaving that in. Of course, at HotWired, that stuff is always edited out. I don't particularly like being edited.

I actually have two Web sites. There is my own Web site, which is complete. It has everything unedited. There is a section of the HotWired Web site called *DaveNet.* It has one piece per week, appearing every Thursday. That goes through an edit cycle. I've probably got three hundred pieces I've written so far, and if you printed them all out, they would probably add up to a two-thousand-page book.

I try not to mix up too much of my business as a software developer and what I'm interested in as a writer. On the other hand, I don't make any pretense of being free of conflicts. I'm a software developer, and that's the perspective I write from. If you're disinterested, you're not interesting, right?

DaveNet was started by accident. I had no idea that it was going to turn into anything at all. I had taken an eight-month vacation from the software business because what I was doing wasn't working, and I was tired. I had a relationship break up, right around the same time, so I wasn't in the mood to work at all. I spent eight months playing and traveling and doing things to feel good. I was getting involved in people's lives, in a nice way. A friend of mine, Marc Canter, was starting up a new company and rolling out a product, and he was going to have a press conference. I had a great Rolodex of electronic mail addresses that I had accumulated over the years, and I had a great set of scripts for distributing email messages. So I sent a notice out to all those people, using these scripts, encouraging them to come and see Marc. Then, at the press conference, he had a list in his press kit: the ten things that he wanted the media to know about multimedia.

Marc, in my book, is the leader in multimedia. He was the developer of Macromedia Director. It's the standard. More importantly, Marc has, and I hate to use the word, *vision*. When Marc says something, I tend to listen. I took his list, typed out the ten things, and sent it out to my list of people. Then I realized I had created a publishing platform that I could use for my own writing. Floating around the industry at the time was the notion that Apple and IBM might get together. I wrote a business plan for them and sent it via email to the executives at IBM and Apple. They did not respond, so I thought, Why don't I send it to the same list I sent Marc's stuff to? So I did, and I got responses from a lot of people.

I wrote a couple of other reports. I'd explored PDAs, drawn some conclusions about what were smart bets, so I wrote a report. Again, it was very opinionated. I published it and got a reply from Randy Battat, an executive at Motorola in charge of PDAs. He wrote a very thoughtful piece, and I published it. I got the idea that I could write something and then, almost like a teacher, call on somebody to respond. This was publishing on the Internet. I was starting to play around with the World Wide Web. I'd gotten an ISP account and was using Eudora. Then I had a flash, a real flash of insight. That flash was coupled with something Bill Gates had said at a conference – that he was betting his company on The Microsoft Network. He denies having said it; he denied having said it at the time, too. His current argument is, How could it be a bet-the-company move for a company that has $18 billion in cash in its pocket? I only meant that it's about the company in the very broadest sense, that Microsoft's position in our industry is vastly diminished today from what it was when I wrote the piece, in late 1994.

My premise was that what had happened was irrevocable, that basically the standards of the software industry were irrelevant at that point. Very quietly, unnoticed by the software industry, the standards of the Internet came along, were effective, were supported by all the vendors, and would be supported by all the platforms in the future. The amazing thing was that none of those standards came from Apple or IBM or Novell.

API stands for application programming interface, a very important concept in software. Software is made out of layers, and the things that connect layers to each other are called APIs. Every important thing in software, if it's going to be built on, has to have an API. The Internet itself really is nothing, yet it's everything. It's all the APIs, all the software written for these standards, but in the end, all it is is a bunch of agreements between people about the way we're going to have our software work together. These open platforms are not done Microsoft style, where it tells everyone what to do after becoming part of these agreements.

Maybe Bill is right, in which case we go back to where we were in 1994, when we were all waiting for Bill to implement new software tools before the rest of us could do anything. As a software developer, I find this extremely boring. I don't want to wait. I'd rather go sailing, or make pottery, or raise a family. I like this world where Bill Gates is one of us. He's a very big one of us, he's a very powerful one of us. I have an enormous respect for Bill, because of the way Microsoft has risen to the challenge of the Internet. I don't want to see him win, but on the other hand I know that if he wins this one and gets his way again, it means a change of direction, a reversal on Microsoft's part: if it makes it through this transition as an important leader, the company will have completely changed, and, I don't *think* he had any desire to completely change his way of doing business.

So far he's trying to compromise by taking "embrace and extend" to a new level – to an embrace of the style of the Net. But few people ask the question, "If Netscape's power is diminished, will Gates revert back to the system that was in place in the early '90s, when Microsoft controlled the evolution of all PC standards?"

In that sense, he decided that Microsoft was going to become an Internet company, and damn it, he didn't know. He was behind the curve. That was the starting point for *DaveNet,* because what I received back then was a very strong response from Gates. Everybody was blown away that you could get this kind of interaction. All I did was use the power that everybody else has on the Internet. I didn't need to be anything or do anything more, other than have an opinion, and state it in a way that it evoked a reply from somebody, and it was interesting. All it has to be is interesting.

I'm delighted that *DaveNet* turned out that way. It gives me a real sense of power, and a way to influence the future. I often have these mini-epiphanies. I'm just frustrated, and I can't stand that the world is a certain way. I have to remind myself that I can do something about it, that I don't have to feel powerless or silent about these things, I can actually make something happen. I want to be the Barbara Walters of the Internet.

Other people are impressed by the size of a company and that guides their choices, but I would prefer to work with great people, and to me it doesn't matter whether they're independent, inside a small company, or inside a huge company.

I would work with Microsoft any day of the week. In January 1996 *DaveNet* was a sparring platform for Bill Gates and Marc Andreessen. My mailbox was filled with stuff from people who were shooting each other. Fascinating. When appropriate I would run the pieces, because this was when things were really moving.

It's very lucky for Apple that Netscape decided to do a Macintosh version. It's also very lucky for Netscape, because if it didn't have the second platform, the company would be controlled by Microsoft now. The fact that Netscape did a creditable if not perfect job supporting the Mac platform means that Microsoft has to do it too. Microsoft's Explorer on the Mac is a very nice piece of software. I wouldn't say that if it weren't true. Leadership is important, and so now that we've got Microsoft investing in the Macintosh platform, which is exciting, leadership makes a difference.

While *DaveNet* comes by email right now, at some point it's going to come via Java. I want a higher fidelity. The nice thing about the Web over email is that I have more control over how things look. That's one aspect of it. The really important one, though, is that I get to link. Linking is an art form that you haven't seen in any other medium, and it's one that we're just starting to explore. You're able to do that in electronic mail, if you have the right kind of an email client.

I have to wear a lot of different hats. In some contexts, I have my opinion and that's what counts. When I wrote about Rick Smolan's project, *24 Hours in Cyberspace,* I gave you exactly what I believed: that this was a friend of mine, that I thought I understood where he was coming from, that he had an opportunity to make history doing what he does, and that I was very disappointed. Then, putting on another hat, here I am promoting free speech on the Internet. All I was asking Smolan to do was to not let Al Gore write about the environment on the same day the administration was clamping down on free speech on the Net, by signing the CDA.

The Clinton administration knows exactly what it's doing. It is maintaining the power structure as it exists without any change. The administration does not want the Internet to change anything. It wants to make it through this whole Internet thing completely unscathed, with no change in the flow of money. You read *The New York Times,* and they talk about the new media industry in New York, and how wonderful it is we've got this new media industry, and they're so damn arrogant about it. Not *The New York Times* particularly, but that whole group of people from the advertising industry believe that this is a one-way medium, just like television is.

What I like so much about it is what they absolutely don't like, the fact that I have no filters on me at all. If I wanted to get on TV, on broadcast or cable TV, I would have to go through a whole bunch of filters that would edit me, and take a lot of the controversy out of it, take the immediacy out of it. Lead times would get introduced, all this stuff would tend to flatten it out. That's really what they want to give us. They want to give us that, and the nature of this medium is that it really isn't controllable. Even if they can put you in jail, they really can't control the broad discussion that goes on this medium.

Next time you talk to Markoff, ask him why the fuck *The New York Times* waited months before they ran an editorial about free speech on the Internet. Ask him what the hell he's doing there – he's supposed to be one of the digerati. Ask Denise Caruso the same question.

Corporate Web sites are going to sterilize everything they can possibly get their hands on. There's got to be a little element of fear that the Web is going to be fun. It's got to provoke a sense of excitement. The kind of things that the corporate people are putting out there on the Web are anachronisms. They're the result of a business plan that says, we're going to do this much business over the Web. What we really need is more experimentation, trial and error, having fun, playing a little bit, losing a few times – that's how technology moves forward.

CNN has a really nice Web site. I go there all the time. Of all of the East Coast media companies, they get it. They understand what their role is in this medium. *The New York Times* totally misses it. That's disappointing to me, having grown up reading *The New York Times* and admiring and respecting it, and thinking, it was going to be wonderful when the *Times* finally showed up in this medium. *Suck* is interesting, but it may have run its course at this point. You can only take so much negativism and sarcasm and adolescent humor. They're very negative people. They're writing about negative things. There never will be a shortage of that on the Web, but I find it's getting boring. I like what the software industry has done in online publications. IDG's *Infoworld Online* is excellent. I keep going back to it. I get what I'm supposed to get out of that, which is more than daily coverage. If something happens, I want to be able to find out about it quickly.

The next killer Web site is going to be one where you can be pretty much sure that if something has just happened, they will have a pointer to what it is that just happened. This is going to be the highest-flow place on the Web. The Web itself holds a lot of news. And the search engines lack the currency, they don't index events immediately. It might take a month before a search engine can get you a comprehensive list of all the places you can go to find information about the Unabomber, who became kind of a Web phenomenon in his own right. Yet you had to go find the information for yourself, and it was not well organized. But if an event such as the Unabomber's arrest is happening, I should be able to find a place where I can go, the Unabomber page, where some group of people is working on getting that story, and the minute something comes online you get a pointer, so this acts like a focal point, a place to come through.

THE MARKETER: <TED LEONSIS> Dave Winer is a curmudgeon. He sends me a daily rant. I would say that every day is a Dave rant day on *DaveNet*. I would encourage everyone to get on his mailing list because he writes funny stuff.

THE PRAGMATIST: <STEWART ALSOP>
"The Lover?" Big change from his early positioning as "The Nerd."

THE GADFLY: <JOHN C. DVORAK> Go to *DaveNet* on the Web. It says it all.

THE CATALYST: <LINDA STONE> He wears his heart (size XL) on his sleeve. He's passionate about what he perceives to be right or wrong, passionate about his beliefs.

<Richard Saul Wurman>
The Impresario

The Scout: <Stewart Brand> *There's a sharp designer and an able business mind behind all that persiflage.*

Richard Saul Wurman is the chairman and creative director of the TED conferences. He is also an architect, a cartographer, the creator of the Access Travel Guide Series, and the author and designer of more than sixty books, including *Information Architects* (1996), *Follow the Yellow Brick Road* (1991), and *Information Anxiety* (1989).

The annual TED Conference is a three-day party of leading people in technology (T), entertainment (E), and design (D). Before anyone had begun to raise the issue, Richard Saul "Ricky" Wurman was smart enough to understand that personal isolation and loneliness would be the fallout from the personal computer revolution and its "enhancement" of personal communications. In TED, he created a conference that could always be described by these adjectives: "warm and fuzzy."

Somebody should have warned me. In 1995, Ricky invited me to appear at TED in Monterey, California, on a panel that followed a group of talks. In TED fashion, these talks are presented without follow-up questions or cross-examination. Feels good, warm, and fuzzy. So what if some of the people who get up on stage are full of shit?

My TED career came and went with a single comment, as I turned to one of the speakers who had just given what, in my opinion, was "The Emperor's New Talk." "I have no idea what you're talking about," I said. "You don't either." A hush fell over the auditorium, a pall over the panel. Ricky quickly put an end to the session.

Later, Kevin Kelly raced up to me in the lobby. He was the most animated I had seen him in fifteen years. "Wow! You bombed big-time! It was as bad as Madonna handing David Letterman the dead mouse. Everybody hated it. You should have been in the audience." Next Linda Stone: "How could you? How could you do that?" Then Denise Caruso: "John, that was completely unnecessary, especially to such a nice guy." Others were as vehement in their approval. This feedback continued for two days, culminating on the last day, when Tom Reilly exhorted the audience from the podium to denounce me by acclamation. Too bad John Markoff wasn't there to cover it for *The New York Times.* (The "Suckśters" were. You can read all about it in *Suck* on the World Wide Web.) By the way, I had a great time. I'll be back.

Some would say Ricky Wurman is an acquired taste. He's an artist in the McLuhanesque vein. He's a sensing device out in front of everyone who sends back signals telling us where we are, and who we are. To make his point, he says, "When I pick up a book, if it's a novel, I know that I have so many more pages to read. I know where I am in the story. When I watch a movie that I know is two hours, I know that no matter what happens in the first five minutes, it's not the end of the movie. It's going to take two hours to go through the plot. I have a sense of where I am. This is not a trivial issue. It gives me a base. It's a centering thing."

In the last few years, he has called himself an "information architect." "That I happen to be an architect," he says, "is only coincidental, because when I use the term *information architect,* it has nothing to do with architecture, the career I was trained in. An information architect is concerned with the systemic but artful organization of information."

Richard Saul Wurman is "The Impresario."

The Impresario: <Richard Saul Wurman> Human beings have a subliminal sense of orientation that makes them feel comfortable. You lose it when you go to a strange city. You don't know if you're landing east, west, south, north of it. You don't know how far it is into the city. You don't know where you are. That lack of orientation makes you feel strange. There is a need for computer information databases that give you this sense of orientation. In a book, in a database, in anything where time and story are involved, this is important. The scrolling of type through a screen doesn't give me that. I never know where I am.

The fundamental task of the information architect is to make information understandable. My passion has always been making the complex clear – clarifying, rather than simplifying it – and I have been talking about this for thirty years. Today, with the explosion of data, there is a crying need for this profession. We are going to have to be able to find patterns in data and organize it in ways that are understandable.

I look for the beginning patterns. I get excited when I have one of those epiphanies, where I see a pattern and say, "My God, that's always been there. I vaguely remember seeing it, but today I understand it." I'm a welter of insecurities. I'm insecure about not understanding what the next person does, about not being as smart as the people listening to me, about teaching in schools that I could never get into, about running conferences where everybody is sharper and faster than I am. The only thing that gives me a nibble of happiness and security is that I'm able to come up with ideas that have the words *of course* attached to them: "Of course, that's the pattern. Of course, that's what's happening." Some of that has to do with the organization of information in my books, and some has to do with the idea of "TEDology" – the merging of the technology business, the entertainment industry, and the design professions.

In this regard, the next three to five years are going to be an important time for business. In the past, it was possible to get along by doing a much better version of what you were doing previously. In the future, you're going to die on the vine if you do only a better version of what you're already doing. It will be increasingly important to explore alternatives, parallel ways of buying and selling ideas, services, products, et cetera, in brief transactions.

When I talk about transactions, the image that comes into people's minds is high-tech transactions on the tube. They think about the future of transactions in a single-dimensional way: the Net, the computer, AOL or some service. It's more complex than that. The image I have in my mind is the barbell that the strong man lifted, the old-fashioned kind with a big round iron ball on either end. In 1984, John Naisbitt talked about high-tech/high-touch and the polarization of these two movements. He gave me reason to feel that my tech conference would always be successful, because the more that people didn't have to come because of high-tech developments in teleconferencing and email, the more they would come. That polarization would make them want to come even more.

Something else is happening that is even more interesting. The fuzzy, warm, high-touch ways of selling are going to be created by high technology. Your ability to get a pair of custom-made Levis, which is a fuzzy, warm thing, is brought to you by the people who bring you technology. It's the kiss of those two balls that will result in the successful selling of services and goods in the next three to five years. What does that mean to the Internet, and how does it affect using your computer or being online? There's no certainty about how you're going to get information. It hasn't happened yet, but we're at the cusp of it happening.

For five years, I've been upset about the fundamental direction in which all interface design has gone. It started with infoclutter and the metaphor of an airplane cockpit. With so many choices on the screen, so many more things than you could possibly use, you can't look at all of them, so you always feel guilty. There's so much stuff that you can't see where you are. I want to figure out how to do an interface that gives you a sense of orientation, provides you with the right amount of information, and allows you to find out what you want to find out without having to push lots of buttons. Solving that interface issue will radically change the material we can be comfortable with on the screen.

I am against the idea of customized newspapers that cut out the serendipity of life. The one moment of serendipity you have on a regular basis is the newspaper, where you can see things you don't look for. God almighty, that's terrific! Serendipity is the open stacks in the library, where you discover a book you didn't go there for. These experiences expand your life, rather than narrow it. They seem like soft and fuzzy things, but they are the basis of how you design, the basis of interface, the basis of conference giving. They're the basis of purchasing and buying. They're the basis of understanding. My search is to find the little things that help you, little things like pagination in a book, which seem so obvious once they've been done. The best comment someone could say about something I invented would be, "We always had that, didn't we? That's the way it was always done."

I am a bit of a voyeur, and I like to observe people coming together in different ways. I am fascinated by the metaphor of a good dinner party. Your respect for and confidence in the host or hostess gives you the desire to make a connection with the person sitting to your left or your right, even though you don't know who they are. Everyone at the party has been invited for a just reason, and there is value in exploring the potential epiphanies that can come from engaging in conversation. There's nothing that human beings do much better than conversation. In fact, my definition of a good marriage is when you'd rather have dinner with your wife than with your wife and another couple. The best reason for companionship is the extraordinary conversation. Marriage is the celebration of conversation.

When we design communication systems, we try to streamline them and take away some of the richness. We edit books so they don't sound like somebody talking. We do these things in the name of good taste and good style, in the name of seeming smart and seeming clear, but I am constantly on a quest for a Holy Grail that allows me, in real time, in print, and electronically, to engage in a wonderful conversation with another human being. That element of excitement that happens in the privacy of a conversation with another human being needs to come into the experience you have when you're sitting in front of a computer. If we can do that, you will be able to find your personal path. We need a computer that can nod – a nod of response, acknowledgment, and understanding.

The Catalyst: <Linda Stone> Ricky Wurman throws the greatest party. How can you not want to go to Ricky's party once a year? Ricky puts people together and he puts events together. He is at once whiny and obnoxious and endearing. He has made so many contributions over the years, as an architect and a designer, in what he's done with books and what he's done with conferences.

THE SCRIBE: <JOHN MARKOFF> Richard Saul Wurman is the guy I'd never met before in my life who had me on stage and gave me a big schmoozy hug in front of six hundred people, making me feel entirely creepy. Then after he gave the other speakers little gift bags, he didn't give me one, so I'm still pissed.

THE IDEALIST: <DENISE CARUSO> Richard Saul Wurman is Richard Saul Wurman. In spades.

THE CYBERANALYST: <SHERRY TURKLE> Richard Wurman shows you how to look at things a little differently, and then, after trying it his way, you usually can't imagine how you did things any other way. Richard's design sensibility has changed the way I hold meetings, plan my travel, and light my office.

EPILOGUE

1996

"Sit down, we have to talk," my wife (and partner) Katinka Matson said to me in a serious tone of voice. It was 2 A.M. and I was just walking in the door from a trip to the West Coast. "You and David have a competitor."

Katinka meant a competitor to Content.Com, Inc., the Internet publishing company I had started with David Bunnell nearly eight months before. Still searching for a coherent revenue model for launching a large-scale publishing venture on the Internet, we had decided to let it rest temporarily, even though we had been successful in persuading dozens of book publishers internationally to participate in a facet of our program which we were calling "Book Channel."

A competitor? I frankly had not seen competition as a problem. My ideas are yours for the taking. Execution is what counts, that's what I get paid for. I believed that no one would be able to duplicate our strategy or our program.

"OK, who is it?" I asked, as I poured a cup of coffee. I could tell it was going to be a long night.

"Shhh," she hushed. "He's asleep," she said glancing at the door to the room of our son Max, who had just turned sixteen.

"Max??" I exclaimed, my voice rising in anger. "OK, let's have it."

"Well," she explained, "your son announced at dinner that he's launching his own channel, on the school Web site, and it involves books."

"So what's the big deal?" I said.

"Uhh," she paused, "it's just that he sent email messages to all the companies doing books on the Net and offered to link with them."

"Using my name??" I exclaimed.

"No," she replied evenly, "he used his name, which happens to be the same as yours."

"That little bastard, I'll kill him," I muttered. (I could have sworn I heard my own father's voice amplified in my head). "Why didn't I get him to sign a nondisclosure?"

"Look," she replied, "be happy you have a son that appreciates your business plan and also knows how to execute."

"OK, but David will sue his butt off," I said.

The next day I had calmed down enough to have a serious talk with Max. I realized that since his "Mac vs. Windows" battle months before with Dr. Eddie Currie, I had scarcely seen him around the house except for meals. The door to his room was usually closed, the red light glowing on the phones indicating he was online. And when he did show his face, he was suddenly (and strangely) disinterested in all matters digital, especially Content.Com, Inc.

"Face it, Dad," Max said calmly when we sat down to talk, "you're too old, and David's too tired. While you guys have been taking meetings I've built a Web site. I'm getting my team together, and we're up and running by the end of the year."

"Now listen to me, –"

"Dad," Max interrupted, "I don't mean to be disrespectful, but it's kids like me that are going to be the pioneers and make this thing happen. We're the digerati."

"Great, go for it," I replied, "but just remember three things. First, pioneers are the guys with arrows in their backs. Second, we learn by making mistakes. Failing young might be a very positive experience; you could make your comeback in college. Third, there is always the very real possibility that you're successful. Then you may want to keep in mind what Gregory Bateson once said to me – 'Of all our human inventions, economic man is by far the dullest.'"

"Sure, Dad. One more thing. You know my Mac," Max said referring to his PowerPC 7500/100. (Yes I did know his Mac, and I was sure he was about to hit me up for a 200MHz upgrade card). "Uh, there's more stuff I could be doing with my site but a lot of the really cool software isn't available for Mac."

"So?"

"So, Dad, let's go 'bi-platform.' How about buying a Windows machine to have around the house. You know, just to use for the Net. There's room in my bedroom next to the Mac. And don't worry about Windows 95. Dr. Currie told me to go right into Windows NT. He'll help me with the setup. Oh, and Dad, I might need just a teeny bit more memory to do my video stuff using Director. Markoff wants me to get at least 80MB. Oh, right, before I forget, Dad, do you remember those new 1GB removable drive cartridges Dvorak told me about? They're really neat for storing multimedia files...."

digerati.edge.org

Digerati is an ongoing project. Digerati, the Web site *(digerati.edge.org)*, carries forward the discourse and presents new ideas from people in the book, as well as introducing the work and thoughts of other digerati. The site will feature audio and video from the encounters in an interactive format that allows readers of the book and others to join the digerati and engage in the discourse. The Digerati Web site is being developed as part of a broader program under the auspices of Edge Foundation, Inc., established in 1988 as an outgrowth of a group known as The Reality Club. Its informal membership includes of some of the most interesting minds in the world.

Since 1981, The Reality Club has had a simple criterion for choosing speakers. We look for people whose creative work has expanded our notion of who and what we are. A few Reality Club speakers are bestselling authors or are famous in the mass culture. Most are not. Rather, we encourage work on the cutting edge of the culture, and the investigation of ideas that have not been generally exposed. We are interested in "thinking smart"; we aren't interested in the anesthesiology of "wisdom." The motto of the Club is "to arrive at the edge of the world's knowledge, seek out the most complex and sophisticated minds, put them in a room together, and have them ask each other the questions they are asking themselves."

We charge the speakers to represent an idea of reality by describing their creative work, their lives, and the questions they are asking themselves. We also want them to share with us the boundaries of their knowledge and experience and to respond to the challenges, comments, criticisms, and insights of the members. The Reality Club is a point of view, not just a group of people. Reality is an agreement. The constant shifting of metaphors, the intensity with which we advance our ideas to each other – this is what intellectuals do. The Reality Club draws attention to the larger context of intellectual life.

The Reality Club is different from The Algonquin, The Apostles, The Bloomsbury Group, or The Club, but it offers the same quality of intellectual adventure. Perhaps the closest resemblance is to the early nineteenth-century Lunar Society of Birmingham, an informal club of the leading cultural figures of the new industrial age – James Watt, Erasmus Darwin, Josiah Wedgewood, Joseph Priestly, Benjamin Franklin. In a similar fashion, The Reality Club is an attempt to gather together those who are exploring the themes of the post-industrial age.

The more than one hundred and fifty individuals who have made presentations at Reality Club meetings or Edge Seminars over the years include a wide range of people in the arts and sciences: philosopher Daniel C. Dennett; scientists Richard Dawkins, Freeman Dyson, Murray Gell-Mann, Stephen Jay Gould, Stewart Kauffman, Benoit Mandelbrot, and Lynn Margulis; psychologists Mihaly Csikszentmihalyi, Howard Gardner, Steven Pinker, and Roger Schank; artists Gretchen Bender, Peter Halley, April Gornick, and Gary Stephan; poets Michael McClure, Paul Mariani, and Gerd Stern; religious scholars Richard Baker-roshi, Elaine Pagels, and Robert Thurman; social commentators Betty Friedan, Paul Krassner, Naomi Wolf, and the late Abbie Hoffman; writers Annie Dillard, Ken Kesey, Steven Levy, and Mark Mirsky.

Edge Foundation maintains an audio and video archive of hundreds of hours of Reality Club meetings and Edge Seminars. The Web site will use these (to the extent that permissions can be cleared) and will advance into new areas such as those explored in *Digerati.*

The mandate of Edge Foundation is to promote inquiry into and discussion of intellectual, philosophical, artistic, and literary issues, as well as to work for the intellectual and social achievement of society. Edge Foundation, Inc. is a nonprofit private operating foundation under Section 501(c)(3) of the Internal Revenue Code. For further information about Edge Foundation, Inc. or the Web site – or for feedback regarding the book – please send email to *digerati@edge.org*.

Index